DEVOTIONS

I will lift up mine eyes unto the hills, from whence cometh my help. My help cometh from the Lord, which made heaven and earth.

—Psalm 121:1, 2

JANUARY

*Photo © **Image Club.***

Y0-DBU-678

Time Alone

Very early in the morning, while it was still dark, Jesus got up, left the house and went off to a solitary place, where he prayed (Mark 1:35, *New International Version*).

Scripture: **Mark 1:35-39**
Song: **"Take Time to Be Holy"**

When we examine our lifestyles and busy schedules, we may find that God is being squeezed out in the rush: "Mom, where's my lunch?" "Honey, I need a different tie." There are Little League, Scouts, youth meetings, Sunday school lesson preparation, and community commitments. When can we possibly find time alone with God?

Jesus understood the problem. When He went away alone, the disciples looked for Him because people were wanting to see Him. They needed Him . . . now! But Jesus knew His ministry depended on staying in close communion with the Father.

Daily time alone with God is vital. Some of us may find the time in the early morning, others late at night. A long commute to work, lunch hour. . . . Whenever, wherever, that period of refreshment will prepare us for our tasks, just as it prepared Jesus for His.

Dear Lord, forgive me when I get so caught up in the busyness of life that I forget about You, my source of strength. Help me order my life to follow Jesus' example. In His name, I pray. Amen.

January 1, 2. **Joyce Anne Munn,** a retired elementary teacher, serves on the national board of Christian Educators International, an organization for public school teachers.

No More Darkness

The people living in darkness have seen a great light; on those living in the land of the shadow of death a light has dawned (Matthew 4:16, *New International Version*).

Scripture: **Matthew 4:16-25**
Song: **"The Light of the World Is Jesus"**

A recent fire at an electrical substation near me created many problems for the community. Within a 45-minute period, authorities fielded 284 calls from concerned citizens. For some, darkness and lack of electricity were simple inconveniences, and they wondered when things would return to normal. Others, however, had more serious concerns. Poultry growers could face financial problems if they lost thousands of baby chicks due to the power outage. Ill people became alarmed, because they depended on a ventilator or oxygen source. Callers were reassured with the words, "We're working on it."

God's chosen people had been without light for hundreds of years. Now, with the beginning of Jesus' ministry, it's almost as if God were saying, "We're working on it."

As Jesus began His task, He recruited men to work with Him in restoring the light. Today, we have that same responsibility. We can work together to share the light of Jesus with those we know who sit in darkness.

Dear Father, *darkness can be a frightening experience. Thank You for sending light to us in the form of Your Son. Help us to dispel the darkness in people around us by telling them of Jesus. Amen.*

Wanting to Change

Jesus reached out his hand and touched the man. "I am willing," he said. "Be clean!" (Mark 1:41, *New International Version*).

Scripture: **Mark 1:40-45**
Song: **"Whiter Than Snow"**

"How many counselors does it take to change a light bulb? Just one, but the bulb has to want to be changed." This old joke masks an important reality that is crucial to the field of counseling—people will change only when they want to change. When the leper came to Jesus, he did not question Jesus' ability to cleanse him. "If you are willing," he said, "you can make me clean." But the leper had to want to be clean and had to come to Jesus.

The fact is that many people say they want to change, but they will do nothing to begin the process. The leper came to Jesus. He showed his desire to change. If we want to be rid of our sins, our bad habits, our insecurities, we must first *want* to be rid of them. Jesus certainly has the ability to cleanse us. If we show a sincere desire for spiritual healing, Jesus will always say, "I am willing. Be clean."

Dear Father, give us the desire to genuinely want to change. We know You have the power and that You are willing. May we have the courage to look deeply into our lives and bring our sins to You and be healed. In Jesus' name, we pray. Amen.

January 3-9. **Dr. James North** is a professor of church history at the Cincinnati Bible College and Seminary. He and his wife, Martha, have two grown daughters.

Bearing One Another's Burdens

Carry each other's burdens, and in this way you will fulfill the law of Christ (Galatians 6:2, *New International Version*).

Scripture: **Mark 2:1-5**
Song: **"They'll Know We Are Christians by Our Love"**

Jesus healed the paralyzed man, but what can be said about the four men who carried him to Jesus? It must have been inconvenient, and if the man had not exercised for years, perhaps he was also a bit overweight. Even for four men, it might have been a heavy load. And then there was the crowd. The house was obviously packed, and the men had to go up on the roof and rip it open to let the man down into the house. Were there indignant stares from those who were showered with debris? Imagine the distress of the owner! Were they chastised for their rudeness? Yet their work was amply repaid when Jesus healed the man.

Paul says we are to bear one another's burdens. These four men carried a physical load. There may be times when our task is physical—driving an elderly friend to a doctor's appointment, mowing our neighbor's lawn as he recovers from surgery, helping newcomers unload their furniture from a rental truck. At other times we are asked to help carry a spiritual or emotional load for others. Such service is fulfilling the will of Christ.

Heavenly Father, *we acknowledge that Jesus bore our burdens. Help us to bear others' burdens and thus become an example of Christian love in action. In the name of Jesus, we pray. Amen.*

Which Is Easier?

Which is easier: to say to the paralytic, "Your sins are forgiven," or to say, "Get up, take your mat and walk"? (Mark 2:9, *New International Version*).

Scripture: **Mark 2:6-12**
Song: **"Trust and Obey"**

We go through life constantly making choices. Many times those choices are based on what is easier. If we need to eat, is it easier to pop a ready-made meal in the microwave or to start a casserole from scratch? If we need to clean out the garage, do we just throw everything in garbage cans, or do we sort things out and save what is still useful? To mow the lawn, do we fix the lawn mower, or borrow our neighbor's machine (again!)? Often we choose the easier route.

Jesus faced a similar question. Which is easier: to forgive or to heal? It would be easy to simply say, "Your sins are forgiven." Who would know whether they were or not? To say, "Get up and walk," however, would mean healing the man and giving him the power to walk. This is more than mere words; this would require a demonstration of power. To utter words of forgiveness would be easy. But Jesus showed His power to heal, thus demonstrating also His power to forgive. He didn't just do what was easy; He did what was helpful.

Lord, we pray that, as we go through life, we may choose to do those things that will glorify You. Guide us to choose service rather than convenience. In Christ's name, we pray. Amen.

Recruitment for Service

I have not come to call the righteous, but sinners (Mark 2:17, *New International Version*).

Scripture: **Mark 2:13-17**
Song: **"Lead On, O King Eternal"**

When Oliver Cromwell was recruiting an army to defend the Puritan/Parliament cause during the English Civil War, he selected men who would work under Christian discipline. In this New Model Army there would be no profanity, no irreverence, no drinking, no gambling, no pillaging of conquered territory. The army set high standards for morality and commitment to the Puritan cause. Military friends told Cromwell the plan would not work—the army needed fighters, not religious fanatics. But Cromwell was convinced that men committed to a religious ideal would make the best warriors to defend that ideal. In the three years of its existence, the New Model Army was undefeated and conquered all of England.

Jesus rewrote the recruitment handbook just as surely as did Cromwell. The religious leaders were looking for persons who were obedient and devoted to religious traditions. But Jesus was looking for sinners, not those who were proud of their righteousness. The religious experts scoffed. But the army of Jesus' followers understood what salvation was all about. In time they conquered all of the Roman Empire.

Dear Father, help us to remember that we are enlisted under a new model of behavior that calls us to live as examples of the kingdom of Heaven. In Jesus' name, we pray. Amen.

Walking in Darkness

Anyone who claims to be in the light but hates his brother is still in the darkness (1 John 2:9, *New International Version*).

Scripture: 1 John 2:9-17
Song: "Sunshine in the Soul"

When I was in Boy Scouts many years ago, a weekend outing at a camp gave us some experience in getting along in the woods. Our scoutmaster took us to an open field surrounded by trees. He wanted to show us what it was like to wander about in the woods without a compass. So he blindfolded several boys and told them to walk in a straight line across the field. It didn't take long for some of the boys to begin to veer right or left, no matter how hard they tried to walk straight. After a while he had them stop and remove the blindfolds. Some were amazed at how curved a path they had traveled.

That is the result of walking in darkness. If we have hatred toward any of our Christian brothers, we are walking in darkness. Trying to walk a straight Christian line while still hating a brother or sister is just as difficult as walking through the woods blindfolded. We need a compass, which is the love of Christ in our hearts. With compass in hand, and blindfold off, we can walk a straight line.

Dear Jesus, guide us so that we may walk in the pathway You have trailblazed for us—a pathway of love and service to our brothers and sisters—above the darkness of this world and in Your heavenly light. In Your name, we pray. Amen.

The Love of God

God is love (1 John 4:8).

Scripture: 1 John 4:7-21
Song: "Love Lifted Me"

Recently I have been doing some reading in Christian mystics from the Middle Ages. I'm not much into mysticism, but I do find some of these writings intriguing. However, one of the elements that bothers me somewhat is the writers' emphasis on "negative theology." This is the idea that we cannot say anything positive about God because He is so much more than whatever we can think. Therefore, the only way to describe God is to talk about what God is *not*. He is not like us; He is not limited; He is not dependent upon anything else. Further, according to this idea, we cannot say that God is strong because He is more than just *strong*. We cannot call Him gracious, for our word *gracious* does not begin to describe what God really is.

This viewpoint is intellectually stimulating, but I find it uncomfortable. Surely there is something positive we can say about God! Yes! John says that God is love. He may be more *love* than we can imagine, but He is certainly love. He sent His Son to die for our sins, He provides our daily needs, and in the end He saves us. God is love.

Heavenly Father, *thank You so much for Your love. Though words may fail us in describing Your character, may we never forget that You loved us all the way to the cross. In Jesus' name, we pray. Amen.*

Speaking Truthfully

Each of you must put off falsehood and speak truthfully to his neighbor, for we are all members of one body (Ephesians 4:25, *New International Version*).

Scripture: **Ephesians 4:25-32**
Song: **"Blest Be the Tie That Binds"**

I am deeply thankful that I generally enjoy good health. Even so, sometimes I get the flu, a bad cold, a stomach virus, or something that makes me feel rather puny. But I have noticed that, whenever that happens, my whole body feels it. If I have the stomach flu, my shoulders ache. In fact, every part of my body feels the effects of the illness.

Imagine what trouble I would be in if one part of my body was ill and then tried to hide it from the other parts of my body. "No, I'm not sick, let's carry on as usual." Or what would happen if other parts of the body denied the illness? "Come on, you're not really ill; let's go!"

The members of my body must speak the truth to one another for an illness to be properly diagnosed and treated. Members of the spiritual body of Christ must do the same. If we are hurting, we should not deny that to other members of the body; nor should we ignore someone else's hurt. We are to speak the truth to one another, for we are all members of one body.

Dear Father, help us to remember that we are all members of Your body, one body. May we treat each other as we treat our own bodies and work together for the health of each other. In Jesus' name, we pray. Amen.

The First Team

Jesus went up on a mountainside and called to him those he wanted, and they came to him (Mark 3:13, *New International Version*).

Scripture: **Mark 3:13-19**
Song: **"So Send I You"**

We must understand that today's verses are more than just a list of names. Each person had distinctive qualities that Jesus could use. Two of those men are particularly interesting: Matthew the publican and Simon the Zealot. Politically, they were as far apart as it was possible to be. The Zealots wanted to overthrow the Romans by force. The publicans worked for the Romans, collecting taxes. The Zealots thought the publicans were traitors. The publicans thought the Zealots were wild-eyed visionaries. Jesus thought He could use both of them—on the same team. The church must always be open to receive people of different political views.

We must also note that, when Jesus called, they came. Each one had other things to do; but each one had such faith in Christ and commitment to Him that he left all else behind. May we also be wholly dedicated and fully committed to the Lord Jesus Christ and to His church.

Dear God, *we do not classify ourselves with Your chosen apostles, but we do believe that You have called us to some specific field of service. We answer, "Yes, Lord, Yes!" Amen.*

January 10-16. **Robert Shannon** is a retired minister living with his wife in Valle Crucis, North Carolina. He conducts revivals and holds interim ministries.

Two by Two

And they went out, and preached that men should repent (Mark 6:12).

Scripture: **Mark 6:6-13**
Song: **"I'll Go Where You Want Me to Go"**

When my wife and I were missionaries behind the Iron Curtain, we occasionally visited a little underground church in Dubrovnik, Croatia. They met in various apartments throughout the city, and they changed the meeting place from week to week. If you missed this Sunday you didn't know where the service would be next Sunday! After one such meeting the leader said, "We will now leave by twos because of the neighbors." Two people left. We waited. Two more left. It gave new meaning to the text "he sent them out two by two" (v. 7, *New International Version*).

In today's Scripture, of course, they were going on an evangelistic tour. They needed the encouragement that comes from working in pairs. Still today, in evangelistic visitation campaigns, the workers go visiting two by two. They encourage one another. It is often difficult to determine when biblical instruction is intended for the immediate listeners then present and when it is intended for all believers in all places at all times. Today we may not be able to heal the sick or drive out demons, but the message we bring is the same message they brought: people should repent. Old Testament and New, prophets and apostles agree on that.

O Lord, as we represent You to a world that desperately needs to repent, keep us faithful in carrying the message. Through Christ, we pray. Amen.

The Extravagance of God

Freely you have received, freely give (Matthew 10:8, *New International Version*).

Scripture: **Matthew 10:5-15**
Song: **"Count Your Blessings"**

Most of today's text is for the twelve named at the beginning of the chapter and not specifically for us. We used to sing a chorus, "Every Promise in the Book Is Mine." Of course, that is not really true. We are not apostles of Christ. We have not been given all the miraculous gifts that were given to them. But we have certainly received freely, and we can give freely.

We serve an extravagant God. On a clear night, with the unaided eye, we can see 2,000 stars. Astronomers think that in the universe as a whole there are 30 billion stars! God made 200,000 kinds of flowers. He made 9,000 kinds of birds. God is so extravagant. We focus so much on what we want that we fail to see what we have. We can see, hear, and think. We can love. The poorest person has received freely. We need to be like God and give as freely as God has given to us. God has entrusted us with material and spiritual blessings. Both kinds need to be shared. If we really appreciate what God has given us, we will give to His cause and to His children. *Freely* must surely refer both to the number of our gifts and to the spirit of our giving.

O Lord, we do thank You for Your bountiful gifts. Forgive us if we take even one for granted. And give us open hearts to share, so that we may be like You. In Jesus' name, we pray. Amen.

Simply Trusting

And they departed, and went through the towns, preaching the gospel, and healing every where (Luke 9:6).

Scripture: Luke 9:1-6
Song: "I Know Who Holds Tomorrow"

It is necessary to distinguish between instructions given to specific people for a specific time and instructions given to all people for all time. Today's verses fit in the first category. But Francis of Assisi did not understand that. The son of a wealthy Italian merchant, he took this passage and the one in Matthew 10 literally. He left home wearing a ragged cloak tied with a rope he took from a scarecrow. He begged from the rich. He gave to the poor. He attracted many followers whom he called Lesser Brothers. Today they are called Franciscans and no longer follow the strict program of Francis of Assisi. Some years ago a minister was talking with his leaders about insurance. One leader said, "A minister should not have insurance. He should believe that God will take care of him. The minister's answer was very wise. He said, "I do believe that God will take care of me. He did it when He put a head on my shoulders!" Following Christ does not mean we cannot be thoughtful and prudent. When Jesus sent the twelve out saying, "Take nothing for the journey," He was giving instructions for a limited mission—not a lifetime.

O Lord, we do recognize the hold that possessions have on us. We ask You to teach us never to put our trust in possessions, but always to put our trust in You. Amen.

The Mind of Christ

Let this mind be in you, which was also in Christ Jesus
(Philippians 2:5).

Scripture: **Philippians 2:1-11**
Song: **"Lord, Make Me Like You"**

We are indebted to the modern English translations of the Bible for making many passages of Scripture clearer. This is true of verse 6 in this chapter. But verse 5 carries greater impact in the more familiar *King James Version*. We are to have the mind of Christ, the same attitude as Christ. That is startling! It is hard enough to be told we should live like Christ. It is harder still to be told we should love like Christ. Here the apostle Paul says we should think like Christ!

Fortunately, he gives us some specifics: humility, obedience, sacrifice. Christ's humility was rewarded by His being exalted to the highest place. And if we will humbly obey, we too will be exalted. We shall reign with Him! (see 2 Timothy 2:12). An old song says, "When the battle's over, we shall wear a crown." In Luke 22:25-30 Jesus speaks at length of this relationship between service here and rewards there. Those who are servants on earth will live like kings in Heaven. Here we may be powerless and put upon, but there we will share the glory of the one whose name is above every name. Every knee will bow, but for some it will be too little and too late. For the faithful, it will be a familiar posture.

Lord of Heaven and earth, thank You for the sacrifice of Your Son, Jesus. Give us grace that we, too, may be humble and obedient, ready to sacrifice and ready to serve. Amen.

Citizens of Heaven

Our citizenship is in heaven. And we eagerly await a Savior from there, the Lord Jesus Christ (Philippians 3:20, *New International Version*).

Scripture: **Philippians 3:12–4:1**
Song: **"This World Is Not My Home"**

The Caribbean islands of Curacao, Aruba, and Bonaire are Dutch. Most of the people who live there have never been to the Netherlands, but they are citizens of the Netherlands. They vote like the Europeans and send representatives to the Dutch parliament far across the Atlantic. The people who lived in Philippi were citizens of Rome, though Rome was hundreds of miles away. Many of them—perhaps most of them—had never even been to Rome; but they were as much citizens of Rome as if they lived there.

That is the background to Paul's statement that we are citizens of Heaven. We have never been there. Heaven is far away. But we are as much citizens of Heaven as if we lived on one of the golden streets. At Philippi Paul claimed the privileges of Roman citizenship (Acts 16:37). And it is to the Philippians that he writes of heavenly citizenship.

We can act like citizens of Heaven even while we are still here on earth. Like Paul, we will never be perfect and must keep pressing on, but like the Philippians we must "stand firm in the Lord" (4:1, *New International Version*).

O God, thank You for so honoring us that You have granted us heavenly citizenship. Help us never to take such a high privilege for granted. We pray in Christ. Amen.

Why Pray When You Can Worry?

Do not be anxious about anything, but in everything, by prayer and petition, with thanksgiving, present your requests to God (Philippians 4:6, *New International Version*).

Scripture: Philippians 4:4-9
Song: "Tell It to Jesus"

The title of today's devotion may look like a misprint. We are familiar with the motto: "Why Worry When You Can Pray?" But sometimes we live as if the opposite were our motto: "Why Pray When You Can Worry?" Anxiety disturbs our sleep and distracts us in our waking hours. The *King James Version* (v. 6) says, "Be careful for nothing." Don't misunderstand; it means, "Do not be full of care."

A young preacher once said that worry was atheistic. After the service a lady attacked him at the door. She said that she worried and she was no atheist. Of course, he did not mean to be taken so literally. There are legitimate concerns and logical worries. But worry should not be allowed to debilitate us. A few people are so consumed with worry that they have panic attacks. Others are so careless that they take needless chances and put themselves in unnecessary danger. We must balance legitimate concerns with living by faith. We must put our trust in God and not allow worry to dominate our lives. We are always safe in the arms of Jesus.

O Lord, forgive us when we fail to trust. Deepen our faith and lift from us the burden of undue worry and anxiety. We pray through Christ, who taught us how to pray. Amen.

Are We There Yet?

I tell you the truth, he who believes has everlasting life (John 6:47, *New International Version*).

Scripture: **John 6:41-51**
Song: **"When We All Get to Heaven"**

Every parent has heard that cry from the back seat of the car. It usually begins about 15 minutes after the start of any family trip. What if you were traveling to Mars? Even at its closest approach to Earth, the red planet is at least 35 million miles away. NASA's estimate is six months there and six months back—at best. Just imagine the number of times the question, "Mom, are we there yet?" could be asked.

More important than any journey to the beach, a vacation hideaway, or even to Mars is our journey to Heaven. It begins with belief in Christ and ends with eternal life. In the middle, it demands both faith and faithfulness. Jesus says, "Everyone who looks to the Son and believes in him shall have eternal life" (John 6:40, *New International Version*).

Our lives are a journey of faith. We must trust ourselves to Jesus. We must listen to the Father and learn from Him (see v. 45)—and thus live lives consistent with God's teaching.

"Are we there yet?" No, but by faith we'll make it.

Father, life's road is often rough. We experience sorrow, grief, and pain. Help us to overcome. Help us to be faithful, so that we may enjoy Heaven with You. In the name of Jesus, we pray. Amen.

January 17-23. **James Moore** teaches philosophy and religion at Georgia Perimeter College and history at Luther Rice Seminary. He lives in Stockbridge, Georgia.

Sharing Life

I am the living bread that came down from heaven (John 6:51, *New International Version*).

Scripture: **John 6:52-59**
Song: **"Hallelujah, What a Savior!"**

There is something very good about supper time. In our house supper time is more than just a time to eat; it is a time for each family member to share the day with the rest of the family. It is a time of homecoming and hearing what everyone else did during the day.

Supper time is warm with happy memories. A day, a time, an hour never stands on its own but is sustained by all the hours that have gone before. Nothing is ever lost—not even the simplest things—for time enhances what has been dear to us. We look back and think about something that, apparently, no longer exists. But it does. It exists in our memories; it exists in the retelling of the story.

This helps us understand something of the nature of Communion. Jesus told us to remember him in the Lord's Supper. At our Lord's Supper time we are to focus our memories on, and retell the story of, His sacrifice for us. When we do, we make Jesus' sacrifice real, in our minds and in our hearts.

Heavenly Father, *thank You for the Lord's Supper. It helps us to remember the death of Your Son, Jesus. Help us never to forget His sacrifice for us. Help us to remember the cross. In the name of Jesus, our Savior, we pray. Amen.*

I Can't Learn to Do That

This is a hard teaching. Who can accept it? (John 6:60, *New International Version*).

Scripture: John 6:60-69
Song: "'Are Ye Able,' Said the Master"

I teach logic at a community college in Georgia. It is one of the courses that students must take in order to transfer to any of the four-year state colleges. For some students, it is the most difficult class that they take. Many pick up the textbook during the first class meeting, look at the alphabet soup of letters, symbols, syllogisms, and terms—and they lose all hope. I tell them that, yes, the class is difficult, but with my help they can and will get through it.

Almost everyone finds some subject or another particularly difficult. Perhaps you aced your English courses but struggled through math. Maybe you found history exciting, but science was incomprehensible. Some teachings are hard!

Some of Christ's teachings are also hard. "Take up your cross and follow me." "Serve me with all your heart and soul and strength. . . ." Sure, such teachings are difficult. Yes, they will take our dedication and commitment. But, with God's help, we can and will get through. If we but ask, Jesus will help us; and we can and will learn to do His will.

Heavenly Father, help us to understand Your way. Grant us the wisdom to see clearly the path that You have laid before us. Empower us to walk it faithfully. In the name of our Lord, Jesus Christ, we pray. Amen.

A Dangerous Question

"But what about you?" he asked. **"Who do you say I am?"** (Matthew 16:15, *New International Version*).

Scripture: **Matthew 16:13-20**
Song: **"Open My Eyes, That I May See"**

"A penny for your thoughts." So goes the old saying. Aside from the issue of inflation demanding more than a penny, the question is really asking, "What are you thinking about?" This is a dangerous question. Do we want the truth or what we want to hear? Guys, if you are out for dinner with your girlfriend, fiancee, or wife and she asks this question, be very careful! This is uncharted territory in your relationship. The right answer is, "I was thinking about how beautiful you look this evening and that your eyes sparkle in the candlelight." The true answer, however, may be, "I was wondering if you're going to finish that steak or could I have some of it?" Which answer should you give?

Jesus asked His disciples, "Who do you say I am?" That too is a dangerous question. We could answer, "Lord and Christ." But saying the words is not enough. We should really mean it. If we mean it we will live in submission to His lordship. That is not easy to do. The question is difficult—the answer is more difficult still.

Father, help us to be vivid witnesses for You and Your Son, Jesus. Help us to be bold when we are given the opportunity to share our faith with others. Help us to live lives that say, "Yes, I am Christian." In the name of our Lord Jesus, we pray. Amen.

He Is Worth It

If anyone would come after me, he must deny himself and take up his cross and follow me (Matthew 16:24, *New International Version*).

Scripture: **Matthew 16:24-28**
Song: **"Alas, and Did My Savior Bleed?"**

At the end of my son's eighth-grade year, Daniel decided that he wanted to try out for the high school football team. At the parents' meeting, the coach focused on "commitment." His message was: "If you want to play the game, you must be willing to commit your time and energy to the game." We agreed but did not understand fully the implications of our agreement. What followed was a grueling program: two weeks of spring practice, summer conditioning in June and July, a "two a day" camp for a week in August, and not getting home till 8 P.M. on school nights in the fall. Some days Daniel was so tired he fell asleep in the car on the way home.

We don't think twice about the need for an athlete to be committed to his or her sport. Our culture says it is worth it because commitment brings rewards.

Serving Christ calls for commitment of time and energy. It is worth it, because Christ is worth it. He died for us. He defeated death for us. He is coming back for us. He is our Lord and God.

Father, help us to dedicate our time and energy to Your faithful service. Help us stay committed when the going gets tough. In Jesus' name, we pray. Amen.

"Is That Your Final Answer?"

Who do you say I am? (Mark 8:29, *New International Version*).

Scripture: **Mark 8:27-30**
Song: **"The Solid Rock"**

We don't hear it so much anymore, but the quizmaster's question from the popular television game show, *Who Wants to Be a Millionaire?* was a common buzz phrase for a while.

So what's *your* final answer?

When we attempt to solve life's problems, we often settle for less than the best solution. Too often we accept the first answer that comes up. Our "final answer" is all too frequently our first answer, and we never find out the *best* answer.

Jesus asked His disciples, "Who do people say that I am?" There were many answers. Even so, people today have many answers. They say that Jesus was a good man, a wise teacher, a rabbi, a teacher of ethics, a prophet, a doer of good deeds, and many other things. All good answers. All correct. But none of them is the best answer.

When Jesus asked His disciples the question, "Who do you say that I am?" Peter answered, "The Messiah." The best answer.

Now how do *you* answer the question?

Father, help us to be faithful to the end—so that, when we stand before You as our judge, we may answer the question, "Who is Jesus?" as we always have. He is the Messiah, our Lord and Savior. In Jesus' name, we pray. Amen.

To Die For

If anyone would come after me, he must deny himself and take up his cross and follow me (Mark 8:34, *New International Version*).

Scripture: **Mark 8:31-38**
Song: **"All for Jesus"**

I love to cook, and I love to eat. So, when I am surfing the Web, I often look for good things to cook and then eat. As I was surfing one day, I came across a review for a book titled, *Desserts To Die For: Chocolate Cookies.* The book is touted as being "from the author of *Death by Chocolate.*"

Now don't get me wrong; I love cookies, and I love chocolate. Cookies give me pleasure in that they taste good. But to die for my love of chocolate cookies—I don't think so! In fact, I can't think of any food item worthy enough to die for.

Now Jesus is another story. He is my Savior. He loved me as none other can. He gave up Heaven for me. He died for me so I can live free of sin's rule in my life. I'm free from the fear of the punishment for my sin. I'm free to live my life in thankful service to Him. I can even face death without fear because I know my life will continue on the other side of the grave.

That makes Jesus worthy enough to die for!

Father, help me to give my all for Jesus. Help me to make every waking moment a time when I serve Him. Grant me the strength to deny self and be lost in service to my Lord. In Jesus' name, I pray. Amen.

Receiving the Little Ones

Whosoever shall receive one of such children in my name, receiveth me (Mark 9:37).

Scripture: **Mark 9:33-37**
Song: **"Thank You"**

Mother was a Christian. Dad, however, was not, and he wouldn't let Mother use our car to attend church. So Mother and we children crowded into Mother's aunt and uncle's car, along with their son, for most church services. Aunt Annie and Uncle Buster took our family under their wing. Many times my sister and I visited in their home, where Uncle Buster baked us warm, perfectly round chocolate chip cookies. They often took us on countryside excursions or out for an ice cream sundae. They prayed consistently for our family. Uncle Buster was a Sunday school teacher who read and studied his Bible faithfully.

During a time of domestic abuse and upheaval in our home, this aunt and uncle became a source of comfort and stability to two small girls. The quiet, nurturing love and support were just what we needed. How the Lord must smile on people like Aunt Annie and Uncle Buster who welcome little children in His name.

Lord, help us to be aware of children who need a kind word, a thoughtful deed, or an invitation into a safe home. May our kindness and love plant seeds of courage and faith in their lives. Amen.

January 24-30. **Phyllis Qualls Freeman** is an office coordinator for a hospital in Tennessee. She and her husband, Bill, have three children and five grandchildren.

Unexpected Answers

The one who received the seed that fell on good soil is the man who hears the word and understands it (Matthew 13:23, *New International Version*).

Scripture: **Mark 10:13-22**
Song: **"I Will Follow Thee"**

A man ran to Jesus, knelt, and asked what he should do to inherit eternal life. Maybe he expected Jesus to pat him on the head with, "Oh, you are doing all the right things," since he already thought he was keeping the whole law. Why did the man refuse to hear Jesus' answer? Was he startled that Jesus required more?

If we ask God for something—for instance, a financial miracle—are we willing to hear His answer? He may give us a miracle, or He may say we need to be more diligent in money management. Or, if we pray for our neighbor's attitude to change, He may show us it is our own attitude that needs to be adjusted.

Are we willing to ask the Lord what He requires of us? If we do, do we really want to hear His answer? It takes courage to ask and courage to follow through with what the Lord impresses upon us to do. What will our response be to Him? We can hear and understand His words. Then, in childlike devotion, we can follow Him.

Lord, *when we pray, we trust You to answer in a way that is best for us. Even if You give us unexpected answers to our questions, help us to continue to follow You. We know Your answers will always be just what we need. Amen.*

Thinking Outside the Box

And they were astonished out of measure (Mark 10:26).

Scripture: Mark 10:23-27
Song: "Awesome God"

Jesus' statements constantly made His disciples really think about what He had said. He wanted them to think outside the box. *Outside the box* thinking means to think in a fresh and a new way. The disciples could have said, "But Jesus, the priest says we should do it this way." Instead, Jesus asked them to look at the heart of each issue.

Religious people of Jesus' day thought in terms of keeping the written Law. However, Jesus wanted them to get to know the one who wrote the Law—since relationship with the Father is what makes it possible to keep the Law.

When they asked Jesus which of the Ten Commandments was the greatest, He did not recite any of the "thou shalt nots." Instead, He astonished them again by talking about loving God.

If I always expect that I know how God will answer my questions and my prayers, then I must believe that God has boundaries or can be contained in a box—and that this one way is the only way He can answer. Jesus wants to work in our lives in fresh and new ways.

Lord, *astonish us with Your words and with Your answers to our questions and our prayers. We want to be receptive to the way You are at work in us and around us. You are an awesome God! Amen.*

It's Not About Me

For I determined not to know any thing among you, save Jesus Christ, and him crucified (1 Corinthians 2:2).

Scripture: **Mark 10:28-31**
Song: **"The Heart of Worship"**

When my two small grandchildren visit, they love to take our little Chihuahua, Poco, out for a walk. "Let me be first," says Beth. "It's my turn," says William. I must help them work out a compromise. Since they are young, their focus is on their own desires and their own wants.

Sometimes adults also have a self-centered focus, a "me first" mentality.

A minister once preached a sermon titled, "It's Not About Me." His message said that we so often only consider what is important to ourselves. For instance, we may say, "No one notices all I've done for the church." This minister said our focus should not be centered solely on ourselves or what we have done, but on the message of the gospel. The focus should be on Christ. It is not about me. It is all about *Him*.

We expect young children to think of themselves first, even though we try to teach them to consider others. Since hearing that sermon, I'm more conscious of my own tendency to be me-centered. My desire is to stay focused on Christ. It's all about *Him*.

Mighty God, help us to lay aside our selfish desires. Help us to avoid tabulating our accomplishments. May our lives inspire people to know You and look to You. We worship You for who You are. Amen.

My Work is His Work

And whatsoever ye do in word or deed, do all in the name of the Lord Jesus, giving thanks to God and the Father by him (Colossians 3:17).

Scripture: **Mark 10:35-45**
Song: **"Let My Life Be a Light"**

As an office coordinator, I may find on one day that my job includes coordinating a meeting for the department director while the next day may involve nothing more than answering the phone. One of my duties is to make the first pot of coffee for the staff. What a little effort it takes, but how important it is to the day's early arrivers.

Is making coffee God's work? Well, that depends. If my motive is to bless others and express God's love to them, then it may indeed be God's work.

Your work for God may be making coffee. Or it may be performing brain surgery, testing automobile parts, playing trombone, directing traffic. . . . Whether the position is complicated or routine, it is God's work—if it is done for Him. One supervisor told her crew, "Clean that hospital room as though your mother would be the next person to check into it." That puts a different perspective on the job, doesn't it?

Whatever our life's work is, we can do it wholeheartedly, in the name of the Lord. Such purpose can make our daily work enjoyable and fulfilling.

Exalted Father, *help us to view our daily work as an extension of Your work, doing it with all our heart. Inspire us to choose excellence so our faithfulness will shine as a beacon of Your light. Amen.*

The Circle of Giving

Remember the words of the Lord Jesus, how he said, It is more blessed to give than to receive (Acts 20:35).

Scripture: **Matthew 20:20-28**
Song: **"Give of Your Best to the Master"**

Margie and her husband had a blended family of ten children. Yet, Margie was never so busy that she couldn't stretch herself a little more to reach out to those in need. She could always fit a neighbor child in her car to go to church. She took children to visit in her home on Sunday afternoons. She fixed meals for an elderly neighbor. On top of all that, almost every weekend, we ended up visiting in their home with our two small children.

Margie didn't know she was mentoring me as I watched her spirit of giving. She did it with such contagious joy. I saw firsthand that it was a blessing to do for others, to serve others, to give to others. Then I tried what she had modeled. It felt good. It seemed right. Once we gave some bags of groceries to a young couple going through a hard time. Later that young wife shared with her peers how it had blessed her. She had been impressed, so that she had later given to a family in need.

Following Jesus' example of service and love, we enter a circle of giving that just keeps growing bigger and bigger.

We thank You, Jesus, that You came to give yourself to us. Enable us to look beyond ourselves and be a part of the circle of giving by sharing the skills and possessions You have given to us. Amen.

Exalted in His Time

And whosoever shall exalt himself shall be abased; and he that shall humble himself shall be exalted (Matthew 23:12).

Scripture: **Matthew 23:1-12**
Song: **"It's Not in Vain"**

Who hasn't watched the glamorous shows on TV when Hollywood's elite are presented with awards and are exalted for their accomplishments? There are Oscars and Grammy awards given to the best actors, actresses, writers, musicians, and others. What productions with all the glitter and high fashion!

An aunt of mine once told my mother that she wanted to see her children's names up in lights some day. She wanted them to succeed, marry well, and be known. My mother repeated this to us, her children. Then she staunchly stated that our coming to celebrity status meant nothing at all to her. What was important to her was that we served God.

Most Christian professionals are not given honors for what they do. There are missionaries, preachers, youth leaders, and others who receive minimum pay and no awards. Even more Christians volunteer their time.

What we do for the Lord is not done in vain. There will be a day when such work and faithfulness will be exalted by the one we serve. In His time.

Father, help us to desire Your approval more than the applause of the world. Let our accomplishments consist of making a difference in others' lives, so that You may be exalted. Amen.

Tears Clean the Soul

Blessed are those who mourn, for they shall be comforted (Matthew 5:4, *Revised Standard Version*).

Scripture: Psalm 6:1-7
Song: "Jesus Is All the World to Me"

Sometimes we cry because we are sad or hurt. Ironically, sometimes we cry because we are overwhelmed with joy. The tears that accompany trouble are often due to an overwhelming sense of doom. Where can we turn but to the Lord?

When we experience the death of a loved one, we can find comfort from our God. When we sin against God and know that we have disappointed Him, we can find relief through His forgiveness. When we are weary from the burdens of life, Christ Jesus says to us, "Come unto me . . . and I will give you rest" (Matthew 11:28).

Tears of joy can be the result of our gratitude for the bountiful blessings of God. Our greatest blessing is the hope for eternity. We know that our tomorrow will be most blessed as we will live it in the very presence of God. The psalmist wrote, "Weeping may endure for a night, but joy cometh in the morning" (Psalm 30:5).

Precious Savior, thank You that Your Holy Spirit interprets our sighs and groans, our tears and our inner sadness, in order that You may know our needs and meet them this day. Thank You for the joy that comes in spite of our tears, because of Your blessings. Amen.

January 31. **Dan Lawson** is executive director of development at a seminary in Johnson City, Tennessee. He and his wife, Linda, have two adult children.

DEVOTIONS

*T*he righteous shall flourish like the palm tree: he shall grow like a cedar in Lebanon.

—Psalm 92:12

FEBRUARY

*Photo by **Chuck Perry**; it features a wooded Kentucky hillside.*

My Times Are in Thy Hand

Trust in the Lord with all thine heart; and lean not unto thine own understanding. In all thy ways acknowledge him and he shall direct thy paths (Proverbs 3:5, 6).

Scripture: **Psalm 31:9-15**
Song: **"Take My Life, and Let It Be"**

Life is not always a bed of roses. We are not immune to illness, financial distress, family problems, death, or any other kind of crisis. So what are we to do in the midst of disappointment and sorrow? How do we deal with the sadness of death? What do we do when a catastrophic illness takes control of our future with no cure in sight?

Our relationship with God is one of trust. The Lord is our strength and refuge, a very present help in time of trouble. In illness He is the good physician. In financial distress our heavenly Father knows what we need before we even ask. In death He is our hope and comfort. In every problem or life crisis our times are in His hand.

Perhaps even today there will be those happenings that seem to bring only grief and sorrow. It is in those moments, when God may even seem far away, that we must trust Him to turn our sorrow into joy.

O Father in Heaven, thank You for working everything in this day together for our good. We trust You and thank You for turning sorrow into a hope that will not fade. In Jesus' name, we pray. Amen.

February 1-6. **Dan Lawson** is executive director of development at a seminary in Johnson City, Tennessee. He and his wife, Linda, have two adult children.

A Comfort in the Time of Storm

God is our refuge and strength, a very present help in trouble (Psalm 46:1).

Scripture: **Psalm 77:1-10**
Song: **"Let the Lower Lights Be Burning"**

Along the coastline of an ocean are hundreds of lighthouses. They mark the shoreline to prevent ships on the sea from running aground, especially in the midst of a storm when vision is impaired by the weather. The lights from the lighthouses also help guide the ships safely in darkness. There are times when the storms on the sea are so severe that the captains of the ships cannot see the light. In the midst of the clouds, foghorns serve the same purpose as the lighthouse. Both the land and the sea can be a places of safety, but both can also be places of danger. Ships are designed to move safely in the sea. The closer they come to land, the greater the danger for such a craft.

Life is like being on a ship. The challenge of life is to dwell in safety and avoid the dangers that surround us. Jesus is the light of the world. He serves as our lighthouse, guiding us through life safely, helping us to walk through the valley of the shadow of death and danger. In our days of trouble, we must seek the Lord. He is our comfort in the time of storm.

Father, hear us today as we call upon You for help. Guide us safely through the difficulties of life. Help us to see and hear You so we will not fear the storms. Thank You for Your steadfast love. Amen.

To Die Is Gain

O death, where is thy sting? O grave, where is thy victory?
(1 Corinthians 15:55).

Scripture: **Ruth 1:1-5**
Song: **"O Love That Will Not Let Me Go"**

Ruth's husband died and then, ten years later, both of her sons died. While death is no stranger to us, it can still be a frightening moment when it knocks on our door.

I visited a lady who was in the hospital battling cancer. Every day I went into her room and asked, "What's the good news today?" Most of the time the news was not so very good. But she was a woman of strong faith. She believed that her time was in God's hands, so she did not worry.

Several weeks had passed, and on one day when I visited, I asked the question of her again, "What's the good news today?" To my surprise she responded, "I'm going home!" I was delighted. But the more we talked, the more I realized that she meant something different that what I had thought she meant. I said to her, "You don't mean 'home' home, do you?" She replied, "I'm going to go to Heaven to be at home with the Lord." O, what good news she had! May our hope be for Heaven, to be at home with the Lord.

O Creator God, thank You for the promise of eternal life. Thank You that You sent Your Son to be our Savior. And thank You that He has gone to prepare a place for us, that we may someday be with You in Heaven. In the name of our risen Lord, we pray. Amen.

My Home Is in Heaven

So whether we are at home or away, we make it our aim to please him (2 Corinthians 5:9, *Revised Standard Version*).

Scripture: **Ruth 1:6-11**
Song: **"The Way of the Cross Leads Home"**

I have lived in so many different places that I simply don't know where home is. When someone asks me where home is, I simply reply with the name of the place where I presently reside. But some people have lived in one place all of their lives. If they travel away on vacation or go away to school or are transferred by their jobs, to return home is indeed special.

Home is a place where special people are, or home is where special memories took place. It is a place of fond relationships. I like this world, and I want to live here as long as I can. But I must remember that I'm just passing through. Lest we become too attached to this world, we must always keep our eyes on Jesus. He is the special relationship that makes Heaven our home.

There is a danger in placing too much treasure and pride in our earthly home to the exclusion of our heavenly home. We must hope for Heaven. To hope for earth is to hope for something that will not last. Heaven is eternal.

Heavenly Father, we long for Heaven, because that is where we can see You face to face. We hope for Heaven, for that is where we can live forever. Turn us toward Heaven, for that is indeed our home. In Jesus' name, we pray. Amen.

What's Yours Is Mine
and What's Mine Is Yours

For where you go I will go, and where you lodge I will lodge; your people shall be my people, and your God my God (Ruth 1:16, *Revised Standard Version*).

Scripture: **Ruth 1:12-17**
Song: **"The Bond of Love"**

The exchange between Naomi and Ruth contains beautiful words of loyalty and kinship. The relationship between these two women was truly that of a loving family. Even after Naomi's son, Ruth's husband, died, the family tie between these two women was extremely close. Ruth clung to Naomi and would not leave her to be alone.

That is the beauty of the Christian family. Husbands love their wives as Christ loved the church. Wives devote themselves to their husbands. Parents love their children. Children honor, respect, and obey their parents.

In the family relationship, we can see love, sacrifice, mentoring, teaching, faithfulness, and all those characteristics of Christ's Spirit. In a day when families are breaking apart, this is a time to recommit. Family relationships do not necessarily come naturally. They require effort and decision. Strong families are the result of a spiritual relationship with Christ as Lord.

Father God, thank You for our blood family into which we were born. Thank You for our church family into which we have been accepted. In Jesus' name, we pray. Amen.

The Cup Half Full or Half Empty

Every good gift and every perfect gift is from above, and cometh down from the Father of lights, with whom is no variableness, neither shadow of turning (James 1:17).

Scripture: **Ruth 1:18-22**
Song: **"Rejoice, Ye Pure in Heart"**

Why does God allow bad things to happen to good people? If every good and perfect gift comes down to us from the heavenly Father, why do evil things happen to Christian people? Naomi's life had been full; but when her husband and two adult sons died, she felt that the Lord had given her emptiness.

I have multiple sclerosis. When I was diagnosed, I thought that I was surely going to die. I joined an MS support group for encouragement. At my first meeting of the group, a young lady with MS said that I was going to experience a lot of anger. She said that she was as mad as could be at God for giving this illness to her. She blamed Him for her illness, for her life's cup being half empty.

When we can see all of the good gifts that God gives to us day by day, what good does it do to see the cup half empty? He has indeed blessed us with hope even in the midst of tragedy, evil, and sadness. He is our help in times of trouble.

Bountiful God, *thank You for the many blessings that You have bestowed upon us. Forgive us when we fail to see the good and choose to focus only on the bad. Forgive us for blaming You instead of thanking You. Help us through this day. In Christ's name, we pray. Amen.*

Cleaning Up Your Soul

Purge me with hyssop, and I shall be clean: wash me, and I shall be whiter than snow (Psalm 51:7).

Scripture: **Mark 7:17-23**
Song: **"Cleanse Me"**

There are government agencies to protect us from contaminants in the air, our water, and food products. If allowed to remain, these contaminants would harm us physically. But who protects us from contaminants that can harm us spiritually? This is exactly the kind of contamination Jesus warns against—contamination that comes from within, from our hearts. Perhaps it is this idea that prompted the apostle Paul to write: "Whatever is true, whatever is noble, whatever is right, whatever is pure, whatever is lovely, whatever is admirable—if anything is excellent or praiseworthy—think about such things" (Philippians 4:8, *New International Version*).

Spiritual pollution is all around us; we cannot escape it. We need a filtering system to protect our souls. The Scriptures provide guidelines that act as a filter—a rating system, as it were—that helps us gauge what is appropriate for us to put into our hearts.

O Lord, give me a clean heart and renew a right spirit within me, that my life may show forth Thy love and my lips may declare Thy praise. In Jesus' holy name, we pray. Amen.

February 7-13. **Ross Dampier** is a frequent writer for Devotions. He is a minister emeritus of Central Christian Church in Bristol, Tennessee.

Beware of Dogs

I will say of the LORD, He is my refuge and my fortress: my God; in him will I trust (Psalm 91:2).

Scripture: **Psalm 59:10-17**
Song: **"God Will Take Care of You"**

I visited a church where the minister was preaching from Philippians 3:2: "Beware of dogs." The entire sermon was the story of six dogs the minister had owned as pets, and how each of them reminded him of certain people or types of people. There was the terrier that could be counted on to sink his teeth into the unwary and so could not be trusted. There was the St. Bernard that could be trusted not to bite a person but could be depended on to slobber all over anyone within reach.

The conclusion was that, in dealing with people, as in dealing with dogs, God does not always protect us from them. The best we can expect is to be given grace to deal with them patiently, and to take seriously Paul's warning to beware of some of them.

The dogs to which David compared his enemies were wild, dangerous creatures that traveled in packs. How frightening! With enemies like that, a person needs God's protection, as well as His grace. Fortunately, this is just what David tells us we will receive. The Lord will be our refuge and strength. He will be our defense.

Lord, protect us from our enemies and give us patience with our friends; and, according to the instruction of Your Word, help us to love both of them. Amen.

God's Judgment on Pride

Wherefore he saith, God resisteth the proud, but giveth grace unto the humble (James 4:6).

Scripture: **Isaiah 13:9-13**
Song: **"When I See the Blood"**

The story has often been told of a soldier in the army of Napoleon who was found asleep at his post. It was his second offense; the penalty was death!

The soldier's mother sought Napoleon and begged for a pardon. The emperor replied that it was a second offense and that justice required the death penalty. "I do not ask for justice," implored the mother. "I plead for mercy."

"He does not deserve mercy," replied the emperor.

"Of course, he does not," cried the mother. "If he deserved justice I would come in pride, demanding justice; but he does not deserve it, so I come in humility pleading for mercy."

Impressed by the mother's love and the simplicity of her reasoning, Napoleon said, "Then you shall have mercy."

Today's Scripture is an alarming passage—for the proud. But the Lord's mercy is great when we are humble before Him.

Father in Heaven, we cannot afford justice, for the price is too high, and we have nothing to pay. Give us mercy, then—the free gift of Your grace, for we come humbly before You in the name of Your Son and our Savior, Jesus. Amen.

Where There's Life, There's Hope

Blessed is the man that trusteth in the Lord, and whose hope the Lord is (Jeremiah 17:7).

Scripture: **2 Kings 5:1-5**
Song: **"My Hope Is in the Lord"**

Naaman the Syrian was a man who had everything, but he was about to lose it all, for he had leprosy. He doubtless tried many cures, but none of them had been effective. The prospect was hopeless. As the disease progressed, Naaman saw all the things that he treasured slipping away from him.

Years ago a successful businessman and his wife adopted a little girl. They provided for her everything that money could buy; but the mother was aware that she needed spiritual direction, too; so she began to go with her to church and Sunday school. The father was much too busy making money to go with them, and he remained indifferent to the claim which Christ had on him.

Then the time came when he became seriously ill, and he believed that he would die. It was his adopted daughter who led him to Christ. His witness was, "She saved my life. She led me to Christ. She gave me hope."

Surely Naaman, with all his possessions, could not have imagined that the most precious thing he had was a little slave girl who gave him hope by pointing him to her God.

Lord, keep us from discouragement. By our trust in You may we never lose hope. Let our faith be confirmed by our experience, for You have never failed us. In Jesus' name, we pray. Amen.

A Lesson in Humility

Humble yourselves in the sight of the Lord, and he shall lift you up (James 4:10).

Scripture: **2 Kings 5:5-10**
Song: **"Sun of My Soul"**

Paul tells us not to think of ourselves more highly than we ought to think (see Romans 12:3)

A successful businessman said to his wife, "Do you have any idea how many great people there are in the world?" She replied, "No dear, but I suspect that there is at least one less than you think!"

A truck driver had driven his big rig under an overpass, and it was stuck tight. He got out and started blaming everyone but himself. He cursed the man who made the truck too high. He cursed that man who made the overpass too low. Then he cursed the mild-mannered man who had just stopped his car. "What do you want?" the trucker demanded. The little man replied, "I just wanted to say that you wouldn't have a problem if you would just let a little air out of your tires."

Naaman needed a lesson in humility. The king of Israel was not glad to see him. The prophet did not come out himself, but sent a servant. Naaman still didn't get it. Sometimes before God can deal with us, we need to learn that He resists the proud and gives grace to the humble.

Dear Lord, we have so much pride. Keep us humble. May we accept with humility the salvation that we cannot earn, but which comes to us freely through the sacrifice of Christ. Amen.

When All Else Fails

Thy word is a lamp unto my feet, and a light unto my path. I have sworn, and I will perform it, that I will keep thy righteous judgments (Psalm 119:105, 106).

Scripture: **2 Kings 5:11-14**
Song: **"Give Me Thy Heart"**

We have all had the experience. The Christmas toy arrives as a box full of parts with the instructions printed in six different languages. It all looks so simple. Who needs instructions? Three hours later it is assembled (sort of), but it doesn't work. It pays to read the directions.

We are trying out a new recipe, while at the same time watching television. We are distracted. The ingredients are mixed, and the batter goes into the oven. The results are far from satisfactory. In fact, the cake is inedible. We used a *tablespoon* of salt and baking soda instead of a *teaspoon*. It pays to focus on the directions.

Naaman was a great general. He understood how to give orders; but he came close to missing a miracle because he would not follow directions!

God's Word gives us a complete set of directions about how to live. Trying to get by without following them, or making up our own rules as we go along, just won't work. It pays to read God's directions and concentrate on them. He knows best.

Father in Heaven, *forgive us when we try to live by our own rules and ignore the clear teaching of Your Word. May we seek Your instruction daily. In Jesus' name, we pray. Amen.*

Taking God Home with You

God hath said, I will dwell in them, and walk in them; and I will be their God, and they shall be my people (2 Corinthians 6:16).

Scripture: **2 Kings 5:15-19**
Song: **"Abide with Me"**

When Naaman was healed, he was converted, but he made a strange request. He asked to take two mule-loads of earth back to Syria. This request was based on the belief in pagan lands that each country had its own gods. Naaman wanted to take some of the earth of Israel with him, so he would be sure that he was taking Israel's God with him.

During a ministry in Pennsylvania I called on a woman who was a member of a church in another state. She had lived in her present home for 23 years, but she refused to move her membership or become active in the local church. When I asked her to consider becoming active, she declined, saying that they would be moving back to North Carolina. "How do you know you are going back?" I inquired. "Oh, we will be going back all right," she said. "We have cemetery lots there." I concluded that she believed in keeping her God, her church membership, and her cemetery lot all in one place!

We can serve God wherever we are because He is with us wherever we are.

Lord, *we know that You are everywhere. We pray that wherever we go we may take You with us. Amen.*

Amazing Grace

For you have been born again, not of perishable seed, but of imperishable, through the living and enduring word of God (1 Peter 1:23, *New International Version*).

Scripture: **1 Peter 1:18-23**
Song: **"Amazing Grace"**

"John Newton, Clerk, once an infidel and libertine, a servant of slaves in Africa, was by the rich mercy of our Lord and Savior, Jesus Christ, preserved, restored, pardoned, and appointed to preach the faith he had once labored to destroy." Thus reads the epitaph of the writer of one of our most loved hymns, "Amazing Grace."

Newton's early life was one of sin, slave trading, and unbelief. Then in the midst of a storm, as he traveled from Africa to England with a shipload of slaves, he heard himself saying, "Lord, have mercy on us!" Why, he pondered, would he call on a God in whom he did not believe? This was the beginning of his journey to a faith that led him into a life of Christian service.

Peter tells us that silver and gold cannot redeem us from our empty way of life. Regardless of our past, may we, like John Newton, accept the amazing grace that sets us free.

Dear Father, *thank You for pardoning and restoring us through Your Son, Jesus Christ. It is hard to comprehend the depth of Your grace. In Jesus' name we pray. Amen.*

February 14-20. **Martha Melton** is a reading consultant in Iowa City, Iowa. She and her husband, Merle, have three sons, two daughters-in-law, and five grandchildren.

The Family of God

How great is the love the Father has lavished on us, that we should be called children of God! And that is what we are! The reason the world does not know us is that it did not know him (1 John 3:1, *New International Version*).

Scripture: **1 John 2:29–3:5**
Song: **"The Family of God"**

We sometimes hear people say, "He is his father's son," or "She is her mother's daughter"—meaning that the son or daughter looks and/or acts like the parent. Responsible parents have high expectations for their children but also bestow love, encouragement, understanding, and forgiveness. Youngsters may think their parents are too demanding at times, but the love and encouragement nurture them as they grow into responsible adults.

These same attributes are present in our relationship with the heavenly Father. We have been born into His family. We should be recognized as belonging to Him. His expectations are high, but the love He lavishes on us far exceeds that given by any earthly parent. The depth of His forgiveness is beyond our comprehension. Parents sustain their children and help them develop in their temporal pursuits, but God's nurturing is much greater as He guides us into Christian maturity. How great is His love that we should be called children of God!

Heavenly Father, *thank You for being our Father, for accepting us into Your family and guiding us in our Christian lives. Thank You for our earthly families, especially our Christian family. In Jesus name, amen.*

Overcoming the World

Who is it that overcomes the world? Only he who believes that Jesus is the Son of God (1 John 5:5, *New International Version*).

Scripture: 1 John 5:1-5
Song: "Faith Is the Victory!"

When a person is self-confident, we may say in jest, "She's out to conquer the world!" History affirms that some people and nations have had that as their goal. In the time of Christ, the Roman Empire ruled most of the world. In the early nineteenth century, Napoleon conquered much of Europe. Slightly over a hundred years later, Adolf Hitler gained control over most of Europe. These nations and individuals sought power.

What a different perspective John has on conquering the world. The world John speaks of is a world separated from God and in opposition to His will. How can we conquer this world? Our defense centers in Jesus Christ. He left Heaven to come to earth and experience the same trials as we. He completely understands our disappointments and frustrations. He gives us strength to face the discouragements and burdens of life. In spite of the world's mistreatment of Jesus, He was victorious—after the cross came the resurrection. We will share in that victory. We are not seeking personal power that conquers nations, but spiritual power that conquers death.

Father, give us the wisdom to realize that earthly power is transient and superficial. Help us to strive for the power that is centered in Jesus and overcomes the world. In Jesus' name, we pray. Amen.

Ye Must Be Born Again

Jesus answered, "I tell you the truth, no one can enter the kingdom of God unless he is born of water and the Spirit" (John 3:5, *New International Version*).

Scripture: **John 3:1-5**
Song: **"Ye Must Be Born Again"**

When my son described the ecstasy of seeing his daughter born, my mind had traveled back to *his* birth. The birth of a child is a momentous occasion. I remember vividly the birth of our sons. I remember as vividly their spiritual births, when their father baptized them into a new life in Christ.

In today's Scripture, Jesus told Nicodemus that no one can see the kingdom of God unless he is born again. Nicodemus was puzzled. How was it possible to be born a second time? Jesus clarified by saying that we must be born of the water and the spirit. We must be cleansed from our sins and then filled with the power of the Holy Spirit, who will guide us in this new spiritual life.

Physical birth produces a new life and brings joy to family and friends. Spiritual birth produces a new life and brings joy to the family of God. What a marvelous creator to have endowed us with the joys of physical and spiritual families!

Father, *Your plan for Your creation is truly amazing. We are so thankful for both our physical and our spiritual families. We are grateful for the Holy Spirit in our lives. Help us, Father, to work together to bring honor and glory to You and Your kingdom. In Jesus' name, we pray. Amen.*

The Mystery of Life

"How can this be?" Nicodemus asked (John 3:9, *New International Version*).

Scripture: **John 3:6-10**
Song: **"I Know Whom I Have Believed"**

"Ah, sweet mystery of life." This phrase from an old song could describe both physical and spiritual birth. How can a small mass of cells develop into a beautiful baby? While it is a common occurrence and we know the scientific explanation, it remains a wonderful mystery.

When Jesus spoke of the new birth, Nicodemus asked, "How can this be?" Again, the concept is shrouded in mystery. The *how* takes us out of the earthly realm and into the spiritual. Just as we cannot fathom the development of a baby in the womb, neither can we fathom how the spirit works within our lives to create a desire for change. Once the baby is fully developed, physical birth translates him or her into the world. When we become truly committed to Christ, baptism translates us into a new life. Jesus compared this birth of the spirit to the wind that blows. We hear its sound, but we cannot tell where it comes from or where it is going. As with physical birth, spiritual birth is a miraculous occurrence that happens many times every day. We see the effects, but the process is a mystery.

Dear heavenly Father, *thank You for the new birth. Even though we do not understand the mystery, we know the effects in our personal lives, and we are grateful. Help us to do Your will. In Jesus' name, we pray. Amen.*

God's Gift to the World

For God so loved the world that he gave his one and only Son, that whoever believes in him shall not perish but have eternal life (John 3:16, *New International Version*).

Scripture: **John 3:11-16**
Song: **"I Gave My Life for Thee"**

A fire raged through the home of a family where the mother and four children were in the house alone. The mother was able to get the three older children to safety. Then, against the orders of the firemen, she rushed back to save her baby. Both perished in the fire. This is a sad story, but exemplary of a mother's love and courage.

In a similar manner, the life of Jesus is one of love and courage. When Jesus told Nicodemus that the Son of Man would be lifted up, He was speaking of His own crucifixion. Moses lifted up the brazen serpent in the wilderness so that the Israelites might look upon it and live. Jesus was crucified so that, by faith, our salvation can be secured. Jesus was willing to suffer a humiliating death for our sins. His resurrection sealed the hope of eternal life for all who believe in Him.

The young mother gave her life because of her love for her children. Jesus gave His life because of His love for all mankind. What a glorious Savior!

Thank You, Father, for securing our salvation through faith in Your Son, Jesus Christ. Just as the Israelites looked upon the brazen serpent and lived, may we look to Jesus Christ, our Savior, and live. In Jesus' name, we pray. Amen.

Sacrificial Love

For God did not send his Son into the world to condemn the world, but to save the world through him (John 3:17, *New International Version*).

Scripture: **John 3:17-21**
Song: **"Wonderful Grace of Jesus"**

The most valued gifts in life cannot be purchased, but come from the hearts of caring individuals. The act of risking or giving one's life for another is the highest gift. The heroism following the terrorist attack on New York City on September 11, 2001, was incredible. Hundreds of people gave their lives to save others. Jesus said, "Greater love hath no man than this, that a man lay down his life for his friends" (John 15:13). In most cases in New York, the sacrifices were made for strangers.

Jesus is the epitome of sacrificial love. God sent His Son into the world to save the *whole world*—not the western world or any specific race. He paid the price for the salvation of every person who accepts Him, including those who have committed the vilest acts.

God loves us, and He loves our enemies. I remember visiting a cemetery in Germany where World War II soldiers were buried. I became acutely aware that the sorrow of those families was just as anguishing as that of American families. They were God's creations, too. Jesus died for all.

Our Father, we become narrow in our own culture and tend to forget that You love equally every person in every part of the world. Help us to become concerned about all people. In Jesus' name, we pray. Amen.

Christ Is All and in All

I press on toward the goal to win the prize for which God has called me heavenward in Christ Jesus. (Philippians 3:14, *New International Version*).

Scripture: **Colossians 3:11-17**
Song: **"I Would Be Like Jesus"**

It is hard to imagine a more comprehensive Bible passage than our text for today. Paul stretches words to their limits to describe the influence that Christ can bring to bear on humanity. Christ destroys national and racial barriers, inspiring a host of virtues that enhance the quality of life.

As followers of Jesus, we are encouraged to incorporate His way into our lives so that we become like Him. This noble aim is not achieved in a day or a year. The important thing is that we make progress in the quest, not becoming discouraged. Compassion, kindness, humility, gentleness, patience, forgiveness, and love are jewels of character that are not attained without effort. But, like sparkling gems, they have great intrinsic value—they're worth having.

We want to be like Jesus. Today's Scripture lists characteristics that tell us what He is like. As we devote each day to living *for* Him, we become more and more *like* Him.

Father in Heaven, we confess that we fall short of our high calling, but we thank You for the presence of the Holy Spirit in our lives whose guidance will lead us into greater Christ-likeness. Amen.

February 21-27. **Dr. Henry Webb,** a minister and retired college professor, and his wife, Emerald, serve Christ and His church in Johnson City, Tennessee.

Jesus Walked in Our Shoes

But [Jesus] emptied himself, taking the form of a servant, being born in the likeness of men (Philippians 2:7, *Revised Standard Version*).

Scripture: **John 4:1-6**
Song: **"What a Friend We Have in Jesus"**

Did the Son of God become tired? Was He ever hungry or thirsty? Was the Son of God subject to such human experiences?

John, who was with Jesus on this journey, notes that He was thirsty. Although He was God's Son, He was also human. As you or I would have become tired on a journey of this kind, so did the Son of God. When He became man, He claimed no exemption from the human experience. Jesus walked in our shoes. He knows what we face when we confront disappointments, sorrow, pain, and rejection. He even went through the forbidding experience of death—and a cruel and violent death, at that! When we go to Him in our distress, it is not to someone who doesn't understand. Jesus even knows what temptation is; He struggled with it, too. He was "tempted in every way, just as we are—yet was without sin" (Hebrews 4:15, *New International Version*). He walked in our shoes. He understands.

Dear Father in Heaven, *how we thank You that we have such a Savior as Jesus, Your Son, who became human and shared our experiences and problems. We confess our sins to Him who knows our frailties and weaknesses. Thank You for the grace of forgiveness. Amen.*

Jesus Speaks About Living Water

Let us therefore make every effort to do what leads to peace and to mutual edification (Romans 14:19, *New International Version*).

Scripture: John 4:7-12
Song: "It Is Well with My Soul"

A mother said to her little boy: "I don't want you to play with that child. They're not our kind." She was building a lasting barrier in the mind of her little boy.

Sometimes it is necessary to shield a child from undesirable influences. But too often we're only reinforcing prejudices in our own thinking and transferring them to our children. Thus prejudices pass from generation to generation.

There were many prejudices in Jesus' day. Prejudices obscure our image of the person who is victimized by prejudice. Honesty, kindness, charity, and other virtues are not the exclusive property of any one clan or race or national people. Jesus surprised the Samaritan woman because He spoke kindly to her, paying no attention to the barrier of prejudice held by Jews against Samaritans. Jesus saw in her a person of value who needed what He could offer. He treated her as a human being created in God's image.

Kindness, good will—and attempting to see people as Jesus did, through the Father's eyes—will help us overcome prejudices.

Heavenly Father, You have created every human in Your own image. Help us to treat every person with proper respect and kindness. Deliver us from hatred. We ask, in Jesus' name. Amen.

The Universal Human Quest

Whoever drinks the water I give him will never thirst. Indeed, the water I give him will become in him a spring of water welling up to eternal life (John 4:14, *New International Version*).

Scripture: **John 4:13-18**
Song: **"Dear Lord, and Father of Mankind"**

A sculpture in a modem art museum portrayed a figure that had scarcely discernable human features and a body shaped like a donut. Two young people came by, gazed at the statue, and one said to the other, "He looks just like me—all hollow inside."

This is a picture of the woman in Samaria, and of many people today. She was restless, frantically pursuing something of enduring value but never finding it. Five husbands and numerous other relationships left her empty as ever.

Then Jesus offered her living water. What could He have meant? We know that water not only quenches thirst but also is absolutely essential for life. What the woman needed was for her life to be rooted in God, guided by His divine truth, and facing the future with hope. Only then would life have purpose and meaning. Jesus' living water could quench her immediate thirst and give her the absolute essentials of life for her future.

None of us wishes to be "all hollow inside." When our needs are met by the living water Jesus offers, we become wells, overflowing with power to bless others.

Heavenly Father, for the presence of Jesus in our lives we are forever grateful. Help us be a wellspring of life to others. Amen.

He Is the Messiah

We did not follow cleverly invented stories when we told you about the power and coming of our Lord Jesus Christ, but we were eyewitnesses of his majesty (2 Peter 1:16, *New International Version*).

Scripture: **John 4:19-26**
Song: **"How Firm a Foundation"**

A Samaritan woman stood by a well conversing with Jesus. She did not know Him. She had neither witnessed the miracles He had performed nor heard His marvelous teaching. But from their conversation she concluded that Jesus was a prophet. When she alluded to a Messiah who would come, Jesus identified himself as that Messiah.

Generally Jesus let people see His mighty works and reach their own conclusions about who He was. But this woman's brief encounter provided her no such opportunity. So He openly identified himself.

How are we to know that Jesus is God's promised Redeemer? We don't see Him working miracles. Or do we? Is He not manifest in His disciples today? Is not the church, His body, revealing Him to the world? How do we explain the countless people whose lives have been touched and changed by Him? How does one account for all the help rendered in His name to the poor, the sick, and the troubled? Who else has power to transform life by giving meaning and hope? Only the living Christ, the same Messiah.

Dear heavenly Father, *we thank You for the gift of the Messiah and for His presence among us. Open our eyes that we may see Your miracles and the beauty of the plans You have for us. Amen.*

Life's Satisfactions

"My food," said Jesus, **"is to do the will of him who sent me and to finish his work"** (John 4:34, *New International Version*).

Scripture: **John 4:27-34**
Song: **"I Love Thy Kingdom, Lord"**

Some of the words of Jesus in today's text challenge our understanding. His disciples invited Him to take food. Food not only satisfies hunger; eating it is also a pleasure. Of course, Jesus needed food for His body, which was like ours and required nourishment. However, Jesus reminded His disciples that there were other pleasures, aside from eating, that bring satisfaction and give meaning to life.

Jesus found great satisfaction in doing "the will of him who sent me and to finish His work" (v. 34, *New International Version*). He had just concluded a most significant interview with the Samaritan woman, and He knew that this woman was at work leading many people out to hear Him. He knew many lives would be influenced toward God, and He rejoiced about it. Jesus found His satisfaction in advancing God's work.

Do we rejoice over victories for the kingdom of God? Do we find satisfaction in the growth of the church, in seeing lives changed, and in the increase of Christian influence in our community? This is "spiritual food" that nourishes our souls.

Father in Heaven, refocus our priorities so that we may place value on spiritual victories. Deliver us from our preoccupation with the things of this world. In Jesus' name, we pray. Amen.

An Instrument in God's Hands

Many of the Samaritans from that town believed in him because of the woman's testimony (John 4:39, *New International Version*).

Scripture: John 4:35-42
Song: "People Need the Lord"

Not everyone can preach. Nor does everyone possess the gift of persuasion. But everyone has enough influence to lead someone to a person who *can* preach and persuade. In today's text we find a woman who, despite her blemished past, led many from her town to meet a remarkable person, Jesus. Many believed, and Jesus spent two additional days in Samaria teaching and giving people hope (see v. 40).

Months and years later the Samaritan woman must have reflected on the difference in the lives of the people in her village—the difference that came about because they had met Jesus. She surely had a deep sense of satisfaction and joy for having had a part in their finding new meaning in life.

Have you ever known that joy? Can you think of a person who needs Jesus? If you aren't gifted with persuasive ability, you could put this person into the company of someone who could lead him/her to Jesus.

Our lives are flawed. But we can still be instruments in God's hands, pointing the way to redemption.

Heavenly Father, use me to lead someone to Jesus. Grant that the influence of my life might serve as a light to help someone who needs to find the way. Amen.

What Does God See?

The LORD looked down from heaven upon the children of men, to see if there were any that did understand, and seek God (Psalm 14:2).

Scripture: **Psalm 14:1-6**
Song: **"Standing in the Need of Prayer"**

When we watch the evening news, what do we see? We see only a tiny portion of what God sees. He sees acts of war, terrorists, snipers, students killing other students and teachers—all the things that terrify and horrify us. But He also sees rescuers, volunteers, students who stand up lovingly and act according to what they believe.

In other words, He sees it all. No good news or bad news is so obscure that it is hidden from Him. My concern—and I believe it is yours also—is what does God see when He looks at me?

I know He sees my imperfections. He sees someone who misses the mark of doing His will every day. But I know that He also sees someone who tries to understand His will and who earnestly seeks Him.

Is that what He sees when He looks at you?

It's me, O Lord, standing in the need of prayer. Help me never to overlook the sin in my own heart. And, when I feel helpless in the face of so much evil that surrounds me, remind me that there is at least one person I can do something about—and that's me, O Lord. Amen.

February 28. **Wanda M. Trawick,** a retired director of Christian education in Aston, Pennsylvania, is active in her church, with Meals on Wheels, and Rescue Mission.

My Prayer Notes

_____

_____

_____

_____

_____

_____

_____

_____

_____

_____

_____

_____

_____

_____

_____

_____

_____

_____

_____

_____

My Prayer Notes

My Prayer Notes

_____

_____

_____

_____

_____

_____

_____

_____

_____

_____

_____

_____

_____

_____

_____

_____

_____

_____

_____

_____

_____

DEVOTIONS

*T*he water that
I shall give him
shall be in him
a well of water
springing up
into everlasting
life.

—John 4:14

MARCH

Photo © Digital Stock

Getting Along Without God?

The wicked, through the pride of his countenance, will not seek after God: God is not in all his thoughts (Psalm 10:4).

Scripture: **Psalm 10:1-6**
Song: **"Must I Go, and Empty-Handed?"**

No room for God?

Children are beset with fears and jealousies at school, pressures to excel to please teachers and parents, and temptations to fit in with others, no matter what.

Teenagers find themselves trying to belong. Thoughts center on being accepted; their place among their peers becomes more important than their place among Christ's disciples. Activities fill the schedule. Temptations abound.

The adult's time and energy are taken up with job and family. Senior citizens grapple with fears of infirmity and dependence, of financial difficulties, and the loss of family and friends their own age.

Throughout life we can be preoccupied with concerns that leave no room in our thoughts or actions for God. "Me-ism"—so natural to the infant and toddler—sticks with us throughout life. When do we make room for God? Today is a good time to start.

Heavenly Father, *our minds race constantly. Give us once again a glimpse of Your Son on the cross, dying for us, and let that image create room in our hearts for You. In Jesus' name, amen.*

March 1-6. **Wanda M. Trawick,** a retired director of Christian education in Aston, Pennsylvania, is active in her church, with Meals on Wheels, and Rescue Mission.

Glass Houses and Stone-throwing

He that is without sin among you, let him first cast a stone at her (John 8:7).

Scripture: **John 8:1-9**
Song: **"Christ Receiveth Sinful Men"**

A sin is a sin is a sin; and while your sin might be different from my sin, we are both guilty of sin. We all are. So, since we are all sinners, we all live in glass houses. If we start throwing stones at other sinners, we just might get stones thrown back at us, shattering those transparent walls through which others see us.

We sometimes make snap judgments about people and make careless remarks. My favorite one used to be, "You call yourself a Christian and then do or say something like that?" I would walk away smugly, having shamed another for some improper behavior. Then later I would find myself thinking, saying, or doing the very thing I had criticized—perhaps just a little more subtly. I was more clever at "hiding" my sins.

God, of course, is not impressed with my subtlety and cleverness. He frequently snatches me up by the nape of the neck like a wayward puppy and sticks my face in a verse like today's.

Why is it so easy for us to see the splinter in another's eye and so hard to discover the log in our own?

Heavenly Father, *deliver us from the pitfall of condemning others, knowing that Jesus has taken our own condemnation from us. In Jesus' name, amen.*

Unashamed

I am not ashamed of the gospel, because it is the power of God for the salvation of everyone who believes (Romans 1:16, *New International Version*).

Scripture: **Romans 1:16-20**
Song: **"Nothing but the Blood"**

Why should we not be ashamed of the gospel? After all, movies and television often make Christians the butt of their jokes, portraying them as unintelligent or fanatical. Writers of secular fiction do the same thing, as do many university professors. It seems to be politically incorrect to criticize or ridicule the beliefs of other religions, but Christians remain easy targets.

In the face of this ill treatment, are we becoming embarrassed to acknowledge our faith in Christ publicly? Jesus' last statement to His disciples was that we would be His witnesses all the way from our hometowns to the ends of the earth (see Acts 1:8). We are not commanded to represent Jesus in a judgmental or argumentative way. But we can be unashamed witnesses of what Christ has done in our lives. We need not apologize for our beliefs about God and the Bible and the church.

Let's pray daily for the gift of discernment in our witnessing efforts—so that we will be loving, but unapologetic.

Heavenly Father, *I am often ashamed of my own failure to be consistent in obeying Your commands, but never let me be ashamed of Your Son and the message of the gospel. Help me to share my faith in an unashamed but loving manner. In Jesus' name, amen.*

You, Me, Us

What shall we conclude then? Are we any better? Not at all!
(Romans 3:9, *New International Version*).

Scripture: **Romans 3:9-14**
Song: **"Breathe on Me, Breath of God"**

Some time ago, the church to which I belonged periodically assisted a nearby rescue mission. A team from the church helped with the evening meal and conducted a brief worship service.

We were pleased that our church was engaged in a hands-on mission project. Eventually, though, one of the team members came to our preacher. He expressed concern over the approach our rather gifted speaker was taking in his work with the congregation at the mission.

Ben was young and idealistic and a bit reticent about appearing to criticize the lay preacher, but he said, "I think he's a good speaker, but it bothers me that he refers to the folks there as "you people"—as though they are different from us. It embarrasses me. They may think *we* think we are better than they are."

Ben was right. It should have made him—and the rest of us—feel uncomfortable. There is no such thing as *you* when talking about sin and sinners. Only one word is appropriate, and that is *we.*

Heavenly Father, never let me forget when ministering to those whose lives have been willfully or carelessly wasted, that there, but for Your grace, go I. Help me have the same understanding of, and compassion for, unforgiven sinners as You do. In Jesus' name, amen.

"I Don't Smoke, and I Don't Chew"

Therefore no one will be declared righteous in his sight by observing the law; rather, through the law we become conscious of sin (Romans 3:20, *New International Version*).

Scripture: **Romans 3:15-20**
Song: **"Just As I Am"**

"I don't smoke and I don't chew and I don't go with boys who do." That ditty and an enthralling tract entitled *30 Reasons Why a Christian Won't Dance* were popular among young Christians during my adolescence. When we reached dating age back in the 1940s and 1950s, rules were in abundance, and some of us tried pretty hard to adhere to them.

There is something comforting in knowing we are "keeping the law" and therefore good citizens; but I wonder if we all realized that avoiding certain pastimes was not going to justify us in the sight of God. I'm sure that, at least in the back of our minds, we hoped for some extra credit for doing so.

There is no doubt that we are much better off living responsibly and striving to please God. But we are not justified or made righteous by obeying the rules of men or the law of God. How grateful I am for God's gift to me in Christ Jesus.

Dear God, thank You for Your law, designed to guide me through life. More than that, thank You for giving yourself to me through Christ, who fulfilled that law for me. In Jesus' name, amen.

What to Do About Sin

If we confess our sins, he is faithful and just and will forgive us our sins and purify us from all unrighteousness (1 John 1:9, *New International Version*).

Scripture: **1 John 1:5-10**
Song: **"Jesus, I Come"**

Most of us fall short of God's will every day—in what we do or fail to do. So what do we do about it?

Some wring their hands in despair while others, at the opposite extreme, easily excuse themselves with, "I'm only human; everybody does it; I'm as good as most people."

The first attitude frustrates the grace of God, and the second makes light of the sin that sent Jesus to the cross. Centuries ago a monk named Brother Lawrence talked about keeping "short accounts" with God. His secret was in confessing all of his day's sins at night, claiming God's forgiveness, and starting the next day fresh. While we ought not to think we fall out of God's forgiveness with each sin until we confess it and find forgiveness anew, Brother Lawrence made good application of 1 John 1:9.

The answer to the sin problem lies in honestly acknowledging our sins of commission and omission, of accepting God's forgiveness, and attempting to turn from our sins. We need not be defeated by them. With God's forgiveness, we have a fresh start every day.

Heavenly Father, *don't let me frustrate Your grace by wallowing in guilt over past sins. Let me live in the fullness of Your grace, rejoicing in the freedom that is in Christ Jesus. In Jesus' name, amen.*

Integrity Check

Judge me, O Lord, according to my righteousness, according to my integrity, O Most High (Psalm 7:8, *New International Version*).

Scripture: **Psalm 7:6-17**
Song: **"I Will Call Upon the Lord"**

David made a request the average believer might hesitate to offer in the Almighty's courtroom: "Judge me according to my integrity." The word *integrity* comes from the same Latin root as *integer,* meaning "a whole number." To have integrity means to be whole.

David was not perfect, but in the struggle he faced at the writing of this psalm—when wicked men had falsely targeted him—he could stand completely honest before God and say, "Help me, Lord. Look in my heart and see that I'm innocent!" His confidence was not in his innocence alone, but in His righteous judge.

God doesn't demand perfection. If we approach His judgment seat with no false front, we can do so with confidence, knowing that Jesus, who lived in human form like us, sympathizes with our weaknesses (see Hebrews 4:15, 16). Whether falsely accused or guilty as sin, search your heart regularly and deeply. Then approach the bench, and make your plea.

Fair and Righteous Father, *judge me according to my integrity. Stand with me as my defender in court. Complete me. In Jesus' name, amen.*

March 7-13. **Jenna Lusby** is a freelance writer, artist, and music teacher. Her most rewarding job has been raising her two daughters, Arian and Andrea.

A Judge Who Can't Be Bought

God himself is judge. . . . Sacrifice thank offerings to God, fulfill your vows to the Most High (Psalm 50:6, 14, *New International Version*).

Scripture: **Psalm 50:1-15**
Song: **"We Bring the Sacrifice of Praise"**

On a wooded hill above Shukugawa, Japan, I saw a Shinto shrine, a stone memorial to dead ancestors who are now thought to be *kami:* gods. On the family gravestone was a snack of food and drink offered to appease the spirit of a departed family member. I couldn't help thinking, "How small a god, who can be appeased with rain-soaked food and watery tea!" In the Land of the Rising Sun—super-advanced in technology and education—ancient beliefs in the power of spirits still hold an entire culture enslaved in obligation and superstition.

Only God is God, and He doesn't need to be fed (see vv. 9, 13.) The animals are His, and the hills on which they graze are His. He doesn't require gifts of obligation and fear. He can't be bought with a meal or with animal sacrifices, which were mere symbols of the deadly price of sin. He paid our debts with His own sacrifice, His Son. He is not appeased by gifts, but He is pleased by our sacrifice of praise and good works.

Dear God, how great You are! How great is Your mercy—from the rising of the sun to the place where it sets. I am so grateful that You alone are my judge. Let my sacrifices to You spring from gratitude and love, not from fear or obligation. In Jesus' name, amen.

God Disdains Moral Superiority

At whatever point you judge the other, you are condemning yourself, because you who pass judgment do the same things (Romans 2:1, *New International Version*).

Scripture: **Romans 2:1-5**
Song: **"They'll Know We Are Christians by Our Love"**

People still worship idols. I was astonished when a Japanese college student would not kill a spider because it could have been the spirit of an ancestor. It amazes me that amulets are sold door-to-door in Japan to ward off evil spirits in the toilet. How can intelligent people believe such things? But what if I had no knowledge of God—absolutely none? What would I believe about the spirit world? Are my beliefs—even as an educated Christian—without quirks?

Christians get truth from every angle: Bibles, Christian radio, sermons, Sunday school, Christian books, Bible clubs. Those of us blessed with the knowledge of God have a great responsibility. To whom much is given much will be required. We can't afford to be snobs.

God is fair, and so must we be. Granted, the Bible does instruct believers to judge moral matters and maintain godly standards in the church (see 1 Corinthians 5, 6). But we must not be so ready to smash others' idols until we have smashed our own.

Righteous Lord, *don't let our evaluation of others be tainted by our own self-righteousness. May we not hoard the riches of Your kindness or pass judgment on those who have not heard. In Jesus' name, amen.*

Judge or Genie?

Will not the Judge of all the earth do right? (Genesis 18:25, *New International Version*).

Scripture: **Romans 2:6-11**
Song: **"He Is Exalted"**

Chuck had gone to church as a child but drifted away as an adult. He broke ties with church altogether when, after his first wife left him, Chuck's preacher refused to officiate at his second wedding.

Chuck was, by most standards, a decent man. But in faith matters he had taken a kind of "term insurance" attitude: "I think God'll be there when you need him." Hmm—You live, you work, you die, and somewhere in there, if you need God, you can call Him up like a genie? He would not have expressed it quite that way, but that was Chuck's attitude.

Chuck was only partly right. God does want to be there for us, but He requires more than a passing nod at His existence. We are accountable to our creator. He will judge us all. This is a very good thing, for without God's sifting good from evil, life would have no lasting consequences: evil would have no retribution, good no eternal benefit. In a word, life would be meaningless.

But life is not meaningless. What we do has an impact on our world for eternity. At the end of his life, Chuck learned that and turned back to the Lord.

Dear God, *we thank You that what we do has consequences, that You esteem us enough to give us work with eternal value. May we never forget that You are judge over everything. In Jesus' name, amen.*

Hearer or Doer?

Do not merely listen to the word, and so deceive yourselves. Do what it says (James 1:22, *New International Version*).

Scripture: **Romans 2:12-16**
Song: **"'Are Ye Able,' Said the Master"**

The Jews were first to receive blessings, first to witness miracles, first to hear God's voice of revelation. And with knowledge and blessing come duty. Paul told the Jews they would receive both reward and punishment before the unbelieving Gentiles would.

To receive God's blessings and do nothing with them is evil. "Anyone . . . who knows the good he ought to do and doesn't do it, sins"(James 4:17, *New International Version*).

Paul suggests that it would be unfair if the Jews of his time (or the Christians of ours) were given the same treatment as unbelievers who have never heard. Pagans don't know God, but so many long for Him! In their longing, they grab for inferior substitutes—desperate attempts to connect to the spiritual.

When we have heard the good news, tasted the blessings of the Holy Spirit, fallen in love with the person of Jesus Christ, the immediate next step is to *do*. Something. Anything. Whatever you see to do in the name of Jesus, do it. Do it today.

Dear Father, today we are reminded of how blessed we are. We have access to Your very words, to forgiveness through Your own Son, and to the indwelling and empowering presence of Your Holy Spirit. Help us to get real with our faith today. In Jesus' name, amen.

Double Standard

God's name is blasphemed among the Gentiles because of you (Romans 2:24, *New International Version*).

Scripture: **Romans 2:17-24**
Song: **"I Have Decided"**

No one likes to be a victim of double standards. Have you noticed how the CEOs who bring down billion-dollar companies get to keep their yachts and penthouses while hundreds of employees go home penniless?

Life's not fair. But God is. He doesn't hold to a double standard. Paul went so far as to call any suggestion that He does "blasphemy"! Some of the Jews in Rome claimed the inherited blessings of the law, but failed to follow it. The New Testament restated what the Old Testament had said: It's faithfulness—not heritage—that identifies one with the heavenly Father. Read the passage and substitute the word *Jew* with *Christian*, and *Bible* with *law*. The thought is the same.

If the Bible says one thing and we do another. . . .

If, like the Jews of the Old Covenant, God's New Covenant people prefer their standards to His. . . .

Paul's message still rings true for us across the centuries: One can't claim God's inheritance and reject His holy Word.

Dear God, *forgive us if we have blasphemed Your name by our actions. We know You despise the double standard. We claim the Bible as our guide for living. May we hide it in our hearts and follow Your precepts. In the name of Jesus, the living Word, we pray. Amen.*

March 13

Are You a Jew for Jesus?

A man is a Jew if he is one inwardly (Romans 2:29, *New International Version*).

Scripture: **Romans 2:25-29**
Song: **"The Family of God"**

Who are the Jews?

One might be a Jew by heritage and be a citizen of France or Russia. An ethnic Jew could be Christian or Buddhist or Hindu in belief. Israelis are so called because they are citizens of the nation of Israel, but that doesn't mean they embrace the ancient faith of Abraham.

Religious Jews, on the other hand, follow Judaism, whatever their citizenship or race—red or yellow, black or white. It's quite confusing.

Paul made it clear. The Jews in his time were proud of their unique standing in God's plan: they claimed father Abraham, the covenant, King David, the promised land. Even in their bodies the men wore a sign of God's ownership: circumcision.

According to the Scripture, a person is a "Jew" if he chooses the God who has chosen Him. "Jewishness" is no longer tied to nationality or geography. Under the New Covenant it identifies people who belong to God. The Bible says if you are for Jesus, then you are a "Jew."

Shalom!

Yahweh, how blessed I am to have the spiritual heritage of the Jews, an exodus from the slavery of sin, citizenship in the New Jerusalem, and the lordship of an eternal king, Jesus! In His holy name, amen.

God Really Loves People

He saved us, not because of righteous things we had done, but because of his mercy. He saved us through the washing of rebirth and renewal by the Holy Spirit (Titus 3:5, *New International Version*).

Scripture: **Titus 3:1-7**
Song: **"What a Friend We Have in Jesus"**

I went to the auction determined to buy one piece of furniture, an old cedar chest. Almost 70 years old and badly in need of repair, the chest had special meaning for me—it was the engagement gift that my mother had received from my dad before they were married. She used to hide my gifts in it so I wouldn't find them before Christmas. Now scarred and dirty, it was to go under the auctioneer's gavel.

When the bidding was completed, the old chest was mine. Other people bidding for it may have wondered about my determination and joy. But they didn't know that it was purchased because of my love, not for the chest, but for the original owners, my parents.

God really loves people. He picks them up, dirty and scarred by sin, and washes them clean by the blood of His Son. Did He pay too much? He doesn't think so.

Dear Father, *we certainly are not worthy of Your great love for us. We accomplish nothing to merit the price paid for our salvation. Thanks for picking us up and cleaning up our lives. Thank You for Jesus! In His name, amen.*

March 14-20. **Dr. David Grubbs** has served as a medical missionary in Zimbabwe and as a Bible college president. He and his wife Eva live in Cincinnati, Ohio.

Glory by Association

Now if the ministry that brought death, which was engraved in letters on stone, came with glory, so that the Israelites could not look steadily at the face of Moses because of its glory, fading though it was, will not the ministry of the Spirit be even more glorious? (2 Corinthians 3:7, 8, *New International Version*).

Scripture: **2 Corinthians 3:4-11**
Song: **"Glorious Things of Thee Are Spoken"**

I opened the letter and spread it before me. The writer was a recently widowed woman whose husband had been a church minister for many years.

She wrote, "Dear President Grubbs, thank you for giving my husband such a wonderful education to prepare him for ministry. He was a good and caring minister and we had a wonderful life of ministry together."

I didn't even know who they were. But since I was president of Cincinnati Bible College and Seminary, she was thanking me for something that happened even before I was enrolled as a student at CBC&S. Letters like that are wonderful. One can receive glory by association, which is better than guilt by association.

As Christians, our faces should outshine the face of Moses. When we serve Jesus, we shine with the glory that belongs to Him. We must let that glory be seen, as He transforms us to become more like Him each day.

Dear God, *thank You for allowing us to share in the glory that belongs to Jesus and to be associated with Him in the wonderful work of salvation. We enjoy what we do not deserve. In His glorious name we pray. Amen.*

Not Just Wishful Thinking

Against all hope, Abraham in hope believed and so became the father of many nations, just as it had been said to him, "So shall your offspring be" (Romans 4:18, *New International Version*).

Scripture: **Romans 4:13-25**
Song: **"All Things Are Possible"**

The night sky in Africa is breathtaking in its beauty. No smog, dust, or light pollution obscures one's view of the heavens. On a moonless night the millions of stars stretch out like tinfoil against the blackness of space. It is exciting to think that it is the same sky that David saw when he wrote "The heavens declare the glory of God; the skies proclaim the work of his hands" (Psalm 19:1, *New International Version*).

Abraham looked at night into the vastness of the millions of stars and heard God say, "Your children will be in number like the stars in the night sky" (see Genesis 22:17). Abraham believed what God said. He was childless and was about 80 years old, but he believed what God said. He had hope.

In the Bible, hope is not wishful thinking. Hope is waiting for God to do what He will certainly accomplish. Hope is believing so strongly that we look for a future that has already been written. In a world that has no hope, we have hope because we have Jesus.

Blessed Father, *thank You that the best is yet to come. We pray that we will be people of hope who will, as Psalm 27:14 reminds us, be strong, take heart, and wait for You. In Jesus' name, amen.*

No Longer Enemies

Therefore, since we have been justified through faith, we have peace with God through our Lord Jesus Christ (Romans 5: 1, *New International Version*).

Scripture: **Romans 5:1-5**
Song: **"Jesus Is All the World to Me"**

Two young men met on the campus of Zimbabwe Christian College in Africa. Both were new students. One was an African and the other a white man. As they exchanged names, the African said, "I seem to know you. Haven't we met before?"

After some discussion, they discovered that they had met once during the war for independence. It was on a rural dusty road where the white student, then a soldier at a roadblock, had held a gun pointed at the African young person. Then they were enemies. But finally peace came.

Peace is not just a good feeling. It is the end of hostilities, a time when enemies learn how to be friends. These two students were now friends, real friends. They were brothers in Christ, both preparing to be preachers of the Word.

That is what Jesus did for us. He ended our hostility against God. He made it possible for us to be friendly to God's call. Faith does that. It stops our war against God.

Father, forgive us for fighting against You, and for treating You like an enemy. Thank You for the peace that came through the cross of Christ. We want to be Your friend and to serve You with love and devotion. Thank You for giving us peace. In Jesus' name, amen.

Always on Time

You see, at just the right time, when we were still powerless, Christ died for the ungodly (Romans 5:6, *New International Version*).

Scripture: **Romans 5:6-11**
Song: **"Anywhere with Jesus"**

When the storm began to blow, the mother bird quickly returned to the nest. Wings outstretched, she carefully sheltered her nestlings. Through torrents of rain, howling winds, wildly thrashing tree limbs, and fierce bolts of lightning, she remained anchored over her young until the storm passed.

Jesus said, "How often I have longed to gather your children together, as a hen gathers her chicks under her wings, but you were not willing" (Matthew 23:37, *New International Version*). That image runs through our Scripture lesson today—Jesus, bent over us in our helpless state, protecting us with His very life. We were utterly and hopelessly unable to save ourselves, but at just the right time Jesus came to shield us with His own body and to receive the blows for us.

God demonstrates His love for us through the death of His own Son. It is beyond imagination. A person may be willing to suffer for a good man, but who would suffer and die for murderers and thieves? Only Jesus!

Father, so many times You have come to our rescue. When there was no way out, You provided a way. Lord, we thank You for a gift beyond measure—Your only Son, Jesus. You are merciful, and Your grace is beyond description. Thank You. In Jesus our Lord we pray. Amen.

Eternity in One Act

But the gift is not like the trespass. For if the many died by the trespass of the one man, how much more did God's grace and the gift that came by the grace of the one man, Jesus Christ, overflow to the many! (Romans 5:15, *New International Version*).

Scripture: **Romans 5:12-17**
Song: **"If That Isn't Love"**

We were all punished. During recess, someone had pushed another student into the neighbor's hedge and badly broke the limbs off at the ground. When the matter was investigated, no one would admit to knowing who the culprits were. So the whole class was made to stay after school.

"If the persons who broke the hedge will confess, I'll let everyone else go home," the teacher said. But no one spoke up, so no one went home. We all suffered because of the behavior of one person.

An ordinary man named Adam sinned, and all people were sentenced to death. Since that time many more people have sinned. Then a unique man, Jesus, stepped forward and said, "Let the guilt fall on me." Through that superior act, God's grace poured down to provide cleansing for all people of all time. Every person who accepts His offer may "go home."

Father of mercy, we give thanks for the grace that came through the one great act of Jesus. Thank You that we do not live fearing death, but anticipating resurrection and joy with You. May it be a gift too precious for us to keep silent. In Jesus we pray. Amen.

Getting the Big Picture

The law was added so that the trespass might increase. But where sin increased, grace increased all the more (Romans 5:20, *New International Version*).

Scripture: **Romans 5:18-21**
Song: **"Open My Eyes, That I May See"**

She was over 70 years old when she decided to go on a short-term mission trip to Africa. Although only a nominal church member, she was a dedicated member of the profession of nursing. She had never offered a public prayer or taught a Bible class. Perhaps it was the mission hospital that called her. Perhaps in some quiet way God spoke to her. Whatever the motivation, she went.

The change was dramatic. On her returning home, she became an army of one and stirred up the whole community, challenging unbelievers and Christians alike to become involved. She was faithful in her service and vocal in her concern about the need to be involved in the things of Christ. Now she saw the big picture and understood what it was all about.

When God gave the commandments, people discovered the horrors of sin in a new way. "Sin increased." But, when Jesus came and died because of sin, our understanding of God's grace increased as well. At last, we got the big picture.

Father, Your grace is so amazing that we confess we still cannot comprehend what You have done, nor do we fully appreciate it. You are amazing, and so is Your grace. Thank You for Jesus, in whose name we pray. Amen.

Change Awaits

Therefore we are buried with him by baptism into death: that like as Christ was raised up from the dead by the glory of the Father, even so we also should walk in newness of life (Romans 6:4).

Scripture: **Romans 6:1-5**
Song: **"He Touched Me"**

Every time Paul says "therefore," we can anticipate change from what is to what will be. Here he likens this change to Jesus' death and resurrection. As Christ was buried and three days later walked out of that tomb, our faith in the living Christ brings newness of life.

God raised Jesus from the dead to transfigure and transform. Once Christ touches us, we are not the same. Nature forms us, sin deforms us, and Jesus transforms us.

A church youth group built a float for a city parade. The float depicted the crucifixion of Christ. Instead of the typical "old rugged cross," they had a beautiful golden cross with lovely flowers around it. Their preacher said it was not like the actual cross of Jesus, and one of the young people replied, "Didn't you tell us nothing Jesus touches stays the same?"

He's right. Habits, attitudes, purposes, plans, life itself, are all transformed when the risen Lord comes to us.

Dear God, I don't want you to change my circumstances. I want you to change me. I know You love me too much to leave me the way I am. Turn me around and put me on a new path. In Jesus' name, amen.

March 21-27. **Dr. Phillip H. Barnhart,** a minister for 45 years, was the founding pastor of Chapel on the Hill in Lake Geneva, WI. He is the father of 4, grandfather of 8.

Grace Happens

For sin shall not be your master, because you are not under law, but under grace (Romans 6:14, *New International Version*).

Scripture: Romans 6:6-14)
Song: "Sinner Saved by Grace"

The condition of grace unveiled in the risen Jesus exists for us. Through faith in Christ, we live in a state of grace.

We do not earn this grace. It is what we don't deserve but get anyway. Law, which came on a mountain, demands the work of personal effort, but grace, which came in a garden, invites the embrace of personal acceptance.

Law is given, not to save us, but to drive us to God's grace. When Moses descended Sinai, he must have been thinking, "How are we going to do this?" Paul, in this letter to the Roman church, points out the superiority of grace over law in dealing with sin. Law sends us off to a lifetime of keeping books with God. Grace wipes the ledger clean.

As a boy, I had a basketball goal in the alley behind our house. One day, my friends and I got in a squabble. I grabbed my ball and ordered them out of my alley with a tirade of angry words. Going up the back walk, I realized Mom had seen it all. "Boy, am I going to get it," I muttered to myself. Instead, Mom said, "It's time for supper, Phillip. I made your favorite."

That's grace!

Dear God, *my sin is outdone by Your grace. The mistakes of my night are crowned with the love of Your glorious morning. Make my heart a receptacle for Your goodness and mercy. In Jesus' name, amen.*

Righteousness Calls

Being then made free from sin, ye became the servants of righteousness (Romans 6:18).

Scripture: **Romans 6:15-23**
Song: **"More Love to Thee"**

Writing to the Romans, Paul promises renewal, recommends grace, and reveals the goal of the life born of grace. We are set free from sin's incarceration to be slaves of righteousness. Let not our appreciation of God's grace dim our desire for righteous character and loving service. We are not called to sit forever at the table but to get up and clear the table for others. We are saved to serve.

The most radical teaching of Jesus was His reversal of the contemporary take on greatness. He found greatness embodied in servanthood. He got up from the table, took a towel, and washed His disciples' feet. Dietrich Bonhoeffer described Jesus as "the man for others."

A missionary spotted a woodcutter in a forest and saw an opportunity to witness for Christ. All day, as the man chopped wood, the missionary shared the story of Jesus. At the end of the day, he asked the woodcutter, "Are you ready to accept Christ?"

The woodcutter replied, "I don't know. All day long you spoke of this Jesus who helps us with our burdens, yet you never helped me with mine."

Dear God, *forgive me when I want to serve You only in an advisory capacity. May I not spend so much time with loaf and cup that I neglect basin and towel. May I give to others and not count the cost to me. In Jesus' name, amen.*

Jesus Rises

As the women were terrified and bowed their faces to the ground, the men said to them, "Why do you seek the living One among the dead? He is not here, but He has risen" (Luke 24:5, 6, *New American Standard Bible*).

Scripture: **Luke 24:1-9**
Song: **"Sing Hallelujah to the Lord"**

The truth of the resurrection of Jesus Christ rises up out of history's pages more formidably than any mountain rises up out of the plain. Historical criticism assaults but does not dislodge it. Demythologizers take their swing but to no avail. Cultural theories seek its demise, but it lives on. The truth of the resurrection of Jesus Christ is an anvil that has worn out many hammers.

A Sunday school teacher auditioned seven-year-olds for an Easter performance, and one boy insisted he play the part of the rock. "Don't you want a speaking part?" questioned the teacher. He didn't, and settled for nothing else. After the presentation, someone asked why he wanted to be the rock. He proudly replied, "Oh, it felt so good to let Him out of the tomb."

God let Jesus out of the tomb. The resurrection announcement in this Scripture is one word—*agertha*—"he has been raised." The passive voice indicates this was the action of God. We have a God who knew His way out of the grave. God buried His undertakers. He always does.

Dear God, *when I am consigned to the shadows of a cross, illuminate my path with resurrection light and help me live in its glow. In Jesus' name, amen.*

Death Loses

At that time Peter and the other disciple did not know that the Scriptures said Jesus would rise to life (John 20:9, *Contemporary English Version*).

Scripture: **John 20:1-10**
Song: **"Christ Arose!"**

Go with me to that place the locals call "the skull," and let us take roll of those present. Jesus is there, of course, as well as His two cross-buttressed companions. The mother of Jesus is there and His aunt and Mary Magdalene. Young John is there. But wait—two others are there also. Death is there. Grave is there.

Death wants to know something from Grave. "I can kill Him, but can you hold Him?"

"Oh, yes," Grave responds confidently, "I can hold Him. I always hold them. I haven't lost one yet."

Death wants to believe Grave, but he's not convinced. Later he returns to Grave and asks, "Is He still in there?"

Grave responds, "None has ever escaped me."

Later in the day it seems Death cannot rest and goes once more to Grave. "He hasn't gotten out, has He?"

"No," Grave shouts, disgusted with Death's doubt.

That is Friday and that is Saturday. But on Sunday Grave is frantic. Running up to Death, he asks breathlessly, "Do you have Him? He got away from me!"

Dear God, impress upon me the transitional nature of death. Help me trust the promise that one day I will cross the threshold of human death into the storehouse of eternal life. In Jesus' name, amen.

Presence Comes

Jesus said to her, "Mary." She turned toward him and cried out in Aramaic, "Rabboni!" (which means Teacher) (John 20:16, *New International Version*).

Scripture: John 20:11-18
Song: "In the Garden"

Mary of Magdala liked having Jesus around. During the Galilean missions He probably was never far from her gaze. Sometimes, during the winter months, she sat with Him around a warm campfire. And, of course, there was the time He placed His hands on her head and relegated her demons to the past. Mary liked having Jesus around, but now He is gone forever. At least that is what she thinks as she plods toward a limestone sepulchre carved in a hill around the corner from where Jesus was murdered.

Minutes later, Jesus counters her gloom with His presence. He'd said a shepherd knows his sheep intimately, and now He proves that He does. He calls her by name. He is near once again.

We are never farther from the presence of Jesus than our faith in Him. A Sunday school class was studying Bible characters and the teacher asked the kids which character they'd like to be. A little girl said she'd liked to be "Lo." The teacher asked her where that person was mentioned in the Bible, and the girl said, "Lo, I am with you always."

He is, you know. Always.

Dear God, *through the Holy Spirit draw close to me now in the risen Lord Jesus Christ. Keep me company this day and always. In Jesus' name, amen.*

Peace Abides

That evening, on the first day of the week, the disciples were meeting behind locked doors because they were afraid of the Jewish leaders. Suddenly, Jesus was standing there among them! "Peace be with you," he said (John 20:19, *New Living Translation*).

Scripture: **John 20:19-23**
Song: **"I've Got Peace Like a River"**

When Herbert Hoover was asked how he coped with his apparently failed administration, he replied with what he described, in good Quaker fashion, as "peace at the center." The presence of Jesus brings us that kind of peace. The company He keeps with us creates an atmosphere wherein we breathe peace.

Two artists painted pictures expressing peace. One painted a calm and tranquil mountain lake. The other painted a violent waterfall crashing down jagged rock. But the second artist added a fragile birch tree in whose branches was a bird nest and in that nest, a bird. No fear possessed the bird because she knew there were wings with which to flee the danger.

Christ in our hearts gives wings to take us beyond any circumstance. No matter what threatens, God can always "peace things together." Without this presence, we weep. With it, we sleep.

Thank You, Father, for being a whatever God. No matter what happens to me, You are there. I praise You for hanging around my difficulties and loving me through them. In Jesus' name, amen.

The Information Age

I am speaking to men who know the law (Romans 7:1, *New International Version*).

Scripture: **Romans 7:1-6**
Song: **"My Redeemer Lives"**

Computers can bring us millions of facts quickly. But I'll tell you a secret: I would rather read a book than use a computer. I recently purchased a book published in 1846—a collection of writings from the early years of the Christian church, roughly the first century and a half after Christ.

Although the writings are not part of the Bible, they tell us much about the early church. In the preface the arch-bishop of the Church of England wrote: "Those writers lived so near to apostolic times, that it cannot be doubted but that they do indeed represent to us the doctrine, government, and discipline of the church, as they received it from the apostles."

The apostle Paul wrote his letter to the Romans to educated men of the day. They were religious; they had read the Old Testament law. But now new information had come: the gospel of Christ—salvation by faith. New ideas. Would they learn? Will you?

Lord, *help us appreciate the truths that have been so carefully preserved by godly believers. In Jesus' name, amen.*

March 28-31. **Beverley Bittner** is retired from a career in publishing and is now working on a series of historical/inspirational novels. She lives in Corry, Pennsylvania.

The Wages of Sin

I would not have known what sin was except through the law (Romans 7:7, *New International Version*).

Scripture: Romans 7:7-13
Song: "The Solid Rock"

My doctor has advised me to avoid certain foods. Now, whenever I see those foods, a desire is triggered in me to eat all I want regardless of what it might do to my health. Sin is like that. God's law, including the Ten Commandments, tells us certain things we are not to do. Perhaps if we hadn't heard the commandments, we might not know that it is wrong to covet, or to lie, or to disrespect our parents. But we *do* know. God gave us the law. Still, desires are triggered within us to sin regardless of the consequences.

Can we earn eternal life by obeying the law? The apostle Paul said, "No!" God does not pay wages. Sin pays wages. "The wages of sin is death" (Romans 6:23). Eternal life is a gift of God through Jesus Christ our Lord.

Jesus said, "My sheep hear my voice . . . and I give unto them eternal life; and they shall never perish" (John 10:27, 28). Jesus will give us "life and peace" (Romans 8:6). What the law could not do, Jesus did on the cross. He made eternal life with God possible, not to be earned as wages, but freely offered to all.

Lord, many feel burdened by past and present sins. Help us know freedom from sin. We were purchased at a great price. Thank You for the blood of Jesus, freely given on the cross. In Jesus' name, amen.

Making Choices

As He who called you is holy, you also be holy in all your conduct (1 Peter 1:15, *New King James Version*).

Scripture: **Romans 7:14-19**
Song: **"Take Time to Be Holy"**

Yesterday I shopped at a store where customers wheel grocery carts to and from the parking lot. I grabbed a cart and hurried toward the store. Then I noticed something in the bottom of my cart that made me stop: cookies! Two packages of chocolate-nut cookies! Now, since my doctor has advised me to avoid sugar, we seldom have desserts at our house. Someone had forgotten these luscious cookies. I looked around the parking lot. There was no one in sight.

Now I had a decision to make. Could I keep the cookies? My mouth watered at the thought. The store had already been paid for them; there was no way to find the rightful owner. It took me a full minute to decide. Then I wheeled my cart inside the store, and handed the cookies to an employee, as I explained. I felt good. I had made the right decision.

A small thing, you say? We have a nature that encourages us to do wrong. God wants us to overcome that carnal nature and be free to serve Him. It is sad to read of the apostle Paul's struggle in today's reading. We struggle also. Making a habit of doing right in small things helps us with important decisions.

Dear God, *forgive us for the times we have failed You in small things. Help us make right decisions that will make us strong. In Jesus' name, amen.*

Jesus Never Fails

To the angel of the church in Smyrna . . . Be faithful, even to the point of death, and I will give you the crown of life (Revelation 2:8, 10, *New International Version*).

Scripture: **Romans 7:20-25**
Song: **"Only One Life"**

Long ago, Polycarp, the bishop of the church at Smyrna, was arrested. Smyrna is a city in modern-day Turkey. Then it was part of the Roman Empire. The Roman soldiers could see that Polycarp was a godly old man. They begged him to deny Christ and save his life, but he refused. A Roman official said, "Recant your faith and worship Caesar, old man. If you refuse, I will cast you to the wild beasts." Again, the old man refused. A crier was sent into the arena of the Roman games to announce the prisoner's name. The crowd knew who he was. They demanded a lion be loosed against Polycarp. The chief officer refused, saying that part of the day's entertainment was over.

"Then burn him alive!" the crowd shouted.

"Eighty and six years have I served Him," Polycarp said, "and He never did me any injury: how then can I blaspheme my King and my Savior?" Polycarp died that day in the flames. His words ring out with truth today, two thousand years later. I have served Christ many years. He has never failed me. How about you? We are perfectly safe, putting our trust in Him.

Thank You, Father, *for the testimonies of believers like Polycarp. Thank You for the firm foundation our faith stands upon. In Jesus' name, amen.*

DEVOTIONS

When he uttereth his voice . . . he maketh lightnings with rain, and bringeth forth the wind out of his treasures.

—Jeremiah 10:13

APRIL

Photo © Digital Stock

Resting in the Lord

Through Christ Jesus the law of the Spirit of life set me free from the law of sin and death (Romans 8:2, *New International Version*).

Scripture: **Romans 8:1-5**
Song: **"He Leadeth Me"**

People attend church for many reasons. Some seek social status or companionship; some go out of habit or a sense of duty. Some go to worship God with other people. Many are seeking a better way of life. God is pleased when His people get together. He said through the palmist, "Sing . . . his praise in the congregation of saints" (Psalm 149:1). Still, many people leave a service with the same burden of sin and despair they hoped to leave behind. Even longtime believers sometimes feel unfulfilled.

Christ Jesus, the Spirit of life, has provided all we need to be free from sin. If we have accepted Christ's sacrifice on the cross, there is no condemnation for us. H.L. Sidney Lear, a writer and preacher of long ago, said: "It may be that recollections of the past hinder you, but you must reject them; anxious thoughts may arise, put them away; your faults seem to raise up a barrier, but no past faults can separate a loving heart from God."

Dear God, help us bring past sins and mistakes to You, so that our hearts may be cleansed as white as snow. Amen.

April 1-3. **Beverley Bittner** is retired from a career in publishing and is now working on a series of historical/inspirational novels. She lives in Corry, Pennsylvania.

Resurrection

He [Christ] was seen of Cephas, then of the twelve: after that, he was seen of above five hundred brethren at once (1 Corinthians 15:5, 6).

Scripture: **Romans 8:6-11**
Song: **"Christ the Lord Is Risen Today"**

Do you know where the Love Chapter of the Bible is located? It is 1 Corinthians 13. There are other chapters with special names as well. The Shepherd's Psalm is one. It is, of course, Psalm 23. And 1 Corinthians 15 is called the Resurrection Chapter. In it the apostle Paul explains the vital necessity of believing in the resurrection of Christ if one wants to be a Christian. In verses 3 and 4 he explains that it is the climax of the essential facts of the gospel: that Christ died for our sins, according to the Scriptures, that He was buried, and that He was raised to life again, according to the Scriptures. The resurrection of Christ is the most significant event in all of history!

We celebrate Easter as a special time to remember Jesus' resurrection. Eggs, spring flowers, special songs, and new clothes remind us of new life. Although Easter is past for this year, our hearts still rejoice as we remember the day the stone was rolled away from the grave where Jesus lay. His resurrection is the evidence that assures us of our own future resurrections.

Hallelujah!

Father God, help us remember the resurrection of Jesus, not only on Easter Sunday, but all through the year. Amen.

The Adopted Child

Ye have received the Spirit of adoption, whereby we cry, Abba, Father. The Spirit itself beareth witness with our spirit, that we are the children of God (Romans 8:15, 16).

Scripture: **Romans 8:12-17**
Song: **"Jesus Loves Me"**

Last year my friends Martha and Paul adopted a little girl from Central America. Sasha's dark skin tells that she was not born to her new parents, who are both white-skinned, blond, and blue-eyed. Martha and Paul love Sasha very much. "Sasha is truly an important part of our family," Martha fretted one day. "How can I tell her she is adopted? Will she be afraid we will not always want her?"

My husband read today's verses to Martha, explaining that all believers are adopted into God's family. We have nothing to fear. We are children of our heavenly Father.

Martha and Paul are not rich. Sasha will not inherit great wealth from her adopted parents. "But," my husband said with a smile, "when we are adopted into God's family we become heirs of God, and joint-heirs with Christ."

It is a wonderful thing to be adopted into a loving family. It is even better to be a member of God's family. When they are sure Sasha will understand, Martha and Paul will teach Sasha how to ask Jesus into her heart. Then they will truly be a real family.

Father, I pray for all adopted children who have found loving parents, and especially for those still waiting for families. May they all find in You the perfect Father. In Jesus' name I pray. Amen.

He Came to Save

For the Son of man is come to seek and to save that which was lost (Luke 19:10).

Scripture: **Hebrews 5:5-10**
Song: **"Jesus Is Lord of All"**

Everyone seems to be talking about purpose today. Corporations and churches alike are developing "mission statements," attempts at defining in succinct statements their purpose for being. The best ones are short enough to be easily memorized and yet comprehensive enough to actually define specific missions.

Jesus expressed His own "mission statement" after His meeting with Zaccheus. It's a mission we can share: "to seek and to save [the] lost." Jesus did many things. He taught the great crowds and He taught His disciples. He healed the sick and released those oppressed by demons. He calmed troubled storms and even provided wine for a wedding. But none of those was the reason He came. Each in some way supported the mission, but none of them was the mission. His mission was to save lost sinners.

The church today does many things as well. She feeds the hungry and clothes the poor. She offers support groups for those who suffer from abuse or neglect. She calls the members together for wonderful times of praise and worship. But her mission is to seek lost sinners and bring them to the Savior!

Heavenly Father, *thank You that Jesus came to save lost sinners like me. May I join Him in that great mission today. In Jesus' name I pray. Amen.*

Inside Out

In his days Judah will be saved and Israel will live in safety. This is the name by which he will be called: The Lord Our Righteousness (Jeremiah 23:6, *New International Version*).

Scripture: **Romans 10:1-8**
Song: **"O for a Thousand Tongues to Sing"**

What makes an item authentic? Is it the package it is wrapped in? The name on the cover? Genuine leather is leather on the inside as well as the outside; real wood furniture is wood all the way through. Authenticity has more to do with the internal than the external.

The Israelites never lacked in zeal, but too often their zeal was on the outside. Before Jesus came, righteousness was mostly understood as keeping the law. But that proved impossible. Once Jesus came, He became the end of the law. He became the way to attain righteousness. It is not attained by doing the right things but rather by knowing the one who is God's righteousness. Righteousness is not something that we do on the outside, it is something that we are on the inside by God's grace. And then our actions on the outside reveal what is on the inside.

How will our words and actions reveal a heart of righteousness today?

O God, we long to be zealous for You. Open our hearts today to hear You. Guard our lips today, that our words will glorify You. In Jesus' name, amen.

April 5-10. **Susan Petropulos** is a writer and a ministry associate at her church in Wexford, PA. She and her husband have two grown children and one grandchild.

No Walls

For he himself is our peace, who has made the two one and has destroyed the barrier, the dividing wall of hostility (Ephesians 2:14, *New International Version*).

Scripture: **Romans 10:9-13**
Song: **"I Love You with the Love of the Lord"**

Watching people at the mall, the airport, or on a busy street reminds us of how unique we all are. Right down to the DNA, each of us is designed by God as a one-of-a-kind masterpiece. However, problems arise when we allow our differences to become walls that separate us.

Webster defines a wall as "an upright structure . . . serving to enclose, divide, or protect." Walls have a purpose when we are building a home or a fort, but God does not intend for us to have walls that stand in the way of our relationships with others. We are not referring here to healthy boundaries that we all need in our relationships. Rather, we are talking about walls that prevent us from sharing the love of Jesus. They are the walls that send the message "No trespassing" and that keep us from reaching out to those who do not think, act, or look like us.

Jesus is the Lord of all. There are no walls in Him. Jesus reached out to the Jew, the Roman, the Samaritan, the woman caught in adultery, and the rich young ruler. Let us tear down any walls that separate us from others, so that His love can flow through us and draw others to Him.

Lord, help us to see the walls in our lives that separate us from others. Open our eyes to see others as You see them. In Jesus' name I pray. Amen.

Selective Hearing

Consequently, faith comes from hearing the message, and the message is heard through the word of Christ (Romans 10:17, *New International Version*).

Scripture: **Romans 10:14-21**
Song: **"Jesus Is Calling"**

Have you ever experienced what I like to call "selective hearing"? For example, you are having a conversation with someone and suddenly realize that you haven't heard a word the other person is saying. Unfortunately, it would seem that often we only hear what we choose to hear.

Over the centuries, God sent prophet after prophet to tell His chosen people of His love for them. But again and again they did not hear. Finally, God sent His Son, Jesus. Surely they would listen to Him. But once again, Israel chose not to hear the one who came to offer them salvation.

God is still speaking to the world every day. Psalm 19:1 says, "The heavens declare the glory of God; the skies proclaim the work of his hands" (*New International Version*). Creation itself speaks to us of God's love, provision, and majesty. Yet so often we are just too busy and preoccupied to listen. God has offered the world the wonderful gift of salvation, a gift that His chosen people rejected simply because they would not hear. Jesus is speaking, always calling us to open the ears of our hearts. Will we listen?

Lord, thank You for the great gift of salvation that You offer to all. Open our ears that we might hear You. Open our eyes that we might see You. Open our hearts that we might follow You. In Jesus' name I pray. Amen.

Amazing Grace

For the law was given through Moses; grace and truth came through Jesus Christ (John 1:17, *New International Version*).

Scripture: **Romans 11:1-6**
Song: **"Amazing Grace"**

It was my privilege to be invited last Passover to the seder of a dear Jewish friend. Every part of the ceremonial meal symbolizes the wonderful provision of God for the Jewish people. I found the experience filled with deep meaning and emotion. The Passover carried an even more passionate meaning for me as a Christian. God truly is the one who makes provision for His people. He is the one who makes a way. And He is the one who continually seeks to draw us to himself.

The history of the Jewish people is the history of God at work, bringing about His plan to bring the Savior into the world. Even their rejection of Him did not thwart His plan.

We live in a world where we can see the effects of rejection all around us. That is why the good news of God's grace renews our hope and restores our joy. Grace accepts, forgives, and continues to offer love and hope in spite of hardened hearts—and yes, even in spite of rejection. Grace is what opened the kingdom to you and to me. And grace will one day bring all of God's people home.

Lord God, *thank You for making a way for the salvation of all people. We pray this day, Lord, for the nation of Israel. May they find the grace that You so freely offer to all who will put their faith in Jesus. May we all live in Your praise forever. In Jesus' name I pray. Amen.*

Grafted by Faith

The words "it was credited to him" were written not for him alone, but also for us, to whom God will credit righteousness—for us who believe in him who raised Jesus our Lord from the dead (Romans 4:23, 24, *New International Version*).

Scripture: Romans 11:13-18
Song: "Christ Is Made the Sure Foundation"

It was an amazing sight. From one branch of the apple tree hung luscious-looking red apples; another branch produced big green pears; and yet another drooped with a different, yellow, type of apple. The owner of the incredible tree had learned from his father the art of grafting branches of different species into one tree. The key to grafting, he said, was to get the grafted branch to accept and flow with the life-giving sap produced by the root.

From the beginning, God has been growing a tree. But His tree became twisted and gnarled by sin. So God sent His Son, Jesus, to bring healing to the sin-sick tree. When many of the branches refused to accept the healing that Jesus came to bring, those branches had to be removed. And God grafted other branches into His tree.

Abraham believed God and "he credited it to him as righteousness" (Genesis 15:6, *New International Version*). Faith in Jesus Christ has been and always will be what gives salvation, to the Gentile and the Jew alike.

Most holy Lord, we praise You for the love that has made us a part of Your family. May those who do not yet know You come to believe in Jesus. In His name, amen.

Yeast of the Pharisees

For if God did not spare the natural branches, he will not spare you either (Romans 11:21, *New International Version*).

Scripture: **Romans 11:19-23**
Song: **"I Am Thine, O Lord"**

A few years ago my husband purchased me a bread-making machine. I am always amazed at the very small amount of yeast that is called for in the recipes. It takes very little of the yellowish fungus to permeate an entire loaf of bread and cause it to raise. The work of the yeast is very subtle and slow, but the result is always the same.

In Matthew 16:5-12 Jesus warned His disciples to be on guard against the "yeast," or "leaven" of the Pharisees and Sadducees. They were the religious leaders, the ones to whom the people looked for spiritual guidance. They were esteemed and respected by those in their communities. But somewhere along the way, they had lost sight of the one they were searching for. So even when He was right before their eyes, they were unable to see Him.

In Romans 11 Paul warned the Gentile Christians to not be arrogant, but to be afraid (see v. 20). Just as yeast permeates bread dough a little at a time, pharisaical thinking and behavior can slowly permeate our lives. If we believe that we cannot fall victim to the unbelief of the Pharisees, we had better listen again to Jesus and to Paul.

Father God, please help us to see any of the "Pharisee" in ourselves. Thank You for making a way for us to know You. Please help us to stand firm in our faith and to look always to You. In Jesus' name, amen.

Dedicated to Prayer

Devote yourselves to prayer, keeping alert in it with an attitude of thanksgiving (Colossians 4:2, *New American Standard Bible*).

Scripture: **Colossians 4:2-6**
Song: **"Sweet Hour of Prayer"**

An Olympic gold medalist once said, "If I miss one day of training, I can tell the difference; two days and my competitors can tell; and three days, the world can tell."

He achieved greatness in his sport through training. He could have been good, even without much training; but commitment to training was what made the greatest difference. Once an athlete is accustomed to training, it becomes enjoyable, and he does not want to miss it.

It is the same in our spiritual lives. If we are committed to communing with God, we will notice a difference if we skip it. (No doubt, the devil also notices and is quick to attack when our defenses are low.)

God's desire is for us to be close to Him and to have great spiritual lives. The more we pray, the stronger our relationship with God will become. We will enjoy spending time with God and will not want to miss our regular times of communion.

Dear God, thank You for the gift of prayer. Help us to see its significance. Lord, please create in us a desire for prayer. Draw us close to yourself through Your Spirit. In Jesus' name, amen.

April 11-17. **James Jordan,** a sports writer for a newspaper in Lexington, SC, created and maintains a Bible study Web site. He and his wife have one child in college.

A Simplified Life

Make it your ambition to lead a quiet life, to mind your own business and to work with your hands, just as we told you (1 Thessalonians 4:11, *New International Version*).

Scripture: **1 Thessalonians 4:1-12**
Song: **"I Am Satisfied with Jesus"**

From television screens, pages of magazines, and billboards along the highway, we are told to get all we can—this will bring us happiness. If we do not have the money to buy what we want, we can use credit cards. Our immediate happiness is the only thing that matters. If only we could be as happy as the actors and actresses appear to be in the advertisements!

The world tells us that it is in possessions, and in doing or achieving things, that we will find happiness and peace. Look better, have more, obtain things more quickly. . . . Yet, many people remain unhappy.

The Bible has a much different outlook on life. Paul encourages people to seek a simple lifestyle, as opposed to one of glamour and fame. He realized there is much more to life than possessions. Perhaps Paul knew that, as we accumulate more possessions and achieve more things, our lives only become more complicated.

A life of simplicity might actually make us happier!

Dear Lord, thank You for all the wonderful things You give us totally without charge. Help us to appreciate them, and to not be caught up in seeking all the things the world tells us we need. Let us seek You instead. In Jesus' name, amen.

Settling the Score

See that no one repays another with evil for evil, but always seek after that which is good for one another and for all men (1 Thessalonians 5:15, *New American Standard Bible*).

Scripture: **1 Thessalonians 5:12-22**
Song: **"God Is My Strong Salvation"**

Before Jesus was crucified, He told His disciples to love each other. He said that was the greatest commandment, second only to loving God. After Jesus' resurrection, His disciples were treated harshly by those who had both religious and civil authority. Even though the disciples received evil treatment, they did not respond with evil, but with love. It was a love that cared for people unconditionally, the same way God cares for us. Even the secular historical writers remarked about the exceptional love the Christians showed.

That powerful love allowed them essentially to take over the Roman Empire within three centuries of Christ's death!

Today Christians may feel that they are losing influence on the world. The early Christians had no rights and certainly no protection from the law as we have today.

What kind of impact would we have if we really loved others as we love ourselves? The world might take notice of love today the same way it did 2,000 years ago.

Dear Lord, we thank You for the tremendous love You have given and continue to give us. Help us to see the people of the world as You see them, so we will not repay evil with evil, but do good and show love. In Jesus' name I pray. Amen.

The Best Runners

No discipline seems pleasant at the time, but painful. Later on, however, it produces a harvest of righteousness and peace for those who have been trained by it (Hebrews 12:11, *New International Version*).

Scripture: **2 Thessalonians 3:6-13**
Song: **"Onward, Christian Soldiers"**

Champion distance runners put a lot of time into running. They rise before daylight and go running, regardless of the temperature or precipitation. They may tire of the routine, and it is often hard to get outside in the cold to run before daylight. On good days, it is a joy to be outside running, but on bad days, it can be painful or even dangerous.

But the best runners keep running, regardless of how they feel about it that day. If they persist in their regimen, they can become great runners. There is a tremendous payoff for such hard work. Even if one does not win a gold medal, the runner finds himself in great health.

It is not easy to keep doing good when you see the world keep doing evil or if you feel unappreciated. We may never see the results of the good we do for God, but God sees and has promised that we will receive a great reward for our efforts. God always keeps His promises, and we will be rewarded, whether in this life or in eternity.

Dear Lord, please give us strength to keep on going when we get tired or feel that the world is against us. Please let us see some results of the good You allow us to do. Help keep our eyes on the eternal reward instead of our circumstances. In Jesus' name, amen.

Knowing Our Value

Through the grace given to me I say to every man among you not to think more highly of himself than he ought to think; but to think so as to have sound judgment, as God has allotted to each a measure of faith (Romans 12:3, *New American Standard Bible*).

Scripture: **Romans 12:1-5**
Song: **"I Surrender All"**

There are programs and books to help people who have too low an opinion of themselves. Low self-esteem can prevent a person from doing what he could if he had more confidence. There are no programs, however, for people who think too highly of themselves. Rather, our culture seems unable to recognize this as a problem.

Paul wanted people not to think too highly of themselves. (Interestingly, he did not feel the need to say they should not think too lowly of themselves.) Both extremes can hurt the person himself as well as those around him. Paul was suggesting a more balanced approach.

In Christ, we are all one, and we recognize that God has given everyone his or her abilities, talents, and position. As a result, there should be no jealousy or envy because God has distributed His gifts as He chose. We all have value and a job in the body of Christ, and each one is important in that body. Let us rejoice in what we have in Christ and not compare ourselves with others in the body.

Dear Lord, we thank You for including us in the body of Christ and for the gifts You have given us. Help us to appreciate our gifts and the gifts others have, and not to let jealousy have a root in our lives. In Jesus' name, amen.

Love Each Other

By this all men will know that you are my disciples, if you love one another (John 13:35, *New International Version*).

Scripture: **Romans 12:6-13**
Song: **"Christian Hearts, in Love United"**

Bird-watchers enjoy getting out into the woods and watching for birds. They get excited when they see a bird that is rare or one they have not seen before. They carry binoculars to help them see the birds more clearly and books to help them identify the kinds of birds they see.

What they are looking for are the birds' conspicuous colors or markings. Some are so obvious even an amateur bird-watcher can spot them and recognize certain types of birds. Others are more subtle, but they are there. Even if a bird could pretend to be a different kind of bird, it would still be known by its markings.

There are also certain markings that identify who Christians are. Often people think the mark is one of religion, but it is deeper. The true marks of a Christian are love for God and for others. Love can be seen especially in the face of trouble, when it actually gets stronger. This kind of love is not something we can do on our own. Just as a bird cannot change its markings, we cannot truly have the markings of a Christian unless God puts them there.

Dear Lord, we thank You for the gifts You have given us and for the love You have put into our hearts. We ask that You give us a greater measure of faith so that the world can see we are disciples of Yours by the love we have for You and our fellowman. In Jesus' name, amen.

Overcome Evil with Good

Do not be overcome by evil, but overcome evil with good (Romans 12:21, *New American Standard Bible*).

Scripture: **Romans 12:14-21**
Song: **"Grace Greater than Our Sin"**

King Saul was jealous of David and desperately wanted him dead. Saul knew David was God's choice to replace him, so he was out to murder David. David had to flee for his life and hide out in the wilderness, even though he knew he had been chosen by God to be king.

Twice (1 Samuel 24 and 26) David had an opportunity to kill Saul, but he refused to do it. Both times, when Saul found out, he repented.

David never let himself get in a position where Saul could kill him, but neither he would take revenge. Though David had the opportunity to get rid of his problem, he refused, trusting God instead. David had no control over Saul, but he did have control over his own actions. David did what he could do and trusted God with the rest.

It is difficult to do as David did, but this is a way that we can overcome evil. There will always be evil in the world, and people will always do bad things to each other. But taking revenge will not solve the problem. Evil can only be overcome with good.

Dear Lord, it is hard not to want to repay evil with evil. Help us to understand Your viewpoint in these things so that we may learn to overcome evil with goodness. Help us to wait on You rather than take our own revenge. In Jesus' name, amen.

Daily Choices

Submit yourselves, then, to God. Resist the devil, and he will flee from you (James 4:7, *New International Version*).

Scripture: **James 4:7-12**
Song: "Humble Thyself in the Sight of the Lord"

Our relationships with others affect our relationship with God. Today's verse gives a formula to help with our choices regarding others.

Our son Nathaniel helped his dad tear down our old garage. His dad guided him through the steps that would allow the roof and rafters to be removed safely and efficiently. I loved watching the two work together, choosing what to save for the rebuilding and what to toss in the trash pile. His dad showed him how and where to set braces around the walls before they removed the last of the rafters and other joints that held the walls together. At just the right moment, they put extra pressure on the side they wanted to cave in first. That resistance made the whole structure fall exactly where they wanted it.

Resisting the devil may seem challenging. If we first submit ourselves to God and His ways, He can help us know how and when to resist the devil.

Dear Father in Heaven, *show us how to resist the devil today, as we humble ourselves before You. Help us notice good qualities in our neighbors. In Jesus' name I pray. Amen.*

April 18-24. **Pam Eubanks** and her husband, Bryan, minister with the Deaf Institute in Cincinnati, Ohio. They are the parents of six children and one granddaughter.

Pictures of Patience

You too, be patient and stand firm, because the Lord's coming is near (James 5:8, *New International Version*).

Scripture: **James 5:7-12**
Song: **"Lord, I Lift Your Name on High"**

The route I usually took from my hometown to college led me past many farms during the two-hour trip. I loved traveling throughout the year from Dewey, Oklahoma, through a corner of Kansas, to Joplin, Missouri. The seasons of farm life fascinated me. I also noticed the effect the weather had on the land, crops, and the farmer's work.

Patience is a quality any farmer has to develop. Many variables, such as the weather and pests, are completely outside of his control. Maybe that's the reason God led James to use the farmer as one of the pictures of patience.

Dealing with other people usually requires heavy doses of patience. Like the weather, their variables are out of our control. As our children have come to us grumbling about a sibling or classmate, we usually remind them they can't change anyone else. They can only change their own attitude and actions about whatever is or isn't happening.

Patience is another "brace" God encourages us to use in resisting the devil. It's also a fruit of the Spirit. And notice how Jesus demonstrated patience during His life on earth.

Dear God, we praise You for the patience Jesus showed throughout His life. Thank You for the patience You have with us daily. Guide us as we allow Your Spirit to help us develop patience in our character. Through Jesus' name I pray. Amen.

The Art of Acceptance

Accept him whose faith is weak, without passing judgment on disputable matters (Romans 14:1, *New International Version*).

Scripture: **Romans 14:1-6**
Song: **"Give Thanks with a Grateful Heart"**

My husband is borderline diabetic. When his sugar problem surfaced, I made a change in how and what I cook. My love for him is expressed in the choices I make for our family's meals and snacks.

For a recent school assignment, our daughter, Maleah, was to make a family recipe that had been passed down by grandparents. I suggested a mayonnaise cake (very moist, chocolate flavor) that I remembered my mother making when I was a child. Maleah didn't remember ever eating it. I realized that I hadn't made the cake in a long time! My mom doesn't make it anymore, either, because she and my dad are diabetic now. So Maleah made two mayonnaise cakes—one with regular sugar and one with applesauce and sugar-free sweetener.

Each person's faith is expressed in a variety of acceptable ways. What a blessing to know God knows our hearts. Acceptance is another "brace" God has given us to resist the devil's temptation to judge others inappropriately. Acceptance is a gift we all need to give and receive.

Dear God, *thank You for accepting us in our journey of faith. Deepen our understanding of others in their journeys of faith. Thank You for the experiences we enjoy because of Your faithfulness to us. We praise You in Jesus' name. Amen.*

How Do We Look?

So, whether we live or die, we belong to the Lord (Romans 14:8, *New International Version*).

Scripture: **Romans 14:7-13**
Song: **"I'll Live for Him"**

People who are both deaf and blind have helpers who are called support service providers. Rod Burke, the preacher at Christ's Church of the Deaf in Cincinnati, is deaf and has very limited sight. He is a powerful leader, teacher, preacher, and friend. He is also working on his master's degree in counseling. He is capable of doing many things in spite of his limited hearing and vision.

Church members help him know who wants to ask a question or share a thought during class. They also direct him around obstacles or move them out of his way. Rod does not drive, but that doesn't stop him from making calls and leading home Bible studies. His wife and other members drive him and help with communication challenges.

We have three choices of how we look at weakness in people's faith: 1) we can look away, ignoring them completely; 2) we can look down on them, condemning their weakness; or 3) we can look down and around them for any stumbling blocks or obstacles we need to remove. Which way will you look today? Are you a spiritual support service provider?

Father in Heaven, thank You for watching over us as we grow in our faith. Thank You for brothers and sisters who encourage us and who need our encouragement. In Jesus' powerful name I pray. Amen.

Sever or Serve

For the kingdom of God is not a matter of eating and drinking, but of righteousness, peace and joy in the Holy Spirit, because anyone who serves Christ in this way is pleasing to God and approved by men (Romans 14:17, 18, *New International Version*).

Scripture: **Romans 14:14-18**
Song: **"What a Mighty God We Serve"**

Sever and *serve* use the same five letters, but they have opposite effects on people. The role of an interpreter illustrates the relationship well. How the interpreter chooses to perform can either *sever* the communication ties between two people or *serve* to connect them. My friend Mary Alice Gardner loves to interpret for deaf and hearing people, conveying the thoughts and wishes of each to the other.

Mary Alice has honed her skills through study as well as placing herself in the mainstream of both worlds. She reads about and experiences a great variety of lifestyles, cultures, sign languages, and traditions around the United States as well as around the world. She continually places herself at the intersection between deaf and hearing. She is thus able to provide a clearer, more understandable communication of other people's thoughts and wishes.

Our freedom in Christ should manifest itself in choices that communicate to others a clearer picture of Jesus.

Father in Heaven, thank You for communicating with us through Your Word and through the Word made flesh. Thank You, Jesus, for visually explaining grace and truth to us. Prompt us to show that same grace and truth to others. In Your Son's gracious and holy name I pray. Amen.

Relationship Building

Let us therefore make every effort to do what leads to peace and to mutual edification (Romans 14:19, *New International Version*).

Scripture: **Romans 14:19-23**
Song: **"Trust and Obey"**

Our ministry with the Deaf Institute gives us opportunities to travel as a family. One challenge in the midst of traveling is maintaining the home. My plants often struggle to survive while I'm away and unable to give them the TLC they need. When I return home, the first step toward the plants' recovery is for me to water them. If I want them to go from "survive" to "thrive," I mix in special plant food with the water. Most of the time the plants respond quickly.

Our choice to live in Christ commits us to loving God and loving our neighbors as ourselves—giving them TLC. The apostle Paul reminds us in these verses that we must make decisions daily that will lead to peace and mutual edification. Bringing peace to relationships requires us to assess what is in the best interest of our brothers and sisters in Christ. Edification is like the plant food I give my plants. We must look for opportunities to build up, strengthen, and encourage one another. This will move the church from surviving to thriving.

Dear Father, thank You for creating each one of us in Your image, yet unique. Help us to live daily in Your peace, encouraged by Your care. Open our eyes and hearts to see how to bring peace and mutual edification to each of our relationships. In Jesus' name I pray. Amen.

Glory

Each of us should please his neighbor for his good, to build him up (Romans 15:2, *New International Version*).

Scripture: **Romans 15:1-6**
Song: **"Lord, Be Glorified"**

One of my weekly jobs growing up was dusting furniture. Mom supplied the tools for the job; I was responsible for using them. One brand of furniture polish was named "Glory." What a descriptive word for the goal of the polish: to bring out the "glory" of the wood. When dust was removed, the oil in the polish caused any light in the room to reveal the wood's natural beauty.

Today's verses show us how to glorify God continuously. God gives us the tools to do our work: endurance and encouragement. When we use these tools to bring unity among the followers of Christ, God is glorified! His character is reflected in our lives.

Glory in American Sign Language is made with both hands in an open-palm shape. The left hand is extended to the front with its palm up. The right hand, palm down, and fingers wiggling, makes a vertical clockwise circle, landing on the left palm as it circles. This sign picture represents light reflecting off a mirror. When we choose to promote unity in God's way, we reflect His character. That's glory!

God, our Father, who gives us endurance and encouragement, give us a spirit of unity among ourselves as we follow Christ Jesus, so that with one heart and mouth we may glorify You. In the name of Christ Jesus I pray. Amen.

Caution, Christians!

Test everything. Hold on to the good (1 Thessalonians 5:21, *New International Version*).

Scripture: 2 Corinthians 11:1-15
Song: "O Word of God Incarnate"

Lemmings are mouse-like arctic rodents. When they cannot find food, groups of lemmings are known to follow one another into oceans where they drown.

Paul warns against being like lemmings. There is danger, he says, in following people blindly. Paul was speaking to Christians with a "sincere and pure devotion to Christ" (v. 3, *New International Version*). Yet they were being led astray by a different gospel. Why? Because they "put up with it easily enough" (v. 4, *New International Version*). They did not test it; they did not fight it (see Ephesians 6:10-18). Sincere Christians were led blindly into oceans of falsehood.

How often are we led astray by attractive messages not from God? Do messages like "spirituality is found within oneself" and "all paths lead to the same end" sound familiar? Caution, Christians! Do not "put up with it easily enough." Hold firmly to the Word of God.

Dear Almighty God, help us to see through the apparent "angels of light" who try to lead us away from You. Give us Your power to test everything. In the name of our Lord Jesus, amen.

April 25-30. **Michelle Webster** is a stay-at-home mom and a registered nurse in Cincinnati, Ohio. She is also involved in the music ministry at her church.

Hold It Together

He is before all things, and in him all things hold together (Colossians 1:17, *New International Version*).

Scripture: **Colossians 1:15-23**
Song: **"Our God Is in Control"**

My head was spinning before I even got out of bed. The baby was crying, needing to be fed. The laundry sat in huge stacks, waiting to be washed. There were phone calls to return, errands to run, rooms to clean, and the list went on. *Hold it together,* I thought to myself as I climbed sleepily out of bed, tired before the day had begun.

Life often seems out of control. It is all we can do to hold it together, keeping our lives in some semblance of order. However, Colossians 1:15-23 reminds us of who really holds it together. These verses describe our Lord Jesus as immensely powerful. He holds the universe— immeasurable by scientists—under complete control. He is the authority over all the rulers of this country and this world. He is the head of His church. He is the author of our salvation. God is in control.

We do not have to be in control because we know who is. We do not live in a world of perfect order. Life is busy, but our souls can be at peace when we trust in the God of the universe to hold it together.

Almighty God, *thank You for being in control. We know that You have the power to hold the universe together, and You have the power to take care of the details of our lives. Please help us today to rest in the peace of knowing You are in control. In Jesus' name, amen.*

Something to Smile About

I bring you good news of great joy that will be for all the people (Luke 2: 10, *New International Version*).

Scripture: **Acts 13:26-33**
Song: **"He Lives!"**

As children, my younger sister Melinda and I were sitting together in church one Sunday morning, trying hard to comprehend what was being said and done. Just as the Communion trays had been passed, Melinda leaned toward me and whispered, "Why doesn't anybody smile when they pray?"

"I don't know," I replied, and often thought about her question later. Why not smile when we pray?

It is certainly appropriate to be reverent before the almighty God, remembering Jesus' death on the cross for our forgiveness. However, it is just as appropriate to smile for joy when we remember that Jesus was raised from the dead to give us hope. Acts 13:26-33 is a solemn account of the death of Jesus, but it is also a joyous reminder of His resurrection! Jesus' death is only part of the gospel. The joy of His resurrection is just as real. This joy is what makes Christians attractive to unbelievers.

We have something to smile about! Let us share it with everyone we encounter by having the contagious and genuine joy that can only come from knowing Christ.

Dear Father, we praise You for the hope we have through the resurrection of Jesus. Fill us with Your joy so that everyone we encounter will want to know why we smile with such genuine gladness. In Jesus' name, amen.

Everyone Who Believes Is Set Free

Therefore, my brothers, I want you to know that through Jesus the forgiveness of sins is proclaimed to you. Through him everyone who believes is justified from everything you could not be justified from by the law of Moses (Acts 13:38, 39, *New International Version*).

Scripture: **Acts 13:34-41**
Song: **"Saved by the Blood"**

One of Aesop's fables tells of a lion who is tightly bound by strong ropes. A little mouse sees the lion's trap and nibbles through those ropes, setting him free. The story does *not* end with the lion tying himself back up! Rather, he leaves that trap, never to return.

We were once trapped in the binding ropes of sin. We could never measure up to God's holiness. How, then, could we be set free? "Thanks be to God—through Jesus Christ our Lord! . . . There is now no condemnation for those who are in Christ Jesus, because through Christ Jesus the law of the Spirit of life set me free from the law of sin and death" (Romans 7:25; 8:1, 2, *New International Version*). We are set free from sin through belief in His saving grace!

Why, then, would we try to tie ourselves up again, working hard to follow the law for justification? There is no need to go back to that trap. Let's rely on His grace alone, not on our good works. Jesus has set us free!

Thank You, dear Lord*, for rescuing us from the trap of sin. Rescue us from the trap of trying to be justified by our own works. We praise you that we are justified by Jesus' precious blood! In His name I pray. Amen.*

No Distinctions

The Lord . . . is patient with you, not wanting anyone to perish, but everyone to come to repentance (2 Peter 3:9, *New International Version*).

Scripture: **Acts 13:44-49**
Song: **"Go, Tell It on the Mountain"**

The Jews were very upset. They felt that they alone met all the requirements to receive God's salvation! They were Abraham's descendants. They followed the Old Testament law. But salvation was being offered to the Gentiles—and they did not meet the requirements!

God's love is limitless. He makes no distinctions among people groups. "There is neither Jew nor Greek, slave nor free, male nor female, for you are all one in Christ Jesus. If you belong to Christ, then you are Abraham's seed, and heirs according to the promise" (Galatians 3:28, 29, *New International Version*).

In the Jews' minds, the Gentiles were not adequate candidates for salvation. How often do we think we are better candidates for salvation than those around us? First Timothy 2:4 says God "wants all men to be saved and to come to a knowledge of the truth" (*New International Version*). If God himself makes no distinctions, shouldn't we be sharing His gracious gospel with all people?

Dear Lord, please help us to share the gospel with all people, not just the ones who seem like better "candidates" in our minds. Remind us that we were all once sinners and that we are all one in Christ when we have come to know You. Through Jesus our Savior, amen.

No Turning Back

I am astonished that you are so quickly deserting the one who called you by the grace of Christ and are turning to a different gospel—which is really no gospel at all (Galatians 1:6, 7, *New International Version*).

Scripture: Galatians 1:1-7
Song: "I Have Decided to Follow Jesus"

I love to run. The routes I follow always go in a loop. There is a time, usually toward the middle of the run, when I want to quit. I become tired, my muscles start to cramp, and I just want to turn around. That is when those looped routes come in handy—I have to press on, heading for home. There is no turning back.

Once we decide to follow Jesus, there is no turning back—in spite of difficulties. We may struggle with sin, with doubt, with evil. It may be tempting to turn away and run toward an easier path—or as Paul says, "a different gospel." Perhaps this different gospel does not require faith; perhaps it allows for sin. Probably it lets us think we can achieve salvation on our own merit.

But there is a reward for those who press on. Hebrews 12:1 says, "Let us run with perseverance the race marked out for us" (*New International Version*). Do not turn from Jesus. Run to Him. He waits for us to come home.

Heavenly Father, *author and perfecter of our faith, help us today to run to You with perseverance, without turning back. Keep us from turning to any other gospel but Yours, and remind us that You are with us as we run, just as You will be with us at the end. In Jesus' name, amen.*

My Prayer Notes

DEVOTIONS

*T*hey that wait upon the LORD shall renew their strength; they shall mount up with wings as eagles.

—Isaiah 40:31

MAY

Photo © Eyewire

Know His Voice

I want you to know, brothers, that the gospel I preached is not something that man made up. I did not receive it from any man, nor was I taught it; rather, I received it by revelation from Jesus Christ (Galatians 1:11, 12, *New International Version*).

Scripture: **Galatians 1:8-12**
Song: **"Be Thou My Vision"**

My four-month-old daughter recognizes my voice. She responds to my voice readily. She knows me.

As God's children, we are can know His voice. Many other people, things, and desires call for our attention; but if we know Him, we can respond to His calling.

Paul says, "Even if we or an angel from heaven" (v. 8, *New International Version*) preach a gospel that is not of God, do not follow it! In other words, no matter who says it, no matter how holy or righteous the person may seem, if that person's words contradict God's words, do not listen!

How can we learn to recognize God's voice? Just as my baby has learned to recognize my voice: by spending time with Him and by observing His ways as written for us in the Bible. The more we know His Word, the more we can distinguish His voice from any other. Listen to His voice.

Dear God, thank You for speaking to us through Your Word. I pray that we will learn to distinguish Your voice from any other, so that we will follow You, the one and only true God. In Jesus' name I pray. Amen.

May 1. **Michelle Webster** is a stay-at-home mom and a registered nurse in Cincinnati, Ohio. She is also involved in the music ministry at her church.

Faith, Not Law

This righteousness from God comes through faith in Jesus Christ to all who believe. There is no difference (Romans 3:22, *New International Version*).

Scripture: **Romans 3:21-26**
Song: **"Once for All"**

A businessman well known for his ruthlessness once announced to Mark Twain, "Before I die I mean to make a pilgrimage to the Holy Land. I will climb Mount Sinai and read the Ten Commandments at the top."

"I have a better idea, "replied Twain. "You could stay in Boston and keep them."

Twain's witty rejoinder may have put that businessman in his place, or at least set him to thinking. But Twain's advice would have been impossible for his friend to follow, even if he were so inclined. The point Paul has been making all along is that law-keeping cannot gain anyone God's favor, because no human being outside of Christ ever has or ever will keep His law perfectly.

The law demanded that we be righteous. Faith in Christ declares us righteous in Him.

Heavenly Father, how beautiful it is to know that we, through Christ, can be clothed in Your righteousness. I praise You for grace so freely bestowed that gives us access to Your holy presence and the promise of a home in Heaven. In Jesus' name I pray. Amen.

May 2-8. **Jean P. Booth** is a motor homer living in Lakeland, Florida. She has written for numerous publications.

It's All Mine

For the grace of God that brings salvation has appeared to all men (Titus 2:11, *New King James Version*).

Scripture: **1 Corinthians 1:3-9**
Song: **"Wonderful Grace of Jesus"**

Every year the residents of my community sponsor a huge yard sale. Families load tables with everything from outgrown clothing to tattered books, which are then offered for minimal prices. The saying, "One man's trash is another man's treasure," becomes a reality. Early in the morning, the park is flooded with people hoping to find bargains.

The first year I lived here, I had not prepared for the sale. Wanting to clean out a shed, I began to put my unwanted items on a picnic table at the side of my house. The bargain seekers saw the articles on the table and wandered over to it. So I made a poster that read: "Free! If you want it take it!" Everything disappeared.

God freely offers His grace and salvation to us. It costs nothing. The Lord Jesus Christ paid it all. Salvation is not only something for nothing—it is *everything* for nothing! "For in [Christ Jesus] you have been enriched in every way—in all your speaking and in all your knowledge"(1 Corinthians 1:5, *New International Version*). Tozer wrote, "Grace is the good pleasure of God that inclines Him to bestow benefits on the undeserving" (*Knowledge of the Holy*, p. 93). How can anyone refuse such a gift?

My Father, how precious that, through accepting Your grace, I am given everything I need for life and godliness. It's all mine! Through Jesus, amen.

Completely Fulfilled

For in Christ all the fullness of the Deity lives in bodily form, and you have been given fullness in Christ (Colossians 2:9, 10, *New International Version*).

Scripture: **Colossians 2:6-14**
Song: **"He Is All I Need"**

People often exclaim when they have had a child, bought a new house, married, or started a new job: "Now my life is complete!" I understand what they mean. Our emotions and feelings of peace, accomplishment, and well-being give a false sense of "all is well!"

God's Word tells us that real fulfillment is not found in material blessings or even in people. Nothing in this world can fill the place in our hearts that belongs to God. When we become aware that we have nothing left but God, we realize that He is enough. He is all we need!

God has given us everything we need, not only for life, but for godliness. God's resources cannot be exhausted. "From the fullness of his grace we have all received one blessing after another" (John 1:16, *New International Version*). Our gifts from God are not simply material things—although He does give those freely. The greatest gift He gives us is His Holy Spirit, who gives us all we need as Christians to live fully the life that is ours in Christ.

Dear Father, *how marvelous is Your love to me. You have filled my life with innumerable blessings. How precious is the gift of Your Holy Spirit. Truly all things are mine in Christ. In Jesus' name, amen.*

Good News for All

And the gospel must first be preached to all nations (Mark 13: 10, *New International Version*).

Scripture: **Galatians 2:5-10**
Song: **"Send Me"**

No people have ever received the gospel except at the hands of a foreigner. It must have been a Jewish believer who brought the gospel to Rome. Roman believers took it to other parts of Europe. Believers from England and Spain brought the gospel to America.

Paul was a Jew with great compassion for his people. But God taught him that the gospel was the power of God for the salvation of *everyone* who believes—first for the Jews, then for the Gentiles (every nation except Jews). Then each convert was to take the gospel to others. God gives us the same commission to tell the whole world about Christ. He says, "Ye shall be witnesses unto me both in Jerusalem, and in all Judea, and in Samaria, and unto the uttermost part of the earth" (Acts 1:8).

"But I have never felt any compelling call to give my life for missionary service," a young man told the conference speaker. "Are you sure you are within calling distance?" was the disquieting reply. We have all been called to be missionaries—wherever we might be. We simply need to be in calling distance.

Father, may we always be mindful of Your great commission and Your plan for us to go into all the world—starting with our own little world—and be witnesses for Your Son who went to the cross for our salvation. Amen.

Believing Faith

Believe on the Lord Jesus Christ, and thou shalt be saved (Acts 16:31).

Scripture: **Galatians 2:15-21**
Song: **"I Know Whom I Have Believed"**

A missionary to a Pacific tribe was translating Scripture into their language. In the course of his work, he found it difficult to find a word for *believe*—in the sense of having faith in or trusting. He finally hit on the idea of leaning one's weight on something. So Paul and Silas's answer to the Philippian jailer's question, "What must I do to be saved?" became, "*Lean your whole weight* on the Lord Jesus Christ and be saved." Believe and obey.

Our little dachshund symbolizes this action. Every morning when she crawls out from under the covers of our bed, where she nestles at night, she stands at the foot and patiently waits for us to lift her down. We open our arms, lean over, and she positions herself on our shoulder, knowing that we will set her on the floor. She trusts us completely to do what she has learned we will do—take her to safety.

Faith believes the Word of God for what it cannot see and is rewarded by seeing what it believes. Faith transcends man's reasoning. Faith is believing that, not only God can, but He will.

Dear Father, *I thank You for Your precious Son who gave His life for my sin and now lives in me. I know that someday I will see Him face to face. In Jesus' name, amen.*

Don't Be Foolish!

Are you so foolish? After beginning with the Spirit, are you now trying to attain your goal by human effort? (Galatians 3:3, *New International Version*).

Scripture: **Galatians 3:1-5**
Song: **"Living by Faith"**

The Gentile believers were yielding to pressure from Jewish zealots to revert to legalistic rules of the Jews, including circumcision. Paul called them foolish. He reminded them that they had been saved by faith in Jesus Christ and that by faith they should continue in the Christian life.

Three boys gave their definitions of faith. One said, "Faith is taking hold of God." The second said, "Faith is holding on to God." A third said, "Faith is not letting go!" Each boy was right.

Faith also can be compared to swimming. A person learning to swim will struggle and fight the water instead of trusting it to hold him. When one rests in the water without moving hands or feet, the water buoys him up. Then, using his own strength, he can soon learn to move in the water. So many people constantly struggle in the Christian life, trying to keep themselves righteous. What they need to do is simply to rest in Christ. He will buoy them up and support them as they move forward.

Father, You have given us everything in Your Son, but still we fail to completely comprehend Your gifts. We struggle and try to do things in our own way. Forgive us and teach us to realize that truly, without faith in Your keeping power, we can do nothing. In Jesus' name, amen.

Consider Abraham

What does the Scripture say? "Abraham believed God, and it was credited to him as righteousness" (Romans 4:3, *New International Version*).

Scripture: **Galatians 3:6-14**
Song: **"Faith of Our Fathers"**

Biblical faith is trusting in God. The power of that faith comes when we put matters in God's hands so that He is able to do what He wants to do in any situation. Abraham had that kind of faith. God told Abraham, "Leave your country, your people and your father's household and go to the land I will show you" (Genesis 12:1, *New International Version*). Abraham went out as God said—by faith. God later instructed Abraham to take Isaac, his son, and offer him as a sacrifice. He tested Abraham's faith, and Abraham passed the test with honors (Genesis 22:1-18). The patriarch believed in the Lord, and God put righteousness on his account. Abraham was justified by faith.

Some say that faith is a gift of God. So is the air, but we have to breathe it. It is not for us to sit down and wait for a sensation of faith to steal over us, but it is for us to take God at His Word—"faith cometh by hearing" (Romans 10:17)—and to act. Abraham believed and was blessed by God, and all nations after him received the blessing of salvation by faith.

Father, You are a God of Your word; You always keep Your promises to us. You are faithful. Sometimes I want to say, "Help thou my unbelief." Help us hold fast to the faith given to the fathers. In Jesus' name, amen.

Living by Law

The law of the LORD is perfect, converting the soul: the testimony of the LORD is sure, making wise the simple (Psalm 19:7).

Scripture: **Psalm 19:7-14**
Song: **"Love Divine, All Loves Excelling"**

Our neighbor, a police officer, describes his job as safeguarding the innocent and protecting the many from the few. Spelled out on his squad car door is the motto, "To protect and to serve." Each day he puts on his bulletproof vest and drives away, placing the safety of others ahead of his own. Although he admits our country's laws aren't perfect, he sees them as essential to the preservation of society. They offer safety and security to those who follow them.

God's laws are more than just rules or safeguards; they are as perfect as He. By carefully following God's law, the Jews were set apart from surrounding pagan cultures. Psalm 119 refers to God's laws as sweeter than honey and more precious than gold (vv. 103, 127). In ancient times, God's people wrote the laws on their doorposts and taught them to their children to guarantee future generations would know to put their trust in God.

What would today's world be like if we did the same?

Dear Lord, help us to remember in this ever-changing world, that Your words are light and life, a firm anchor to which we can cling. In Jesus' name, I pray. Amen.

May 9-15. **Linda Zielinski** volunteers as the associate teaching director at an interdenominational Bible study. She is a freelance writer and plays the violin and piano.

A Shadow of Things to Come

And you, being dead in your sins . . . hath he quickened together with him, having forgiven you all trespasses; blotting out the handwriting of ordinances that was against us . . . nailing it to his cross (Colossians 2:13, 14).

Scripture: **1 Timothy 1:3-11**
Song: **"Father, Lead Me Day by Day"**

By the time of Jesus' birth, the Pharisees and scribes had taken God's laws and distorted them into a long list of *do*s and *don't*s. Mercy, justice, and honesty were set aside—replaced by a form of legalism that made the Pharisees look good on the outside, while their hearts were filled with hatred and contempt for others.

Those who truly love God don't just follow rules and regulations. They desire to please Him as a lover seeks to bring joy to her beloved. The law was given to show us how much we needed a Savior. It was a shadow of what was to come. But the Pharisees and scribes chose the shadow over the substance, and to wander in darkness instead of living in God's light.

Even today men seek to deceive God's children with man-made rules and false teaching. The truth is clear for those who earnestly study God's Word. When we accept Christ into our hearts and put Him first in our lives, we'll naturally seek to do His will.

Dear Lord, *I pray for your leading in all that I say and do. May your love direct me to walk in Your ways and to live in Your will. In Jesus' name I pray. Amen.*

God's Law Fulfilled

Think not that I am come to destroy the law, or the prophets: I am not come to destroy, but to fufil (Matthew 5:17).

Scripture: Matthew 5:17-22
Song: "Pass Me Not, O Gentle Savior"

The trial was long, the evidence overwhelming. The jury reentered the courtroom, and the defendant trembled as he stood to hear his fate. Twelve sets of eyes were carefully averted; not a single juror dared look toward the accused. The man shuddered as the judge's gavel slammed down once, twice, and again.

The verdict handed down was unanimous: guilty as sin. The judge looked toward the condemned man with sorrow. "I have no choice," he said. "The law demands this verdict." And so the prisoner was sentenced to death. As the spectators watched aghast, the judge himself stood and calmly stated, "I'll die in your place. You will receive the mercy I long to give, and the law will be fulfilled as well." Then he marched away to the executioner.

An incredible story, for sure; but those who've placed their faith in Christ recognize that it is a true one. Each one of them is the defendant in the story!

The good news of the Bible is that God himself came to earth to live—and die—for us. It wasn't in response to our righteousness that He came, for we had none. Instead, He did it out of love.

__Dear Father,__ thank You for sending Jesus to live and die for our sins. Help us always to remember Your great love for us. In Jesus' name, amen.

Christ and the Banner of Faith

Knowing that a man is not justified by the works of the law, but by the faith of Jesus Christ, even we have believed in Jesus Christ, that we might be justified by the faith of Christ (Galatians 2:16).

Scripture: **Romans 3:27-31**
Song: **"Rock of Ages"**

Abraham was 99 years old when God promised he'd be the father of many nations. Upon hearing this startling announcement, Abraham fell on his face in laughter; so the Lord directed him to name his son Isaac, a word that means laughter. (See Genesis 17:17-19.)

"Is any thing too hard for the LORD?" God asked later (Genesis 18:14). The answer Abraham chose to believe was a resounding "No." His faith was counted to him as righteousness.

As we step out in faith, believing God's promises, we too are justified, forgiven, made right with God. As we walk by faith, trusting in our heavenly Father, the Holy Spirit will live within us, giving us the strength and desire to do His will.

No one can be saved by following the law. "For it is by grace you have been saved, through faith—and this not from yourselves, it is the gift of God—not by works, so that no one can boast" (Ephesians 2:8, 9, *New International Version*).

Dear Lord, help us to remember You are a God of joy. Thank You for the freedom You've given through faith in Christ Jesus. In His name, amen.

In Protective Custody

But before faith came, we were kept under the law, shut up unto the faith which should afterward be revealed (Galatians 3:23).

Scripture: **Galatians 3:19-23**
Song: **"Under His Wings"**

When I was a young bride, the first gift my husband brought home to me was a cookbook (a not-so-subtle hint). As God looked at His people and their lives, He, like my husband, determined that they needed direction. He gave them the law to provide the perfect "recipe" for successful and productive living.

Usually when we think of the law, we think in terms of *do*s and *don't*s, but God also included times of rest, thanksgiving, and even celebration. Through the law God made himself known to His people. They learned of His character traits: mercy, justice, love, holiness, and so much more. Under the umbrella of the law they were kept safe until they received the promised Messiah.

The decrees, offerings, and sacrifices all combine to point the way to the one final atoning sacrifice: Christ, the Lamb of God. Every part of the Bible directs us clearly and unmistakably to Jesus, our Messiah. The more we study God's Word, the clearer our understanding becomes. Christ is the fulfillment of the law, the perfect sacrifice to atone completely for all our sins.

Lord, *thank You for loving us so much that You sent Jesus to atone for our sins. In Jesus' name I pray. Amen.*

The Law—Our Bodyguard

He that hath no rule over his own spirit is like a city that is broken down, and without walls (Proverbs 25:28).

Scripture: **Galatians 3:24-29**
Song: **"Abide in Me, O Lord"**

When Nehemiah returned to Jerusalem after being held captive in Babylon, his first priority was to rebuild the walls, the defenses of the city. Just as earthly fortifications provide safety, God's Word is our moral defense. The self-discipline and spiritual character, built by studying and obeying God's Word, serve as a strong armor around us. They keep us save from the fiery darts of Satan. Then the Holy Spirit, who lives within every believer's heart, convicts us of God's truth and warns us to avoid earthly temptations and steer clear of places where sin abounds.

It's said that the New Testament is concealed within the Old, and the Old revealed in the New. God's Word unfolds like a road map. Beginning in Genesis and ending in Revelation, the roads on this spiritual map are clearly marked in the brightest crimson—and all head in only one direction, to one destination. The law points to our sin and our need of a Savior. It directs us clearly to Jesus, the ultimate, complete, and final sacrifice: God's law fulfilled.

Thoughtful believers study the Old Testament carefully. They find Jesus on nearly every page!

Dear God, *thank You for so clearly marking the direction we must take to find You: through Jesus, Your own Son. In His name I pray. Amen.*

Children of the King

But when the fulness of the time was come, God sent forth his Son . . . to redeem them that were under the law, that we might receive the adoption of sons (Galatians 4:4, 5).

Scripture: **Galatians 4:1-7**
Song: **"True-Hearted, Whole-Hearted"**

Did you know you can do nothing to earn an inheritance? The possessions we fall heir to are always the product of someone else's work and usually aren't received until that person's death. As Christians, we've been grafted into God's family, making us heirs of Jesus. Because of Him we're no longer slaves to sin, but rather the adopted children of our heavenly Father. Christ died to secure our inheritance. Then He rose again so we'd receive not just a dead man's goods, but His victory over death as well. We live with the presence of God in our lives right now and the assurance of Heaven when we die!

God's legacy to us includes a change of heart and mind, transforming us by the indwelling Holy Spirit, remaking us from the inside out. We begin by believing in Christ's atoning work at Calvary. Then as we permit more and more of God to live in our hearts, we find that our desires, thoughts, and even deeds begin to change. The things that used to seem attractive no longer appeal to us; our focus is more and more on God.

Because of Christ, our sin debt is marked "Paid in Full."

Dear God, *there is nothing better than knowing You as our Father. Thank You for Your abundant love. In Jesus' name I pray. Amen.*

The Chains of Freedom

Then you will know the truth, and the truth will set you free (John 8:32, *New International Version*).

Scripture: **John 8:31-38**
Song: **"Make Me a Captive, Lord"**

Rows of heavy chains hang on the outside wall of a monastery in Toledo, Spain. There, for many years, Christians had been enslaved by the Moors until the armies of Ferdinand and Isabella freed them. The freed Christians then fastened their chains on the wall in commemoration. The chains of slavery became chains of freedom.

To those who think freedom has no limits, the term "the chains of freedom" may seem to be a contradiction. But if we live without proper restrictions, we will become completely enslaved by sin, evil habits, and self-indulgence from which only God can free us. By choosing to serve God we can become free, just as God created us to be.

Because of our faith in Jesus, Christians are free from the enslavement of sin, from the penalty of sin, and from guilt. Wearing "the chains of freedom" liberates us to enjoy the abundant life, to love others unselfishly, and to do joyfully all the good we can. That's real freedom!

God of freedom, we thank You for the freedom You give us through faith in Christ Jesus. May "the chains of freedom" guide us so that we will not become enslaved again by sin but live life to the fullest. In the name of Jesus, amen.

May 16-22. **Virgil Fry** is an author and a retired professor/minister. He and his wife, Kathryn, live in Francisco, Indiana. They have one son and one granddaughter.

The Responsible Use of Freedom

Live as free men, but do not use your freedom as a cover-up for evil; live as servants of God (1 Peter 2:16, *New International Version*).

Scripture: **1 Peter 2:11-17**
Song: **"Make Me a Blessing"**

When a certain teenage boy received his driver's license, his father gave him the car to drive alone for two hours. He considered the thrill of driving 100 miles an hour or of running some traffic lights. But he could not bear to break the trust his father had in him. So he did not use his freedom as an excuse to drive recklessly.

Like this teenager, we Christians are to exercise our freedom in Christ in a responsible manner. If we misuse our freedom, it will become a license or excuse to sin. Then we will become enslaved by sin (see Romans 6:20; John 8:34). The only way we can be free from such bondage is to become servants of Christ by a full commitment of ourselves to Him and His lordship.

One way to use Christian freedom responsibly is to subordinate ourselves to others. We demonstrate our freedom by preferring to give rather than to receive, and to serve instead of being served. A responsible use of freedom in Christ is to be gracious, honest, friendly, and loving.

How responsible are we in the use of our freedom?

Heavenly Father, *we thank You for our freedom in Christ. Help us to be responsible in the use of this freedom. May we never misuse it as a license to sin. In the name of Jesus we pray. Amen.*

Free as Slaves of Christ

For he who was a slave when he was called by the Lord is the Lord's freedman; similarly, he who was a free man when he was called is Christ's slave (1 Corinthians 7:22, *New International Version*).

Scripture: **1 Corinthians 7:17-24**
Song: **"Since I Have Been Redeemed"**

In the United States Army I was free—outwardly, as long as I followed military regulations and obeyed the orders of my superiors; and inwardly, as long as I followed biblical teachings and obeyed the will of God.

All Christians are free as long as we obey the commandments of our Lord. Christ has bought us with a price, delivering us from the tyranny of sin. Now we belong to Christ totally. Yet we live free as His slaves because of the profound change He has made in our inner lives. These truths explain how easily Paul could identify freedom in Christ with being the slave of Christ. Living by the law of Christ, the law of love, gives us true freedom.

Freedom in Christ gives our lives a much deeper and fuller meaning. We are free from fear, selfish desires, and sinful thoughts and actions. We are free to do right, to love one another, and to take Christian friendship to the workplace.

How well do we demonstrate that we are free as slaves of Christ?

Lord, we are so thankful that You have freed us from the tyranny of sin. May we use our freedom in a way that those who are enslaved by sin will see how free we really are as Your slaves. In Jesus' name, amen.

Free from the Fear of Death

Since the children have flesh and blood, he too shared in their humanity so that by his death he might destroy him who holds the power of death—that is, the devil—and free those who all their lives were held in slavery by their fear of death (Hebrews 2:14, 15, *New International Version*).

Scripture: **Hebrews 2:14-18**
Song: **"My Redeemer"**

In the ancient world, enslavement to the fear of death was widespread. For people who did not believe in life after death, the most a good person could expect was to live on in the memory of those who knew him. Death also terrorizes many people of modern times—even professing Christians. They are afraid even to mention death directly.

But Jesus, through His death and resurrection, defeated the devil—who had the power of death—and freed us from bondage to the fear of death. Now we have eternal life in Christ.

Therefore, natural death will not open the way to condemnation in the judgment (see Hebrews 9:27), but to *commendation* for living life in Christ. Neither will physical death end in eternal separation from God, but in eternal presence before Him.

We rejoice in this marvelous freedom!

Dear Father, *we praise You for the freedom You have given us from enslavement to our fear of death. We adore You for wrenching the power of death from Satan. We thank You for giving us eternal life through Your grace. In the name of Jesus, our Redeemer, we pray. Amen.*

Standing Firm in Freedom

It is for freedom that Christ has set us free. Stand firm, then, and do not let yourselves be burdened again by a yoke of slavery (Galatians 5:1, *New International Version*).

Scripture: **Galatians 5:1-5**
Song: **"Free from the Law, O Happy Condition"**

When a certain man takes a vacation, he reminds himself that he has no constraints of time and may do whatever he desires. Yet his activities make him feel somewhat uncomfortable; he even longs to return to his normal activities. They would offer him direction, make him productive, and give him satisfaction.

Similar to the vacationer, the Christian Gentiles of Galatia were uncomfortable with their freedom in Christ. They were used to external rules to guide them. So Paul urged them to "stand firm" in their freedom in Christ and to reject the Jewish law as a means of salvation. The law would only enslave them. Christians are free because the Holy Spirit lives within our hearts. He enables us to discern and to obey the will of Christ.

Christ not only liberates us from bondage, but He also frees us to do what is right. We are free to control our anger, to forgive others, to shock people with kindness, and to yield the fruit of the Spirit. Freedom in Christ brings us joy, peace, and satisfaction. What a wonderful life!

Dear Lord, *You are the liberator of all who want to be free. We praise You for freeing us from the bondage of Law, sin, and death. May we stand firm in this freedom. In Jesus' name we pray. Amen.*

The Essential Element of Salvation

For in Christ Jesus neither circumcision nor uncircumcision has any value. The only thing that counts is faith expressing itself through love (Galatians 5:6, *New International Version*).

Scripture: **Galatians 5:6-10**
Song: **"Make Me a Channel of Blessing"**

The parable of the sheep-and-goat judgment is troubling to many believers. If salvation is by faith and not by works, why does the judge use works as the basis for judgment in the parable?

Paul answers the dilemma when he says what really matters in salvation is not a ritual, but faith expressing itself by practical deeds done for others through love. Essential to salvation is faith that expresses itself by good deeds and not by good words only. Good deeds are the natural, instinctive response of a living faith and a loving heart. God's love for us motivates us to love Him and people. Thus love is the channel through which our faith works.

Faith may express itself by giving food and drink to the needy, cheering up the sick, visiting the imprisoned, practicing hospitality, and inviting nonbelievers to become Christians. Is this the kind of faith we have?

Gracious God and Father, may You keep reminding us that saving faith shows itself by good deeds done through love to help others. May the love that motivated You to give Your life on our behalf inspire us to give freely of ourselves to benefit others. We pray in Jesus' name. Amen.

Love Without Limits

Love your neighbor as yourself (Galatians 5:14, *New International Version*).

Scripture: Galatians 5:11-15
Song: "Help Somebody Today"

A small Christian lady walked without fear among the toughest prisoners in an Illinois prison. She smiled at them, hugged them, listened to them, read the Bible to them, and assured them of God's powerful, unlimited love, which was able to meet the worst offender's need. The woman clearly loved these prisoners as herself—and they loved her without reservation.

Thinking of God's unlimited love for us makes it easier to love our coworkers, our neighbors across the street, our fellow-worshipers, and our families as ourselves. Doing such ordinary deeds as visiting shut-ins, running errands for the elderly, and reading to the blind suggests that we love them as ourselves.

God also wants us to go beyond what we consider a *reasonable* level of love. We are to love as ourselves the person who passionately hates us, the one who tells lies about us, and the one who betrays us. Come to think of it, some of us were at one time like that! Yet God loved us without reservation, for love without limits is His nature.

Has this kind of love become our nature?

Dear Father, *with deep sorrow we acknowledge our shortcomings and ask Your forgiveness. Continue to challenge us until loving our neighbors as ourselves becomes our nature. In the name of our loving Lord we pray. Amen.*

A Good Tree

He is like a tree planted by streams of water, which yields its fruit in season (Psalm 1:3, *New International Version*).

Scripture: **Matthew 7:15-20**
Song: **"I Long to Glorify Thee"**

His name was John Chapman, but the settlers called him Johnny Appleseed. Barefoot, wearing poorly fitting clothes, Chapman roamed America's frontier in the early 1800s. Convinced of the value of apple trees, he planted seedlings all over the country.

Johnny Appleseed was right. Trees benefit people by providing fruit to eat, wood to burn, and a filter for the air we breathe. The Bible says a person who obeys God's Word is "like a tree." With kind words, prayers, and positive actions, a believer's life can benefit each person he encounters.

A tree may bend in a storm, but when the wind stops, a strong tree remains erect. So, also, storms don't easily sway a Christian, nor do they uproot his faith.

If a tree is to bear fruit, its roots must sink deep into the soil, pulling out necessary nutrients. A Christian also, to be productive, depends upon a source outside himself for strength. That source is God's Word. As we sink our roots deep into its truth, we will have good fruit to share.

Loving Father, may Your love sink deep into our hearts so we will be strong, fruitful in Christlike actions and words. In Jesus' name, amen.

May 23-29. **Jewell Johnson** is a retired registered nurse who teaches first and second graders in Sunday school. She and her husband have 6 children and 6 grandchildren.

The Prayer Chair

For where two or three come together in my name, there am I with them (Matthew 18:20, *New International Version*).

Scripture: **Matthew 18:15-20**
Song: **"I Must Tell Jesus"**

Our daughter was struggling with an eating disorder. Our family prayed—but nothing changed. As Jenny's mother, I felt isolated in a jungle of guilt and worry.

I began attending a ladies' prayer meeting, where I shared our daughter's need. The group prayed for Jenny for months, then years. As the problem worsened, I wondered, *Will she ever recover?* The prayer group became a shelter for me, a place of hope.

One day Jenny called me. "I was thinking today that I have nothing to live for," she said. "Then in my mind I 'saw' the ladies in the prayer group place me in a sedan chair, the kind people in the Orient are carried in. As they picked up the poles, I asked, 'What are you doing?' The ladies said, 'We are carrying you on the chair of prayer.'"

The ladies continued to "carry" our daughter, praying for her until her eating problems were overcome. And I, with the group's support, received strength to go through the trial. As He promised, Jesus truly was in our midst as we came together to pray.

Thank You, God, *for Your presence that is with us at all times. We appreciate the special promise You give to us when we meet in Your Son's name. Thank You for brothers and sisters in Christ who support us in trying times. In Jesus' name, amen.*

The Power of Encouraging Words

Do not let any unwholesome talk come out of your mouths, but only what is helpful for building others up according to their needs, that it may benefit those who listen (Ephesians 4:29, *New International Version*).

Scripture: 1 Timothy 6:11-19
Song: "Take My Life, and Let It Be"

Words of encouragement can change a person's life—even the course of history. It happened to George Washington Carver. Having been denied entrance to a Kansas college because he was black, George went home and eked out a living doing laundry, cooking, and janitorial work.

While George lived in Winterset, Iowa, a white couple took an interest in him, often inviting him to their home. When Mr. and Mrs. Milhollander realized the young man's passion for an education, they encouraged him to follow his dream, suggesting that he apply to Simpson College in Indianola, Iowa. George eventually received degrees in agricultural science from Iowa Agricultural College (now Iowa State University) and later earned worldwide acclaim for inventing more than 300 products from the peanut. Much credit for his success goes to the obscure couple who encouraged him.

As we share encouraging words, God will use us to spur others forward to realize His purposes for their lives.

Dear God, may we be sensitive to people around us who have suffered disappointments. Allow us to speak words of cheer until their despair turns to hope. In Jesus' name, amen.

A Fat Soul

Dear children, let us not love with words or tongue but with actions and in truth (1 John 3:18, *New International Version*).

Scripture: **1 John 3:18-24**
Song: **"I Would Be Like Jesus"**

I left my garden that day, my arms loaded with freshly picked sweet corn and tomatoes. Under a willow tree, I settled into a lawn chair to husk the corn for my family's noon meal. A yellow butterfly flitted nearby. As I brushed it aside, a Bible verse flashed into my thoughts: "The liberal soul shall be made fat" (Proverbs 11:25). "Where did that come from?" I wondered.

Glancing at my watch, I noticed it was time to start lunch. The thought returned. "Why does this verse keep coming back?" "The *liberal soul*," I pondered. Then I got it. Garden produce! I filled a grocery bag with corn and tomatoes and, calling our son, I instructed him to deliver the produce to a family who didn't have a garden. In the kitchen I smiled as I dropped corn into boiling water.

"A fat soul! You thought my soul needed some fattening up, Lord? You're right!" I thought. "This full-to-the-brim feeling that comes from sharing is definitely a fat-soul feeling."

God has blessed us with two hands—one for receiving and the other for giving.

Dear God, help us to think beyond our circle, reaching out to the homeless, people suffering from hunger, and those in countries torn by war. In Jesus' name I pray. Amen.

A Fruitful Bough

This is to my Father's glory, that you bear much fruit, showing yourselves to be my disciples (John 15:8, *New International Version*).

Scripture: Galatians 5:22-26
Song: "All for Jesus"

I became a Christian at age 17. The day after I'd made the decision to follow Christ, doubts began to flood my mind. "Nothing happened to you when you prayed," a voice seemed to say. "You're not good enough to be a Christian." I became bewildered and believed the doubts. Then I met with a Christian friend. As Ardyce and I talked, she shared Bible verses with me. She assured me that Jesus' blood covers all my sin. Her concern, her joy, and the assuring words she spoke that day helped me hurdle the first temptation of my new life.

Barnabas also knew how to help novice believers. When newly converted Saul tried to join the disciples in Jerusalem, everyone was afraid of him; they did not believe he really was a disciple (Acts 9:26). But Barnabas befriended Saul and became a bridge between him and the apostles.

Recent converts need Spirit-led people like Barnabas and Ardyce—people who will accept them, encourage them, and introduce them to other believers.

Dear Father, a new convert may be struggling with doubts today. Lift him up. Give him assurance from Your Word. And if our paths cross, give us the words to say that will help him move forward in his spiritual walk. In Jesus' name, amen.

Carry the Burdens of Others

We who are strong ought to bear with the failings of the weak and not to please ourselves (Romans 15:1, *New International Version*).

Scripture: Galatians 6:1-5
Song: "Take Up Thy Cross"

At my mother's memorial service I was pleased to see a friend whom I hadn't seen since childhood. Lois had traveled a great distance to be there. When I voiced my appreciation, she said, "I'm here to help lighten your load."

Lois was fulfilling the law of Christ. On the eve of His death He said, "My command is this: Love each other as I have loved you" (John 15:12, *New International Version*). He went on to demonstrate how far this love can take us—to lay down our lives for our friends.

Most of us won't be compelled to die for another person, but there are countless other ways to lay down our lives for others. One way is to help bear their burdens. Picture two travelers walking on a road, each with a large bundle on his back. One traveler becomes tired beneath his load. The stronger traveler takes the bundle from the weaker, thus renewing the strength of the weary one.

In the church, no person need be worn out by his trials, temptations and sicknesses. We, as fellow "travelers" can, in love, step forward to help carry the load.

Kind Father, *how thankful we are that You bore our burdens on the cross. Help us to follow in Your footsteps and aid those who are weak. Let us be willing to carry the burdens of others. In Jesus' name, amen.*

No Good Work Is in Vain

Always give yourselves fully to the work of the Lord, because you know that your labor in the Lord is not in vain (1 Corinthians 15:58, *New International Version*).

Scripture: **Galatians 6:6-10**
Song: **"Speak, My Lord"**

On May 14, 1796, Dr. Edward Jenner made two small cuts in the arm of eight-year-old James Phipps and placed cowpox exudate into each cut. Dr. Jenner believed if he exposed James to this mild disease, the boy's body would make antibodies to keep him from contracting the often fatal disease, smallpox. After James recovered from cowpox, the doctor placed smallpox serum into his arm. The disease had no effect. Though Dr. Jenner did not know it at the time, his experiment would save millions of people from the dreaded scourge.

In our walk with God it is also possible to perform humble acts that have far-reaching effects while being unaware of the good they will eventually accomplish. In the Bible account, a boy gave his lunch to Jesus, and more than 5,000 people were fed (John 6:1-15). A woman poured a fragrant ointment on Jesus' feet, and 2,000 years later people remember her sacrificial act of love (Matthew 26:6-13).

How important to listen to God's voice, to be ready to obey—no matter how unimportant the deed seems to us—and to pray as Jesus did in Gethsemane, "Your will be done."

Dear Father, it overwhelms us to think of the power our lives have for good. Lead us to love and influence people for Your kingdom. In Jesus' name, amen.

The Son—Our Brother

You are my Son; today I have become your Father (Psalm 2:7, *New International Version*).

Scripture: **Psalm 2:7-12**
Song: **"I Belong to the King"**

What does it mean to say that God has a Son? Does it mean there was a time when the Son did not exist? Is He somehow less than the Father? In the ancient Middle East, the position of "son" described the person who would receive the inheritance and all the authority of the father. A king designated his chosen heir by announcing: "This is my son." The heir wasn't necessarily a biological son and could even be the same age as the "father."

We understand from John 1:1 and other passages that the Son has existed eternally and is one with the Father. Today's passage warns that we must treat the Son with respect, for He represents God himself.

When we understand the role of the Son, isn't it amazing that God would call us His sons! (Even "daughters" are legally "sons"—heirs—in God's house!) When we consider that our fellow Christians are also God's adopted sons, we should treat them with great respect and love in order to show honor to the Father.

Father, thank You for my big brother, Jesus. I want to be just like Him. Teach me how to be a good child of the Father. In Jesus' name I pray. Amen.

May 30, 31. **Andrew Wood** is a former missionary to Ukraine and is currently teaching at Cincinnati Bible College.

Living the Message

Clothe yourselves with humility (1 Peter 5:5, *New International Version*).

Scripture: **Mark 1:4-8**
Song: **"Seek Ye First"**

When people flocked to the desert to see John the Baptist, did they want to hear a great sermon on repentance, or were they merely curious about a weird guy? What they discovered was a man whose lifestyle backed up the message he was teaching. His humble food and clothing were consistent with a message of repentance and dependence on God.

Every Christian would agree that people are more important than things; but in practice, we may not show that we really believe it. We tend to work long hours in order to accumulate material things we don't need. We sacrifice time with family and ministry, because we have absorbed the message of a materialistic culture. When people look at Christians, do they see a remarkable lifestyle— or do they see something very much like the way they are living, with the addition of some church activities?

What would happen if Christians today began living a simpler, more purposeful lifestyle? Such a life would raise the world's curiosity, and preach the clearest message possible—a sermon of action, not words.

Father, thank You for Your provision. May our lifestyles witness to the world of our dependence upon You. Help us remember that we are not permanent residents of this world. In Jesus' name, amen.

DEVOTIONS®

As for man, his days are as grass: as a flower of the field. . . . But the mercy of the Lord is from everlasting to everlasting.

—Psalm 103:15, 17

JUNE

Photo © Diamar

Healthy or Hollow?

He is like a tree planted by streams of water, which yields its fruit in season and whose leaf does not wither (Psalm 1:3, *New International Version*).

Scripture: **Matthew 3:7-12**
Song: **"The Church's One Foundation"**

My grandparents' farmhouse was surrounded by 200-year-old oak trees. They shaded the yard and provided a great place for us kids to climb and swing. Scattered throughout were a few dead and rotten trees, empty inside except for bugs. In strong winds, branches or even entire trunks toppled unexpectedly to the ground.

What happened to kill these magnificent oaks? Some were attacked by colonies of bugs or microscopic diseases. Others failed to develop a good root system. Being poorly anchored, they could not withstand strong winds.

The religious leaders in today's Scripture were similar to dead oaks. They appeared magnificent in their legalistic righteousness, but their hearts were eaten up with pride. Lacking good fruit, they were fit only for the woodpile.

With the proper care, even a stump can produce a vibrant new tree. With a gardener like God to care for us, it's never too late.

Lord Most High, we approach You in Jesus' name, asking You to prune away the deadness in our lives. Help us grow and produce spiritual fruit. Amen.

June 1-5. **Andrew Wood** is a former missionary to Ukraine, currently teaching at Cincinnati Bible College.

The God Who Asks for Help

"I need to be baptized by you, and do you come to me?" (Matthew 3:14, *New International Version*).

Scripture: **Matthew 3:13-17**
Song: **"So Send I You"**

John was flabbergasted, and rightly so. Jesus Christ, the spotless Lamb of God, had come to him for baptism. This was the first of many such instances throughout the Gospels in which we see Jesus asking for help from people who are unworthy to give it. He asked for a cup of water from a sinful Samaritan woman. He requested the prayers of unspiritual disciples in Gethsemane.

It is amazing that God seeks the help of weak and frail human beings to accomplish His purposes. Whether the task be administering a kingdom or spreading the good news to the world, God entrusts jobs to His children rather than supernaturally intervening to do it all himself.

Obviously, an all-powerful God doesn't need our help; so why does He ask for it? As a good Father, He gives His children the opportunity to learn by experience and give something back to Him. Tasks are given, not because the Father needs the help, but to help the children grow. We can be grateful for what God gives us to do—feeling neither proud of our sufficiency nor unconfident in our ability. God chooses appropriate opportunities to help us grow.

Wise God, *thank You for seeking a relationship with us and for giving us the opportunity to participate in Your work. May we take joy in working at Your side. In Jesus' name I pray. Amen.*

Between Animals and Angels

He was with the wild animals, and angels attended him (Mark 1:13, *New International Version*).

Scripture: **Mark 1:9-13**
Song: **"Yield Not to Temptation"**

Caught between the animals and the angels—that's where Jesus found himself immediately after His baptism. He wandered in the wilderness, tired, hungry, tempted by Satan at every turn, and wary of the desert beasts. At the same time He drew strength from angels sent by God to minister to His needs.

Caught between the animals and the angels—isn't that where we find ourselves as well? We hear the howling of the wolves in the distance; we feel the hot breath of temptation on the back of our neck. At the same time, we find that God sends messengers to provide strength and call us to holiness and faithfulness.

One of Satan's craftiest tricks is to convince us we are outside of God's will, that we wouldn't be going through trials if we were good Christians. Satan used this trick on Jesus, questioning whether He really was the Son of God.

When tempted, we need to keep a clear focus on the fact that we are saved children of God, whom no one can take out of His hand. When it seems the "animals" are drawing near, there are also ministering angels close by.

Father, thank You that we are Your children and that You protect us from all harm. Help us to trust You today and to resist the temptations of the evil one. In your Son's name I pray. Amen.

Jesus the Reformer

He will proclaim justice to the nations (Matthew 12:18, *New International Version*).

Scripture: **Matthew 12:17-21**
Song: **"We've a Story to Tell to the Nations"**

How do you start a social reform movement? In the days of prohibition you might have taken up an ax and smashed liquor stills and bars. In the days of the women's suffrage movement you might have carried a sign and marched in protest. During the civil rights movement you might have joined a march on Washington. How about firing off a letter to the editor, going on strike, engaging in civil disobedience, making speeches?

By this standard, Jesus doesn't seem like much of a reformer. According to Isaiah, He didn't quarrel or cry out; He didn't proclaim His message in the streets as modern activists do. His way was one of gentleness—bearing with the weak, the hurting, and the helpless. He changed the world by changing the hearts of people. His unorthodox methods for proclaiming justice to the nations would result, today's Scripture says, in leading justice to victory.

A few gifted individuals have been able to make an enormous difference in our world through political activism. But none has ever had so great an impact as the quiet and gentle Jesus, healing one person at a time.

Lord, *give us a genuine concern for the problems of the poor and oppressed. Help us contribute to changing this world—one person at a time. In Christ's name I pray. Amen.*

The Temptation of Impatience

Wait for the Lord; be strong and take heart and wait for the Lord (Psalm 27:14, *New International Version*).

Scripture: **Matthew 4:1-11**
Song: **"In the Hour of Trial"**

The microwave oven is an amazing invention. Pop in a cold meal and take it out piping hot in just 30 seconds! Somehow, though, 30 seconds now seems like a long time to me. I find myself cooking food repeatedly for 10 seconds at a time, because I don't want to wait so long!

It's in our nature to want instant gratification. Like children, we react to the answer "Wait" as if it were "No." Wise parents realize that children develop maturity through learning to delay gratification.

Everything Satan tempted Jesus with in the wilderness was something that Jesus eventually received anyway. Jesus eventually did receive bread to satisfy His hunger; He did survive death in such a way that the world knew He was God's Son; and He did inherit the kingdoms of the world. The temptation was to use illegitimate means to bypass God's plan and achieve the goal immediately.

Many of our own temptations are things to which God has not said "No," but "Wait." God has a legitimate plan for our needs to be met in good time. Waiting on Him will give true satisfaction in a way that Satan's shortcuts never can.

We praise You, God, that You provide abundantly. Help us to wait patiently for Your timing rather than seeking quick and easy ways to fulfill our desires. Through Your Son, Jesus, I pray. Amen.

God Is My Driver

"Go home to your family and tell them how much the Lord has done for you, and how he has had mercy on you" (Mark 5:19, *New International Version*).

Scripture: **Mark 5:1-13**
Song: **"I Surrender All"**

The disciples had experienced a terrifying boat ride in a storm, in which Jesus displayed His power over nature. Upon landing, they must have been frightened as Jesus stepped from the boat, knowing that the tombs cut into the steep cliffs before Him housed the dead and demon-possessed. Imagine the disciples' horror as a wild man came running and shouting from the eerie shadows!

The legion of demons—a Roman legion was a regiment of up to 6,000 men—resisted Jesus' command to yield control of the man. Finally, Jesus gave the evil spirits permission to go into a herd of 2,000 pigs feeding on the hillside; they rushed down the steep bank and drowned in the lake.

Whether one is filled with unclean thoughts or possessed by evil spirits, the result may be the same. By refusing to surrender control of his or her spirit and will to the Lord, a person has allowed Satan to take up residence. If you invite the devil for a ride, he'll want to drive!

Dear God, *I surrender my spirit and my will to You. Please guide me along the road of righteousness. In Your name I pray. Amen.*

June 6-12. **Dr. Judith Hebb** is head of the humanities and general studies department and director of the writing program at Atlanta Christian College.

Back to the Beginning

"He has done everything well," they said. **"He even makes the deaf hear and the mute speak"** (Mark 7:37, *New International Version*).

Scripture: **Mark 7:31-37**
Song: **"This Is My Father's World"**

In this passage, we find the detailed report of healing for a man who was deaf and mute. Any powerful words Jesus might speak to heal infirmities would be lost on a man who could not hear. So Jesus devised a method suited specifically to this individual. First, Jesus demonstrated consideration for the man as they quietly withdrew to a private place. Because the man was deaf, Jesus used outward, visible signs of healing. He put His finger into the man's ears, spit on His fingers, and touched the man's tongue. Then Jesus looked to Heaven to acknowledge the source of the healing power. Finally, Jesus sighed deeply to indicate His genuine sorrow and sympathy for the man. The man comprehended the miracle of his opened ears and his loosened tongue even before he heard a single word.

The crowds were "overwhelmed with amazement" and exclaimed, "He has done everything well." This declaration echoed the assessment of God's handiwork at creation: "God saw all that he had made, and it was very good" (Genesis 1:31, *New International Version*).

Almighty God, open my eyes that I may see and my ears that I may hear the beauty of Your creation. Thank You for renewing me in Your image. In Jesus' name, amen.

The Bread of Life

"Therefore I tell you, do not worry about your life, what you will eat; or about your body, what you will wear. Life is more than food, and the body more than clothes" (Luke 12:22, 23, *New International Version*).

Scripture: **Mark 8:1-5**
Song: **"Break Thou the Bread of Life"**

After feeding the five thousand (see Mark 6:30-44), Jesus declared to the crowds, "I am the bread of life. He who comes to me will never go hungry" (John 6:35, *New International Version*). While many of His followers deserted Jesus after His hard teaching (John 6:66), Jesus could still draw a crowd—even in remote places without easy access to food. So when Jesus suggested that this second hungry crowd be fed, the disciples were incredulous: "Where in this remote place can anyone get enough bread?" (Mark 8:4, *New International Version*). Apparently, the disciples had forgotten Jesus' earlier lesson on food, both physical and spiritual. In the first miracle of the loaves, the disciples raised objections based on the cost (John 6:7); this time they protest the inconvenience. How could they have forgotten that the first meal was not provided through human intervention?

Like the disciples, we don't always learn our lessons the first time. When we put Jesus first in our lives, we won't have to worry about food; we will be satisfied—both physically and spiritually!

Father, give us this day our daily bread and the spiritual food to supply all of our needs. In Jesus' name, amen.

Hampers of Blessing

Now to him who is able to do immeasurably more than all we ask or imagine, according to his power that is at work within us, to him be glory in the church and in Christ Jesus throughout all generations, for ever and ever! Amen (Ephesians 3:20, 21, *New International Version*).

Scripture: **Mark 8:6-10**
Song: **"There Shall Be Showers of Blessing"**

In the second miracle of the loaves, Jesus fed four thousand men (not counting women and children) with seven loaves and a few small fish. Not only were all the people satisfied, there were seven baskets of leftovers! But these weren't hand baskets; they were hampers, like the basket in which Paul was let down from the wall of Damascus.

Before Jesus fed each crowd, He asked the disciples how many loaves they had. He did not need the information himself; He wanted to show the miraculous nature of the feeding. Before breaking the loaves, Jesus gave thanks for the abundance of food, and He presented a visual image of the nature of His love. Later the apostle Paul would pray that the Ephesians (and we) would "grasp how wide and long and high and deep is the love of Christ" (Ephesians 3:18, *New International Version*).

If we reflect on all the things God has given us, we will see that He showers us with hampers full of blessings beyond measure.

Loving Lord, thank You for showering me with blessings beyond my imagination. To You be the glory. In Jesus' name, amen.

Footsteps of Service

"I tell you the truth, whatever you did for one of the least of these brothers of mine, you did for me" (Matthew 25:40, *New International Version*).

Scripture: **Mark 3:1-6**
Song: **"Footprints of Jesus"**

When Jesus entered the synagogue, the Jewish leaders were watching for an excuse to discredit Him (Mark 3:2). Doing any kind of work on the Sabbath, including healing, was forbidden under the contemporary understanding of Jewish law. Saving a life was the only exception. The man with the paralyzed hand was not terminal.

But Jesus had recently challenged the Pharisees' understanding of the Sabbath: "The Sabbath was made for man, not man for the Sabbath" (Mark 2:27, *New International Version*). The Pharisees watched Jesus closely for His response to this test case. When confronted with the dilemma between doing good (healing the man) or doing evil (leaving the man in his wretchedness), the Pharisees had nothing to say. They were completely defenseless. Jesus was angered at their stubborn hearts.

Is religion about ritual or service? William Barclay wrote:

> Our Friend, our Brother, and our Lord,
>   What may Thy service be?
> Nor name, nor form, nor ritual word,
>   But simply following Thee.

Heavenly Father, *gently remind me when I forget that loving You and others takes precedence over regulations and rituals. In Jesus' name, amen.*

A Heavenly Call

It is not the healthy who need a doctor, but the sick. I have not come to call the righteous, but sinners (Mark 2:17, *New International Version*).

Scripture: **Mark 2:1-5**
Song: **"The Great Physician"**

To the Jews, disease was considered punishment for sin. When Jesus and His disciples passed a blind man, the disciples' question was natural: "Rabbi, who sinned?" (John 9:2). When the four men lowered the paralyzed man on a mat through the roof of a house where Jesus was preaching, Jesus immediately saw their faith. Jesus didn't tell the man he was healed, but that his sins were forgiven (v. 5). The man's soul needed healing even more than his body.

Jesus is in the business of healing souls as well as bodies. Spiritual healing—forgiveness of sins—is more important than physical healing. Physical healing is temporary—everyone whose body Jesus healed has since died! But spiritual healing is good for eternity.

In our world, we tend to put more faith in the medical profession than in the Great Physician. The doctor's phone number is programmed into speed dial. Even then, however, we have to negotiate through a menu of options, punch buttons, or be put on hold. When we "dial" the Great Physician, we are immediately connected to Heaven's healing power!

Dear Lord, *thank You for Your power to heal all of me—body, mind, and soul—and make me whole. In Jesus' name, amen.*

Walking Billboards

Hide your face from my sins and blot out all my iniquity. Create in me a pure heart, O God, and renew a steadfast spirit within me (Psalm 51:9, 10, *New International Version*).

Scripture: **Mark 2:6-12**
Song: **"More Like the Master"**

When Jesus told the paralyzed man that his sins were forgiven, He was openly inviting criticism of His ministry. If Jesus could forgive sins, He was equating himself with God. For anyone but Jesus, that was blasphemy!

Unfortunately for the Pharisees, Jesus knew their thoughts and their plans to entrap Him. He pointed out that it is easy for a charlatan to say that sins are forgiven, because there is no visible proof of forgiveness. On the other hand, the miracle of healing is an outward manifestation of the power of God. So when Jesus told the man to take up his mat and walk, He was declaring His authority both to forgive and to heal. He was also publicly affirming that He was the Son of God.

The man got up and walked out in full view of all who were gathered there. He became a walking billboard advertisement for Jesus, the Son of God.

When God works in our lives, we are accountable for earthly endorsements. By our words and actions we proclaim to the world the power of God to forgive and to heal.

Mighty God, *please help me to remember that I may be the only image of You that others see on this earth. Thank You for Your power to forgive my sins and heal my body. Amen.*

Beyond the Denial

Peter declared, "Even if all fall away, I will not" (Mark 14:29, *New International Version*).

Scripture: **Mark 14:26-31**
Song: **"O Jesus, I Have Promised"**

A monument in Schuylerville, New York commemorates the Revolutionary War battles of Saratoga. Niches in the monument hold statues of battle heroes, yet one niche is empty. The hero whose statue should have been there is Benedict Arnold, who betrayed the new American nation.

When we compare Peter's denial of Jesus and Benedict Arnold's story, there are similarities but a great difference. Both Peter and Arnold betrayed the causes they'd formerly supported. Arnold, however, was then rejected by his country, while Peter's denial brought only a short-term separation. Arnold fled to exile in England, but Peter resumed his place among the disciples and became a major leader in the first-century church. Peter's second chance came because of forgiveness from a Savior who continued to love.

We may not actually deny or betray our Lord, but we do fail Him. We may experience the same regret Peter did. Yet God is always ready to offer His loving forgiveness. Our failure doesn't end our service for Him.

Father, give us the strength to follow You as devotedly as did Peter after his restoration. In Christ's name I pray. Amen.

June 13-19. **Anne Adams** is a writer/teacher in Houston, Texas. In the past thirty years she has been published in both secular and Christian publications.

Waylaying God?

Then one of those standing near drew his sword and struck the servant of the high priest, cutting off his ear (Mark 14:47, *New International Version*).

Scripture: **Mark 14:43-50**
Song: **"Guide Me, O Thou Great Jehovah"**

Sarah sighed in frustration. "Oh, Marie, I did so want that promotion at the office, but they gave it to someone else. I even took those extra classes. I tried so hard, but it didn't do any good."

"Did you ever think that maybe it wasn't God's plan? Maybe all that extra effort was just your own idea," Marie answered.

With her disappointment, Sarah learned the futility of jumping into a new situation without seeking God's will. That's what Peter did when he attempted to defend Jesus and prevent Him from being arrested. (Peter is identified in the John 18 account.) But Peter was actually interfering in God's plans, for Jesus' arrest was, of course, the first step toward the cross. But Peter didn't consider that—he had his own ideas and acted on them.

There are times when we jump ahead and forget to include God in our plans. Often nothing goes right, and the challenge becomes a disappointment. God has a perfect plan. Seeking His will may at times bring challenges and even difficulty, but ultimately it brings His blessing.

Father, help us constantly be aware of Your plans and purposes for us. In Jesus' name I pray. Amen.

True Witnesses

The chief priests and the whole Sanhedrin were looking for evidence against Jesus so that they could put him to death, but they did not find any. Many testified falsely against him, but their statements did not agree (Mark 14:55, 56, *New International Version*).

Scripture: **Mark 14:53-59**
Song: **"Jesus, We Just Want to Thank You"**

In 1804 Aaron Burr, vice president of the United States, shot and killed political rival Alexander Hamilton in a duel. Though he completed his term as vice president, his political career was ruined. Eventually he joined in a plan that seems to have been to create a new nation out of the western territories. When word of the plot reached the authorities, Burr was brought to trial for treason. Despite his unpopularity and probable guilt, he was acquitted. The authorities lacked the two witnesses the Constitution required for conviction of treason.

Jewish law also required two witnesses for a criminal accusation (Deuteronomy 19:15). The Pharisees failed to find the required number of witnesses to testify against Jesus. The reason was simple: Jesus had never committed a crime.

Had the Jewish leaders looked for witnesses who could speak in *favor* of Jesus, many would have testified gladly of His loving care and compassion. What do our lives and lips testify of Him?

Lord, *help us testify not only what You have done for us, but also all that Jesus can mean to the world. In His name I pray. Amen.*

The Real Thing

But Jesus remained silent and gave no answer. Again the high priest asked him, "Are you the Christ?" (Mark 14:61, *New International Version*).

Scripture: **Mark 14:60-65**
Song: **"Stand Up, Stand Up for Jesus"**

In the early 1700s a stranger who called himself George Psalmanazar fascinated London society with exotic stories of his native homeland of Formosa (now Taiwan). Sponsored by a London cleric, the visitor told elaborate tales, including stories describing the bizarre practices of cannibalism, human sacrifices, and polygamy. Gold, he said, was so common it was used to cover roofs. As he described a distant land few had ever visited or even heard of, he was the center of attention.

Yet there were skeptics. They questioned Psalmanazar's tales and eventually exposed him as a phony. He had fabricated his own identity as well as the details of Formosa.

London society believed a phony was the real thing. The Pharisees had the opposite situation: they saw Jesus as an imposter. But He really was who He said He was, the very Messiah for whom they were waiting.

Our world today has to make a similar choice. The Jesus they see will be the Jesus we display in our lives and in our words. Will the world see the real Jesus?

Father, when we consider all that You have revealed about Your Son and all that You want to offer us through Him, we have no choice but to try to be true witnesses for Him. Help us achieve that. In His name I pray. Amen.

From Cowering to Conquering

He began to call down curses on himself, and he swore to them, "I don't know this man you're talking about" (Mark 14:71, *New International Version*).

Scripture: **Mark 14:66-72**
Song: **"Grace Greater Than Our Sin"**

A story is told about brilliant inventor Thomas Edison and his associates when they were developing the light bulb. The men worked for hours to produce a prototype, which Edison handed to a young assistant to put away. Nervous at handling such an important item, the young man stumbled—and the precious bulb shattered.

Edison's team worked long and hard to make a duplicate bulb. When it was finished, Edison gave it to the same assistant to put away. That was true forgiveness.

When Peter denied his Lord, we would think that it was certainly the end of everything. How could he make up for what he had done? How could he ever recover? Yet despite his failure, Peter's denial was not the end, but a new beginning. The cowering disciple from the dark courtyard became, just weeks later, the dynamic representative for Jesus' church in a hostile and unbelieving world. What had happened? Jesus had forgiven and forgotten. He had kept loving Peter even though he didn't deserve it.

Father, we can never truly understand the love and acceptance we have as Your children, but help us to remember that, because of it, we have a personal relationship with the perfect God of the universe. In the name of Jesus, who made it all possible, amen.

Unspoken Judgment

But Jesus still made no reply, and Pilate was amazed (Mark 15:5, *New International Version*).

Scripture: **Mark 15:1-5**
Song: **"Abide with Me"**

The board of directors of a small company was deciding on new directions and procedures. The discussions had been intense and sometimes bitter. Each director was eager to express his own opinion. However, one older man, deeply respected for his experience in the company, had been unusually quiet. Finally, someone turned to the older man. "You've not said anything during this discussion, sir. But I'm sure we'd all like to hear what you think."

"I have found," the man said, "that in this case silence is an opinion."

In the midst of the clandestine trials and behind-the-scenes chicanery of the Pharisees, Jesus, by keeping silent, was expressing His opinion or view of the situation. He was silent because He knew that nothing He said could change the situation or the intentions of those who intended to eliminate Him. At the same time, Jesus knew that He was in the middle of God's will, so words were unnecessary. Nothing else mattered.

Sometimes silence is a mark of fear. But sometimes it shows supreme confidence. Do we know the difference?

Father, we are so often prone to jump in with unnecessary words or explanations. Help us to trust You and Your plans for us. In Christ's name I pray. Amen.

The Substitute

Wanting to satisfy the crowd, Pilate released Barabbas to them. He had Jesus flogged, and handed him over to be crucified (Mark 15:15, *New International Version*).

Scripture: **Mark 15:6-15**
Song: **"Great Is Thy Faithfulness"**

During the American Civil War, a potential draftee could pay a substitute to fight in his place. A draft replacement could earn as much as $300—a great deal of money in those days. While the original purpose was to enable vital craftsmen to continue working or to establish crucial war industries, there was much fraud. Sometimes the substitutes were physically unqualified; some would desert and apply elsewhere to be paid again. Sometimes foreigners were drugged and installed in the army while unconscious!

When Pilate offered to release Barabbas, he thought he could accomplish his real purpose of securing the release of Christ. Perhaps he hoped that the people would cry out for the release of the innocent teacher so many loved, and not the criminal, Barabbas. Yet the crowd went along with the Jewish leaders and shouted for the death of Jesus— and it was God who accomplished His purpose!

Jesus was the substitute for Barabbas, who was set free. And He was the substitute for all mankind, bearing the sins of the world to set us free.

Father, throughout the accounts of Jesus' last days we've constantly seen You at work accomplishing Your purpose—to provide our salvation. We stand in awe of Your perfect plan. In Jesus' name, amen.

God's Security System

We have this hope as an anchor for the soul, firm and secure (Hebrews 6:19, *New International Version*).

Scripture: **Matthew 27:62-66**
Song: **"Great Is the Lord"**

During the first few weeks after we moved into our new home, we were besieged by salespersons offering us "free" security systems. We accepted none of them because we knew they were not free; and we did not feel we needed or wanted a security system.

The men who went to Pilate wanted and got the best security system available in their day. They wanted to keep Jesus' disciples out of the tomb area. They wanted to prevent them from stealing His body and saying He had risen. Their security system would have prevented that. They were watching on the outside. It seems no one was expecting to be overpowered from the inside. While they were guarding against human intruders, God's power was patiently waiting within. What an impossible task they had been given!

How blessed we are to be able to read this story, know the outcome, and place our eternal futures in the keeping of the One who can give real security.

Dear Father, *in this uncertain world, thank You for being our constant point of security. In Jesus' name I pray. Amen.*

June 20-23, 25, 26. **Wanda Pelfrey** is a freelance writer and a Montessori teacher. She is a wife, mother of two, and grandmother of two.

A Positive Negative

Now faith is being sure of what we hope for and certain of what we do not see (Hebrews 11:1, *New International Version*).

Scripture: Matthew 28:1-6
Song: "My Faith Looks Up to Thee"

It seems every prayer list is filled with them—loved ones, friends, and acquaintances being tested for or fighting cancer. We pray for a negative: "The results were negative." "The tumor is gone." Those are the reports we want to hear. Often we seem surprised when we *do* hear them. We have prayed, but we did not want to get our hopes up.

Did the women going to the tomb have their hopes up on that Sunday morning? Did they remember Jesus' promises, or were they just going to minister to His body? Were they hoping for a negative—an empty tomb?

From all appearances they were not. They had no expectation of Jesus' resurrection. It does not even seem that they considered it a remote possibility. Like the two on the road to Emmaus, they "had hoped" in Jesus (Luke 24:21), but they hoped no longer.

Isn't it wonderful that we have a God with whom we can trust our hopes? Since Jesus did not stay in the tomb, God can provide our needs. Since Jesus did not stay in the tomb, God can fulfill our dreams. Since Jesus did not stay in the tomb, God can save our souls.

Dear God, thank You for allowing us to bring our dearest hopes to You. We praise You for having the power to make them reality. In Jesus' name, amen.

A Positive Positive

"Death has been swallowed up in victory" (1 Corinthians 15:54, *New International Version*).

Scripture: **Mark 16:1-8**
Song: **"Easter Song"**

When my daughter asked for my late father's gumball machine to help with our grandson's toilet training (it's a long story), I was sure I knew where it was—but it wasn't. It also was not in any of the other possible places I looked. I know I did not sell it or give it away, but I cannot find it. It has not helped my grandson, and it has frustrated me.

What if Jesus simply had not been in the tomb when the women arrived. What if the angel had just said, "He is not here"?

The women could see that Jesus was not there. From that point they could have jumped to several conclusions. In fact, they did. They seem not to have heard the angel's words, "He has risen." Mary assumed some unknown persons had moved Jesus' body (John 20:2, 13).

God is so good. He asks us to have faith, but He gives us so many positives on which to hang that faith. The truth that Jesus "has risen" changed the doubt and despair. Jesus' appearances to Mary, the women, and others proved that God was at work. Hope was alive again. Salvation was a possibility.

It still is!

Dear Father, thank You for proving Your power by raising Jesus from the dead. Help us always to trust that power. In Jesus' name I pray. Amen.

Wow!

Suddenly, when they looked around, they no longer saw anyone with them except Jesus (Mark 9:8, *New International Version*).

Scripture: **Matthew 28:6-10**
Song: **"We Would See Jesus"**

Before our grandson Grayson's second birthday, we kept asking him if he was excited about his birthday party. He must not have known what to expect, because each time we asked, he replied, "Don't want party."

In view of his attitude, we were glad only a small family gathering had been planned. After supper, as Grayson was entertained in his room, his mother brought out balloons, a cake, and gifts. When he entered the dining room, his attitude was transformed. His eyes grew large, and he uttered a word we did not know he knew: "Wow!" Grayson enjoyed his party.

The women who went to the tomb that Sunday morning did not know what to expect. They went to anoint the body of a dead man. Later, we are told, they were afraid but filled with joy. They must have been confused!

Their attitudes were transformed as soon as they saw Jesus. Fear and confusion fell away, and they worshiped.

The world and even the church can often confuse and frighten us, but when we see only Jesus, we can worship.

Wow!

Dear Father, please help us keep our eyes focused on Jesus. In His name I pray. Amen.

Not Successful, but Faithful

Do not be afraid of what you are about to suffer. . . . Be faithful, even to the point of death, and I will give you the crown of life (Revelation 2:10, *New International Version*).

Scripture: **Mark 16:9-13**
Song: **"I Love to Tell the Story"**

Imagine having the greatest news imaginable, but no one will believe you. What do you do? If you discovered a cure for cancer, but no one would accept your credentials, would you say, "Oh, well, I guess they'll figure it out for themselves eventually"? If you discovered an inexpensive and renewable energy source, but no one would give it a try, would you just give up and keep on buying expensive fossil fuels with everyone else?

Mary Magdalene had good news—great news. Jesus was alive! She had seen Him. But no one would believe her. That didn't matter; she told her news anyway. We, too, have the same great news. Jesus is alive; He is Savior of those who accept His grace. But very often we find people do not believe us. They reject our testimony and may even ridicule us. But no matter!

We have not been called to be successful; we have been called to be faithful. As He did with the disciples, He will deal with those who do not believe (Mark 16:14). Let's just share the good news as eagerly as Mary did.

Dear Father, *we confess that we have sometimes been intimidated by the doubters and have ceased to share the good news. Help us to remember our call is to be faithful and to leave the rest to You. In Jesus' name, amen.*

The Constant

Jesus Christ is the same yesterday and today and forever (Hebrews 13:8, *New International Version*).

Scripture: Matthew 28:16-20
Song: "Jesus Never Fails"

My employer and mentor at the Montessori school where I teach died within two weeks of the death of my mother. Neither knew of the sickness or death of the other. One day it went through my mind that, if they ran into one another in Heaven, they might exclaim simultaneously, "But you're supposed to be taking care of Wanda!"

In this life, no matter how well intentioned we are, we cannot promise always to be there for those we love, and they cannot promise to be there for us. It's not simply a matter of the uncertainty of the length of our lives. Many other situations can come up that interfere with the best of our plans. The simple truth is things change: life, health, politics, circumstances—everything changes. Nothing ever remains the same—except for the Lord.

God knew people needed a constant in their lives. When finances fail, Jesus is there. When health leaves, Jesus is there. When friends disappoint, Jesus is there. When loved ones die, Jesus is there. Through bad times and good times, Jesus is there.

Father, You made us and know our earthly needs as well as our eternal needs. Thank You for providing abundantly for both. In Jesus' name I pray. Amen.

Equipped to Work

May the God of peace . . . equip you with everything good for doing his will, and may he work in us what is pleasing to him, through Jesus Christ, to whom be glory for ever and ever. Amen (Hebrews 13:20, 21, *New International Version*).

Scripture: **Mark 16:14-20**
Song: **"Send the Light"**

The child looked confused. I did not understand. He had done that work before. Then I looked at his work mat.

When I had put out his morning work, I had given him the wrong materials. I had given him a job to do—but the wrong tools with which to do it. The lesson that day was "Teachers make mistakes." My pupils learn that frequently.

When Jesus went back to Heaven, He left us work to do. He promised to be with us. He promised a comforter in the person of the Holy Spirit. He gave us the Bible. He promised the right tools for the right job.

I may not need to be able to drink poison with no ill effect today, but God will equip me for whatever task I do have. If I need to speak to someone, I have the Bible to provide truth. If I need to share in someone's grief, I have experienced grief to soften my heart. Perhaps what happens today will equip me for a task still years away. The joy comes in having a job to do and being able to approach it with the confidence of having the tools I need to do it. God does not make mistakes.

Father, thank You for trusting us with Your work and for equiping us to do it. I pray in Jesus' name. Amen.

Happy Hunger

Then he said to them, "Watch out! Be on your guard against all kinds of greed; a man's life does not consist in the abundance of his possessions" (Luke 12:15, *New International Version*).

Scripture: **Luke 6:17-23**
Song: **"A Child of the King"**

A college student once sent the following note to his father: "No mon! No fun! Your son." The father replied in a similar way: "How sad! Too bad! Your dad." It is easy to assume that money—lots of it—is necessary for fun, contentment, and happiness.

King Solomon was one of the richest men in history. Ecclesiastes 2:4-11 describes his quest for happiness through a variety of possessions and amusements. He finally decided that "everything was meaningless, a chasing after the wind" (v. 11, *New International Version*).

In contrast, many believers in Christ enjoy a "happy hunger." They lack material riches, but focusing their hunger and thirst on spiritual realities, they are filled. When we hunger and thirst for righteousness, we discover the satisfaction only God can give.

Are you hungry?

Our dear God and Father, *sharpen our perception regarding the relative emptiness of material wealth. Guide us as we focus our heart's hunger on that which provides eternal satisfaction. In Jesus' name, amen.*

June 27-30. **Kenton Smith** ministers with the Dunreith (Indiana) Christian Church. He and his wife, Eileen, have four daughters and three grandchildren.

Positively Pure-Hearted

Finally, brothers, whatever is true, whatever is noble, whatever is right, whatever is pure, whatever is lovely, whatever is admirable—if anything is excellent or praiseworthy—think about such things (Philippians 4:8, *New International Version*).

Scripture: **Matthew 5:1-8**
Song: **"Cleanse Me"**

A bumper sticker posed this question: "How much can I sin and still go to Heaven?" Too many of us are satisfied with setting our own standards for purity. We are vaguely aware of what the Bible says, but we dismiss that. In our opinion, eighty percent purity or sixty percent or something less should suffice to gain entrance into God's presence.

Old-timers remember when Ivory soap was touted as being "ninety-nine and forty-four one hundredths percent pure." That was supposed to be as close to absolute purity as a soap could be. As fallible human beings we are certain to fall short of perfection, but we can make a positive effort to practice purity.

Let us be pure in thought, our minds unsullied by greed and lust and selfishness. Let us be pure in word, avoiding the slander and abuse too many tongues employ. Let us be pure in deed, imitating our Savior through honest, compassionate, loving behavior. Jesus calls us to nothing less.

Our Father in Heaven, *thank You for calling us to purity of heart. Help us to avoid mere human standards of purity and focus on those You have revealed in Your Word. In Jesus' name I pray. Amen.*

Peacemaking Without Pretense

[Jesus made] peace through his blood, shed on the cross (Colossians 1:20, *New International Version*).

Scripture: **Matthew 5:9-16**
Song: **"Peace, Perfect Peace"**

The teacher of a weekday religious education class was guiding her fifth-graders in a discussion of Matthew 5:9. "Who are the peacemakers today?" she asked.

One child answered, "Policemen." Another said, "Firemen." Still another said, "Ministers." The teacher smiled her approval at each response. One lad meekly raised his hand and suggested, "Soldiers." The teacher disagreed with the lad, but he was right. Making peace involves dealing with sin, hatred, aggression, and conflict. Jesus brought us peace "through his blood, shed on the cross."

Being a peacemaker is, therefore, more than mouthing flowery phrases about peace. It goes beyond taking part in marches and writing to politicians to plead for peace. Even handshakes and hugs and happy greetings among human beings offer no guarantee of harmony and peace.

We are true peacemakers when we urge people to face up to the sin in their lives and acknowledge their need for a Savior. We are peacemakers when we are "soldiers of the cross," waging war against the real enemy: Satan-inspired rebellion against God.

Our gracious heavenly Father, we praise You for Jesus, who is our peace. While the world clamors for an unrealistic peace, separated from faith and holiness, help us to point to the genuine path to peace. In Jesus' name, amen.

Sunshine and Rain

A cheerful look brings joy to the heart (Proverbs 15:30, *New International Version*).

Scripture: **Matthew 5:43-48**
Song: **"Sunshine in the Soul"**

God gives the sunshine and the rain even to those who ignore Him or rebel against Him. How can we imitate Him?

Our smiles are like warming sunshine. A cheerful look brings joy to the giver and the receiver. When we smile, we lift up the heavy hearts of those who see us. At the same time we may benefit from a smiling response on their part. And, yes, even our enemies can benefit from our glowing faces.

Our words of praise are like the refreshing rain. We can find something to praise in even the most prickly person. Perhaps it is the way she dresses or fixes her hair. It may be the zeal he puts into his work or the care he lavishes on his car. If we rain down sincere verbal praise, we may effect some changes. Her attitude toward us may soften. His harshness toward us may give way to kindness. At least the unhappy one will have experienced some brightness.

We have no control over the weather. But we do have the power to bless others with our own brand of sunshine and rain.

Smile!

Our heavenly Father, *thank You for Your kindness to all people. Help us to imitate You by giving our own sunshine and rain to others. We ask this in Jesus' name. Amen.*

My Prayer Notes

_____

_____

_____

_____

_____

_____

_____

_____

_____

_____

_____

_____

_____

_____

_____

_____

_____

_____

_____

DEVOTIONS

*T*he harvest truly is plenteous, but the laborers are few; pray ye therefore the Lord of the harvest, that he will send forth laborers into his harvest.

—Matthew 9:37, 38

JULY

Photo © *PHOTODISC*

Amazing Mercy

God . . . is rich in mercy (Ephesians 2:4).

Scripture: **Luke 6:32-36**
Song: **"Depth of Mercy! Can There Be"**

Two books by Elisabeth Elliot combine to tell a remarkable story of mercy. *Through Gates of Splendor* describes the martyrdom of her husband and four other missionaries in the jungles of Ecuador. The five were attempting to evangelize the fierce Auca Indians. Their bodies were found on a remote beach where they had landed their plane and commenced an effort to communicate with the Aucas.

The second book is entitled *The Savage My Kinsman*. In it Elliot tells of her personal sojourn, along with her young daughter, in the Auca village. She completed her husband's mission, bringing Christ's love and mercy to a people hated and avoided by others.

This is a level of human mercy that reflects, however dimly, the depth of mercy that God has extended to us. Do we have opportunities to reflect and extend that divine mercy? What a privilege is ours when we do!

"Be . . . merciful, as your Father also is merciful" (Luke 6:36).

Our Father, how we bow in awe and amazement at Your mercy toward us! Open our eyes wider to the marvel of Your mercy, and help us to reproduce it in our response to those who abuse us. I pray in Jesus' name. Amen.

July 1-3. **Kenton Smith** ministers with the Dunreith (Indiana) Christian Church. He and his wife, Eileen, have four daughters and three grandchildren.

God Alone Is Judge

You, then, why do you judge your brother? Or why do you look down on your brother? For we will all stand before God's judgment seat (Romans 14:10, *New International Version*).

Scripture: **Matthew 7:1-5**
Song: **"I Would Be True"**

A crime has been committed. The police arrive and begin to interview the eyewitnesses. They find that they must sort out conflicting testimonies. One eyewitness claims the perpetrator was over 6' tall. Others, however, describe him as between 5' 6" and 5' 9". A woman reports that he was wearing a gray jacket. The rest of the witnesses say he had on a white tee shirt and no jacket. Some say he drove away in a Chevrolet, but some say it was a Buick.

We should not be surprised when eyewitnesses give conflicting testimony. Jesus said human beings sometimes have logs in their eyes. For one it's a log of prejudice toward people whose race or language is different from his. Another has a log of self-centeredness that makes her indifferent to other people's needs. Still another has a log of fearfulness that hinders him from being open and honest toward others. Whatever it is, it keeps them from seeing others clearly.

How careful we must be when we make judgments regarding others on the basis of what we see.

Our Father, we praise You for Your wisdom and patience toward us. We confess to You our proneness to sit in judgment on our fellow human beings. Make us aware of our limitations, the "logs" in our eyes, which make us poor judges. In Jesus' name I pray. Amen.

Judging Ourselves First

Brothers, if someone is caught in a sin, you who are spiritual should restore him gently. But watch yourself, or you also may be tempted (Galatians 6:1, *New International Version*).

Scripture: Luke 6:37-42
Song: "Help Somebody Today"

It was mealtime, and the family gathered around the table. They bowed their heads, and the father offered a prayer of thanks. When they raised their heads again, Jane focused an accusing look on her younger brother. "Jerry had his eyes open during prayer!" she declared.

Children are not the only ones who can harshly accuse others of wrongs when the accusers are equally guilty. Paul's "watch yourself" in his counsel to the Galatians is an exhortation we can all take to heart. If we take notice of our own faults and weaknesses and make an effort to deal with them, that will require much of our attention. And, if an occasion arises when we must call someone else to task for wrongdoing, we will be better prepared to do so. We will more likely be that "spiritual" person who can administer gentle restoration.

Restoring gently someone who has stumbled—what a glorious prospect! And we can do it, if we will practice judging ourselves first.

Our Father, we praise You for gently restoring us to fellowship with You. Help us to avoid setting ourselves up as judges of others. Guide us in the practice of sincere self-examination. May we become gentle spiritual restorers. In Jesus' name I pray. Amen.

A New Nation United Under God

Blessed is the nation whose God is the Lord (Psalm 33:12).

Scripture: **James 5:13-18**
Song: **"God Bless Our Native Land"**

In the summer of 1787, Congress gathered in Philadelphia to debate issues of the Constitutional Convention. Some feared bigger states would have more power; larger states argued that they had more people, therefore the right to greater representation. Tempers flared up; men stormed out of the room. Rather than binding the new nation together, the debate was tearing it apart.

On June 28 Ben Franklin spoke up. He reminded the men that, when they faced eminent danger from the British, they prayed daily for God's protection. Why had they forgotten to do that now? "God governs in the affairs of men," he said. "Is it probable that an empire can rise without his aid?"

On July 4, William Rogers preached to the delegates and prayed for wisdom and strength to work in unity. Men's hearts changed. They created a strong government for the good of the country. Today, Congress opens each day's business with prayer led by a chaplain. This prayer becomes part of the congressional record.

Lord, we are thankful for a country where we can worship in freedom. Thank You for being the guiding light to our founding fathers. Remind us of the importance of prayer in our own lives. In Jesus' name I pray. Amen.

July 4-10. **Jeannie Harmon** is a freelance writer, speaker, conference teacher, and author. She and her husband have two children and two granddaughters.

July 5

Nothing Is Impossible

If you have faith as small as a mustard seed, you can say to this mountain, "Move from here to there" and it will move. Nothing will be impossible for you (Matthew 17:20, *New International Version*).

Scripture: **Mark 11:20-25**
Song: **"O, for a Faith That Will Not Shrink"**

Hannah was a persistent pray-er. She wanted a child, and she knew where to get an answer: the house of God. Year after year, Elkanah took his two wives, Hannah and Peninnah, and Peninnah's children to worship at Shiloh. They offered sacrifices to the Lord Almighty. And, every year, Peninnah taunted Hannah because she had no children. Removing her barrenness became Hannah's main prayer request.

Hannah was fervent in her resolve. She made her way to the tabernacle. In bitterness of soul, she wept before the Lord, promising that if He would answer her prayer, she would give the child to the Lord all the days of his life. She never wavered in her belief that God and God alone could answer her prayer.

Has your faith ever wavered in the face of adversity? Take courage from Hannah's story. Nothing is impossible for God.

Heavenly Father, thank You for being there to hear our prayers. Increase our faith so that we can believe for the answers we need. Our faith often falters, but You are strong. You never change. Nothing is impossible for You, dear Lord. We can trust You completely. In Jesus' name, amen.

The Blessing of a New Generation

Therefore I say to you, whatever things you ask when you pray, believe that you receive them, and you will have them (Mark 11:24, *New King James Version*).

Scripture: Matthew 7:7-11
Song: "Only Believe"

One of the greatest joys of growing older is to rediscover life with my grandchildren. Each "first time" experience—putting on their own clothes, learning to write their names or draw a picture, discovering a bug or butterfly—brings a new freshness to my well-worn sense of awe. When I explain how things should go, they believe me unconditionally because I am the grandma and must surely know about these things. When they ask for a drink or snack from my kitchen, they know that I will provide whatever they need. Their trust in me is unquestioning.

We are raising up a new generation of potential believers. Every verse we quote, every Bible story we tell, and the models we provide with our lives can bring a child closer to believing in a God who is bigger than any problem he or she will face. All that child has to do is believe.

God tells us simply to ask, seek, and knock. He will do the rest. We need not be encumbered by past doubts and fears. Rather, as children, we can believe in the infinite wisdom and knowledge of God and accept that He can provide for our every need.

Father, help us to have a simple, childlike faith. May we encourage faith in those around us so that they will believe in You also. In Jesus' name, amen.

When the Going Gets Tough

Be joyful always; pray continually; give thanks in all circumstances (1 Thessalonians 5:16-18, *New International Version*).

Scripture: **Luke 11:5-13**
Song: **"I Need Thee Every Hour"**

Recently I sat across the table from a friend who had been unemployed for over a year. Despite her efforts, the situation was becoming desperate. The determination needed to eke out a living for her and her teenage daughter seemed to be ebbing.

"I have prayed every day for God to intervene," she said, "but nothing changes."

Where is God when the heavens seem silent? I could not give my friend the money she needed, nor could I solve her problem. But I offered reassurance that God is still where He always is: close. He loves us and cares about our needs.

Even though God hears our prayer the first time we pray, sometimes He requires that we persevere and keep asking. He doesn't turn a deaf ear or forget to answer. He sees a bigger picture. As we seek His face, our circumstances take on a different look and don't seem larger than life. Keeping our eyes on God, we'll find we won't be able to focus on our problems. His perspective will help us know that God is truly in control.

Lord, some days the cares of this life overwhelm me and cause me to doubt Your ability to direct my path. Help me see that You have me tightly in Your hand. Give me the assurance that help is on the way. I turn my situation over to You. In Jesus' name, amen.

A Secret Only God Knows

Thy Father which seeth in secret himself shall reward thee openly (Matthew 6:4).

Scripture: **Matthew 6:1-8**
Song: **"Lord, Be Glorified"**

Why are we drawn to seek public recognition? As a child, I did extraordinary things to obtain some little trinket for friends' birthdays. Then, at the parties, I anxiously awaited the opening of my gift—so I could hear the *oohs* and *aahs* of the group. These efforts brought only a brief reward.

As I grew older, I came face to face with biblical principle. Christ admonishes us to do our praying and good deeds in secret, not to be seen by others. The things done in secret, He will reward openly.

I had an opportunity to see the principle in action. It was getting close to Christmas. A single parent coworker of mine, struggling financially, was facing a meager holiday. The Lord planted the desire in my heart to give her $100 anonymously. I slipped the money in an unmarked envelope and put it on her desk. Did I receive accolades from the department? No. But I knew a secret that, otherwise, only God knew, and I felt great joy in my heart. God's way always brings the greatest reward.

Lord, Your ways are always best. Thank You for helping us know that any prayer we pray or deed we do for others is not unseen by You. Help us to keep our hearts in tune with You so that we may follow Your leading. In Jesus' name I pray. Amen.

A Prayer Sandwich

Lord, teach us to pray (Luke 11:1).

Scripture: **Matthew 6:9-15**
Song: **"The Lord's Prayer"**

Knowing how to pray is so important to our Christian walk, but where do we start? One of my early remembrances of Sunday school is of my teacher helping me learn how to pray. She used a sandwich (something I already knew about) to illustrate what we should say.

"First," she said, "start with a piece of bread. This is our praise to God. We tell Him He is wonderful and thank Him for all the good things He does for us. Then, add the meat. The mayonnaise, cheese, and meat represent our requests before God. We ask Him to help us with the things that are troubling us. Finally, top it off with a second piece of bread. We end with praise and thanksgiving, telling God we love Him."

The truth of that simple message was engraved on my heart that day. Jesus was a storyteller. He used everyday things to illustrate principles that would confound the wise, yet be understood by a child. My teacher had done the same. Nearly fifty years later, each time I eat a sandwich, I am reminded that my spiritual food comes from God when I meet with Him in prayer.

Thank You, Lord, for providing a sample of how we should pray. Keep us ever mindful that our strength and guidance come from You. Never allow us to become so busy that we forget to go to You in prayer. We love You. In Jesus' name, amen.

The Treasure of Fasting

Then your light will break forth like the dawn, and your healing will quickly appear; then your righteousness will go before you, and the glory of the Lord will be your rear guard (Isaiah 58:8, *New International Version*).

Scripture: **Matthew 6:16-21**
Song: **"Open My Eyes, That I May See"**

We live in a world that loves to eat. McDonald's—the world's leading food service retailer—recently reported that it has more than 30,000 restaurants in over 100 countries and serves 46 million customers each day. That is a lot of people eating hamburgers and fries!

In contrast, the Lord admonished us to fast in order to focus on Him. And, to ensure the focus remains on Him, He urged us to dress and behave as usual—not advertising our fast.

How does fasting bring us closer to God? When we are full and content, our spiritual vision may be dimmed. Our eyes may also be dimmed with too much TV watching or too many activities—a "fast" may involve something other than food. God wants us to separate ourselves from anything that desensitizes us, spending time with Him to find the true riches, to find out how He thinks, and to discover our own weaknesses. If we take the time to draw close to God, we will discover where the real treasures lie.

God, please forgive the times that my humanness takes my mind off You. Help me to set aside a special time of fasting and prayer so that I may know Your heart. Teach me Your ways, O Lord. In Jesus' name, amen.

Remembrances of Faith

I will remember the deeds of the Lord; yes, I will remember your miracles of long ago (Psalm 77:11, *New International Version*).

Scripture: **Psalm 78:1-7**
Song: **"Wonderful Words of Life"**

As I unpacked boxes from an old storage unit, I came across several crocheted items I had inherited from my grandmother. Her precision, craftsmanship, and love of color was evident in every stitch. She taught me this art when I was a young child.

But more importantly, she taught me the art of being honest, the value of hard work, the importance of keeping one's word, and the value of tending to details. She taught me how to create something beautiful out of seemingly nothing. Crocheting was just one way my grandmother taught me the lessons of life.

By what methods do you teach the way of righteousness, the practice of honesty, the need for purity? Will your lessons last for generations? When we love God and His children, our faith will be evident. We can be remembered for our faith.

God of all ages, please help us to be aware of the things we teach others. Let our every act be to Your glory. Keep us humble, make us pure, and empower us to be good examples for others to follow and remember. In Jesus' name, amen.

July 11, 14-17. **Malinda Fillingim** and her husband live with their two daughters in Rome, Georgia. She is "still learning what it means to be a faithful follower of Jesus."

Awesome God! Awesome Grace!

O Lord, our Lord, how majestic is your name in all the earth! . . . What is man that you are mindful of him, the son of man that you care for him? (Psalm 8:1, 4, *New International Version*).

Scripture: Isaiah 6:1-10
Song: "Awesome God

One of the most amazing facts ever recorded is the truth that God—the almighty creator of the universe—desires to keep company with human beings. It's a truth we can easily take for granted. In fact, there are some who seem to have the opinion that God is lucky to have them around!

Isaiah had no such egocentricity. He was used to royal courts and kingly splendor, but they were nothing compared to what he saw when God revealed himself to the prophet. "High and exalted" is how the *New International Version* describes Him, and we feel it must understate the case immensely. Isaiah felt "ruined"; the contrast between him and the exalted God was too much to bear.

But God had the solution. He sent His messenger to purge Isaiah's uncleanness. He has done the same for us. This same high and exalted God has sent His Son to purge our own uncleanness. What an awesome God!

What an awesome grace!

Dear Father, I am amazed at Your power, Your holiness, and Your wisdom. More than that, I am amazed at Your grace and Your love, by which You welcome me into Your presence. May I never be proud of my own righteous deeds, but count wholly on the righteousness of Your Son and on the grace that applies it to me. In Jesus' name, amen.

A Great Harvest

He that goeth forth and weepeth, bearing precious seed, shall doubtless come again with rejoicing, bringing his sheaves with him (Psalm 126:6).

Scripture: **Mark 4:1-9**
Song: **"Bringing in the Sheaves"**

"What's a sheave?" Bill asked. "We sing, 'Bringing in the sheaves,' but what's a sheave?"

Between the urbanization of American society and the vast changes in farming methods, the foundation for understanding the hymn—and perhaps Jesus' parables—had not been laid for Bill. His preacher explained first that the word was *sheaf,* the singular for *sheaves.* He explained that "bringing in the sheaves" was a reference to harvest. The standing grain would be cut and tied into bundles, called sheaves, and then carried to the threshing floor to have the grain separated from the straw and chaff.

Farming has changed since the days of "bringing in the sheaves." Today large combines cut, thresh, and pour the grain into wagons to be hauled to large storage bins. The newer methods allow one farmer to till, sow, and harvest much more land, resulting in bigger harvests. Have we been as diligent to improve our methods of spiritual farming? Are we still working to bring in the thirty-, sixty-, and hundred-fold harvest?

Dear Father, thank You for the seed of the gospel, which makes the harvest possible. May we be diligent to sow, cultivate, and harvest—bringing in the sheaves—for You. In Jesus' name, amen.

The Value of Words

Jesus used many stories like these to teach the crowd God's message (Mark 4:33, *New Century Version*).

Scripture: **Mark 4:10-20**
Song: **"I Will Sing the Wondrous Story"**

I was a new teacher mid-year for a fourth grade class—a class that was known for poor behavior and even worse grades! The students had been allowed to rule the roost. I had a great challenge ahead of me!

Traditional teaching methods did not seem to work with this class. I had to come up with new and creative ways of conveying information in order for the students to listen and comprehend. We played educational games, gave prizes for high grades and good behavior, and enlisted community leaders as mentors. Eventually this class became a wonderful group of high-achieving students who all loved school!

Jesus had a challenge in teaching the people something new, unconventional, and earth-shattering! He often used storytelling as His means of conveying heavenly truths. And the people listened! They listened to stories about everyday things to which they could relate—and it worked!

Jesus was (and remains today) the greatest teacher of all times. Are we high-achieving students who love school?

Father, we want to sow the seed of Your Word. Give us creative ways to spread the good news. In Jesus' name I pray. Amen.

Hearing Aids

Be still, and know that I am God; I will be exalted among the nations, I will be exalted in the earth (Psalm 46:10, *New International Version*).

Scripture: **Matthew 13:1-9**
Song: **"Rise Up, O Men of God"**

As a chaplain in a retirement home, I often helped the residents look for lost hearing aids. Eventually, we would find them stuck under a pillow, lost on the floor, or still in a case on the nightstand. Without the hearing aids, the residents often felt lost and left out!

When Jesus shared the story of the farmer and the seeds, the people were given a hearing aid of sorts. They were given the unique gift of a story that illustrated the need for God's children to listen, learn, and live for Him. When our hearing is clear, we can truly listen to God's Word. Then we know what to do that will benefit the kingdom.

"He who has ears," Jesus said, "let him hear" (Matthew 13:9, *New International Version*). Sometimes our ears need a little help—a hearing aid. Prayer, meditation, service, and discipleship are all good spiritual hearing aids that will help us to hear what Jesus is saying.

Don't lose yours!

Lord, we want to receive Your Word. We want to be good hearers of Your Word and to share it with others. Sharpen our hearing so that we hear Your voice clearly. And help us to be both hearers and doers. In Jesus' name I pray. Amen.

20/20 Vision

Jesus said, "For judgment I have come into this world, so that the blind will see and those who see will become blind" (John 9:39, *New International Version*).

Scripture: **Matthew 13:10-17**
Song: **"Be Thou My Vision"**

One of my jobs in seminary was reading to a student who was blind. He was a smart man, with a keen sense of humor. Every day he told me that his goal in life was to see Jesus—both in the lives of others and then on resurrection day, when he would come face to face with our Lord. This man's physical impairment didn't interfere with his spiritual vision!

Many of us who have 20/20 vision physically are often blinded by sin. We fail to heed God's Word, fail to live righteously, fail to confess our shortcomings. When we do these things, we lose sight of what is really important, and that is Jesus.

Jesus says we will be blessed when we choose to see and hear Him. And it is a choice. Some have closed their eyes and have forfeited the blessing. The blessing comes through our intimate walk with Him and our efforts to proclaim Him.

Spiritual blindness can be cured when we look up and see Jesus.

God of all, Lord of my life, illuminate my heart with Your Word. Open my ears to Your Word. Cure me of my spiritual blindness so that I can see Jesus clearly. In Jesus' name, amen.

What Type Are *You?*

I meditate on your precepts and consider your ways. I delight in your decrees; I will not neglect your word (Psalm 119:15, 16, *New International Version*).

Scripture: **Matthew 13:18-23**
Song: **"People Need the Lord"**

I took a personality test recently and discovered I was an extrovert who likes to control things (and, yes, people). I also find comfort in having things organized. That test slotted me as being a certain type of person.

The Scripture today offers a spirituality test:

#1 Seeds fall on people who hear but do not understand God's kingdom! Do they need someone to clarify the message?

#2 Seeds fall on shallow followers who impulsively accept the message but fail to grow deeper. Do they need someone to mentor and disciple them?

#3 Seeds fall on those who worry. Do they need someone to assure them they need not worry over the cares of this world but can trust the God who cares for them?

#4 Seeds fall on people who really want to grow in the Word. Their soil is fertile and ready to produce a good harvest.

What type of Christian are *you*?

Lord, we ask that You help us not to be dull, shallow, or worried in our walk of faith, but to grow daily as strong believers who will produce a harvest. May we be ever diligent to be fruitful and to help others to be fruitful as well. In Jesus' name, amen.

Giving God Our Full Attention

We have not listened to your servants the prophets, who spoke in your name to our kings, our princes and our fathers, and to all the people of the land (Daniel 9:6, *New International Version*).

Scripture: Daniel 9:4-10
Song: "In the Garden"

"Hello, anybody home in there?" my wife said. She wasn't knocking on the door to the neighbor's house; she was looking at the blank expression on my face. I was pre-occupied—again. I apologized and made a better effort to give her my full attention.

Distractions keep us from hearing important things. It's so hard to listen that our local college offers a course dedicated entirely to the subject of listening. I'm afraid my wife may secretly enroll me!

In today's Bible passage, Daniel is heartsick over his own sin and the sin of the people nearest him. "We have not listened," he said (v. 6). Maybe they were distracted, too. Daniel recognized the failure to listen to God as sin.

Maybe the best thing we can do for God today is to ask forgiveness for failing to listen to His Word—and then give Him our full attention.

Dear God, forgive me for the times I have been too distracted to hear Your words clearly as I read the Bible. Today I want to start fresh and hear Your gentle whisper to me. In Jesus' name, amen.

July 18-24. **Greg Swinney** is the ministry director for the Christian Student Fellowship of Nebraska. He and his wife, Laurie, have two children.

In Prison but Set Free

I said, "I will confess my transgressions to the Lord"—and you forgave the guilt of my sin (Psalm 32:5, *New International Version*).

Scripture: **Psalm 32:1-5**
Song: **"Whiter than Snow"**

The worship service at the state penitentiary was especially full this Sunday. A group of us had traveled to the prison, filled out the necessary forms, and were escorted into the large auditorium where nearly a hundred prisoners gathered. When I asked whether anyone wanted to share a favorite Bible passage, a young man near the front stood and recited Romans 8:1. He didn't just say the words; he quoted them from the depth of his heart: "Therefore, there is now no condemnation for those who are in Christ Jesus" (*New International Version*). I don't know what crime he had committed to be put in prison, but I do know he felt the freedom of forgiveness because he had come to Christ.

God does forgive our sin. He frees us from the guilt and pain of our bad choices and sinful behaviors when we come to Him in repentance and confession. In His loving mercy, God looks beyond the sin to the attitude of our heart and extends His grace. When we confess our shortcomings to the Lord and seek His forgiveness, the freedom we find brings unlimited joy.

Dear God, our lives are so far from perfect. Today, as we recognize You are forgiving and merciful, we pray You would forgive us and free us from the guilt we feel. Thank You, Lord. In Jesus' name, amen.

Let's See Who God Really Is

You are forgiving and good, O Lord, abounding in love to all who call to you (Psalm 86:5, *New International Version*).

Scripture: **Psalm 86:1-7**
Song: **"Jesus Loves Me"**

Sociologists and researchers have discovered that different people have different views of God. To some, God is a cosmic Santa Claus. He showers gifts on those who have been "good." To others, God is a sort of Aladdin's lamp. "Rub the lamp three times" (pray) and get a wish. Others view God as a vengeful policeman. He roams the world looking for people who are having fun—and then tells them to stop!

These views of God are worse than inadequate, they are wrong. It's no wonder that some people reject God and don't come to church. Most of us would reject such a mistaken image of God.

The biblical view of God is the accurate one. God is described as a loving Father, a gentle shepherd, and a merciful Lord. The psalmist in today's Bible passage tells us God is loving and forgiving. He longs to forgive us and bless us, if we only will call to Him.

How do you see God? What is the distinguishing characteristic of His nature? Do you feel you can run into His arms as the prodigal son did? Why not run to Him today?

Dear Lord, we thank You today that You abound in love. We have felt so much of that love. We are so blessed because of Your goodness. Thank You for being a heavenly Father we can always turn to. In Jesus' name, amen.

Letting Go for My Own Good

If he sins against you seven times in a day, and seven times comes back to you and says, "I repent," forgive him (Luke 17:4, *New International Version*).

Scripture: **Luke 17:1-5**
Song: **"Jesus, Keep Me Near the Cross"**

Forgiving others doesn't come easily. It's difficult to let go of things someone has said or done against me or against someone in my family. Jesus' disciples struggled with this, just as we do. Today's Bible passage points out the need to forgive—and hints at our tendency to hold grudges.

An unforgiving heart does more harm to us than we can imagine. Not forgiving someone is like drinking poison and waiting for the other person to die. We are hurt much more than the other person is.

"I forgive you" may just be the most healing words a person can ever hear. One may have been wronged by a friend, a spouse, a coworker, someone in the church family, a parent, or someone else. Harboring bitterness will only make matters worse.

Jesus' words to us today urge us to make forgiveness an everyday habit. He tells us to forgive, not once or twice, but up to seven times in one day! Forgiveness heals relationships, heals the hurts of others, and heals our own hearts—to the glory of God.

Dear God, You know how hard it is for us to forgive. The things others have said and done against us seem so cruel. Help us realize today, Lord, our need to forgive others—and teach us how. In Jesus' name, amen.

God's Loving Hug

I urge you, therefore, to reaffirm your love for him (2 Corinthians 2:8, *New International Version*).

Scripture: **2 Corinthians 2:5-11**
Song: **"Bind Us Together"**

Jim was trying to overcome his bad temper, but he was having a tough time. He was the pitcher for the church softball team, and a losing season only made matters worse. Things came to a head when he yelled at an umpire—and sat the rest of the night on the bench. Then Hank sat down by Jim, put his arm around Jim's shoulder, and said, "Jim, you're a bigger man than this. I know you struggle, but with God's help you can overcome. I believe in you."

Paul wrote to Christians in Corinth about a brother who was struggling with sin. Paul had written earlier with orders to take strong disciplinary action against this one (1 Corinthians 5). The sin was serious, and the church's reputation had been damaged as well. Still, Paul urged the church to forgive.

The church is a hospital for sinners, not a museum for the saints. People hunger for God's love and the forgiveness and acceptance of other Christians. Reaffirm your love for someone else today. You may just be the person God has prepared to restore someone to a right relationship with Him.

Dear heavenly Father, we know the church family is only as strong as the individual members. Help us to set the example of forgiveness as You have set the example for us. In Jesus' name, amen.

The Formula for Forgiveness

Then came Peter to him, and said, Lord, how oft shall my brother sin against me, and I forgive him? till seven times? Jesus saith unto him, I say not unto thee, Until seven times: but, Until seventy times seven (Matthew 18:21, 22).

Scripture: **Matthew 18:21-27**
Song: **"Sinner Saved by Grace"**

Black and white—that's the way Peter wanted it. He wanted to know just how many times he was required to forgive someone. He wanted to know that the eighth time someone sinned against him he wouldn't have to forgive any more. He was looking for justification for his self-righteousness.

Jesus responded with a black and white answer, a formula for forgiveness. Some say these numbers really mean 77 times. Others point out that seventy times seven is 490. Still others say the language suggests seventy to the seventh power, which would equal 8,235,430,000,000 times. In that case, calculating would take more effort than forgiving!

Would we want God to stop forgiving us after we've committed the same sin five times? Ten times? How about a hundred times? No. We trust in God's unending grace and limitless forgiveness. Otherwise, how could we ever have a hope for Heaven?

Keep on forgiving—and don't keep track. That's the command of Jesus.

Dear Lord, *You forgive us time and time again. Help us to forgive others no matter how many times we feel wronged by them. In Jesus' name, amen.*

About Forgiveness

Bear with each other and forgive whatever grievances you may have against one another. Forgive as the Lord forgave you (Colossians 3:13, *New International Version*).

Scripture: **Matthew 18:28-35**
Song: **"Amazing Grace"**

Forgiving others as God forgives us is a recurring theme in the teaching of Jesus. When Jesus gave His disciples the model prayer (what many call "the Lord's Prayer"), He taught us to pray: "Forgive us the sins we have done, just as we have forgiven those who did wrong to us" (Matthew 6:12, *New Century Version*). This is a frightening prayer! Do we really want God to forgive us "just as we have forgiven" others? For those of us who struggle with an unforgiving attitude, it means trouble!

Obviously, Jesus compels us to forgive over and over again. That's how we desire to be treated by the Lord, and we need to begin by taking the first step in forgiveness.

A man recently loaned some money to our campus ministry. Some time later he wrote us to say, "Don't worry about paying the loan back; I just want you to have it and to use it for the ministry." His generosity and humility taught us a great deal about the debts we owe and the debts others owe us. The Lord used our friend's gift to bless us and then to teach us!

Dear God, please help me to be able to say the model prayer and really mean it—especially the part about forgiving others. As I let go of the past, I realize, Lord, that You've planned a great future. In Jesus' name, amen.

Measuring Wisdom

The Lord looks down from heaven upon the children of men, to see if there are any who understand, who seek God (Psalm 14:2, *New King James Version*).

Scripture: **Psalm 14**
Song: **"Turn Your Eyes Upon Jesus"**

We often measure intelligence by IQ points, SAT scores, college honors, and career success. By those measurements many atheists are brilliant. Indeed, they have proven themselves shrewd enough to force society to prohibit mention of God in the schools and to remove the Ten Commandments from public buildings!

God doesn't measure intelligence by the world's standards. Psalm 14 begins: "The fool hath said in his heart, There is no God." When we look at history, we understand. The books of Kings and Chronicles contain fascinating accounts of all the kings of Israel. Godless rulers always brought chaos, poverty, and bloodshed on the land. The kings under whom Israel prospered were all men who turned their hearts toward God. Psalm 111:10 says, "The fear of the Lord is the beginning of wisdom." That's why wise men still seek Him.

Dearest heavenly Father, how grateful we are for Your Word, which keeps us on the right path. We praise You and thank You that, whenever we lack wisdom, we can ask You for it. In Jesus' name, amen.

July 25-31. **Maria Anne Tolar** is a Christian writer who lives with her husband in Portland, Oregon.

In Good Time

Do not withhold good from those to whom it is due, when it is in the power of your hand to do so (Proverbs 3:27, *New King James Version*).

Scripture: **Proverbs 3:27-33**
Song: **"Others"**

When my brother was in junior high, he had a paper route in our small Oregon town. The end of each month brought a chore he dreaded: collecting. In terrible weather, my mother sometimes drove him around his assigned territory, to stop at each customer's door and ask for the monthly newspaper payment.

There were wonderful people who either had the cash waiting in an envelope or quickly wrote a check. But there were many other customers who didn't want to bother with finding their purses or wallets. These customers always found excuses to have him come back some other time, and then again, and again. How discouraging it was for him—and for the local newspaper waiting to be paid.

Sometimes what we withhold from others is as simple as a word of encouragement, of thanks, of acknowledgement. I regret friendships in my life that have disappeared, not through harsh feelings, but from my failure to pick up a pen and simply write back. When we use our power to do good, both sides benefit.

What good can you do today?

Dearest Father, I pray for a heart eager to help others, eager to go the extra mile. Let me be quick to seize opportunities to do good. In Jesus' name, amen.

Salt of the Earth

You are the salt of the earth; but if the salt loses its flavor, how shall it be seasoned? (Matthew 5:13, *New King James Version*).

Scripture: **Luke 6:27-31**
Song: **"Pass It On"**

Why is ocean water so salty? Isn't it a pity that nearly three-fourths of the earth's surface is covered by water that is undrinkable, unusable?

Well, no! That salt may be a far greater blessing than many of us ever knew. A recent study from Hebrew University concludes that there is an amazing benefit from the saltiness in the air around oceans. As winds constantly move back and forth from ocean to land, the salt in the air removes practically all the pollutants in the air. Even in desperately polluted areas, people breathe clean air because oceans are salty.

In the Beatitudes Jesus called believers to be salt and light to the world. I once heard a minister mention how much money the church saves local and state governments. Christians reach out to meet an immense variety of needs—not only with local missions providing food and clothing and jobs, but with counseling and hope, prayer and friendship. Special ministries work with addicts and prisoners to give them a future. All this to save souls, who will also become the salt of the earth.

Dearest Lord, *help us to be excellent purifiers, preservers, and seasoning in the world. Thank You for the responsibility and the privilege of being salt and light. In Jesus' name, amen.*

Treasures in Heaven

Command them to do good. . . . In this way they will lay up treasure for themselves as a firm foundation for the coming age, so that they may take hold of the life that is truly life (1 Timothy 6:18, 19, *New International Version*).

Scripture: 1 Timothy 6:13-19
Song: "My Tribute"

Not long before my mother died at age 81, she spoke wistfully of all she had missed out on in life. She'd never been on an airplane, had seldom traveled, and had lived a narrow life. She had done so little, she said. She and my father had always lived comfortably, but frugally.

Looking at her financial records after she was gone, I was amazed at how she had divvied up their limited resources. Month after month, in addition to tithing, she gave a little bit, ten dollars, to each of several ministries. She had selected these ministries with great care, as though buying valuable stocks and bonds. She read their newsletters, listened to their programs, and prayed for them. I was touched she had taken those meager donations so seriously. But it was so little, I thought—until I multiplied it by twelve and saw how it allowed her to be faithful and generous far beyond her means to so many causes during the year. And not just one year, but steadily, year after year.

Mom had not missed out on life. She had taken hold of the life that is truly life!

Dear Lord, *help me be faithful in small things, to store up treasures in Heaven. May I grasp the life that is truly life. In Jesus' name, amen.*

World Views

Do not marvel, my brethren, if the world hates you (1 John 3:13, *New King James Version*).

Scripture: **1 John 3:11-17**
Song: **"A Mighty Fortress Is Our God"**

A national survey was conducted to determine which were the most respected and the least respected of all groups in the country. The most respected? The military. And next to dead last, those least respected and most disliked? Evangelicals.

That shocked me. But the next morning as I read the Bible, I noticed something: the hatred of the world system toward God and His people is a recurring theme in both the Old and New Testaments. Being an Old Testament prophet, for example, was a very dangerous occupation. Throughout the two-thousand-year history of Christianity, millions of Christians have suffered and died for their faith.

A Christian brother in China said, "Christianity is confrontational." He pointed out that Jesus boldly proclaimed an unpopular message in His time despite opposition from the authorities. That example gave the Chinese Christian the boldness and determination to do the same.

We Christians were not put on this earth to be loved. We were put in this world to share the truth in love.

Dearest Lord, *thank You for drawing each one of us out of darkness into Your marvelous light. Grant us such compassion for the lost that we cannot help but be bold in proclaiming Your truth. In Jesus' name, amen.*

Family Matters

I tell you the truth, whatever you did for one of the least of these brothers of mine, you did for me (Matthew 25:40, *New International Version*).

Scripture: **Matthew 25:31-40**
Song: **"I Would Be Like Jesus"**

Does *brothers* in this verse refer to all people?

Some commentaries suggest not, that Christ's reference is specifically to *Christians* who were hungry, thirsty, ill, and in prison. We know Jesus had deep concern for His disciples, because it is through their testimony that the world would come to hear about Him. But He's also concerned because they belong to Him and are under His protection. He loves them.

Sometimes it seems our focus is so intent on saving the lost, that we take those who are found for granted. Do we assume that, because our brothers and sisters in Christ are saved, they have all the answers and resources they need?

Are there hurting Christians among us, sheep of His fold who are spiritually hungry and thirsty and lonely and ill and in prison? As we pray for the mission field, do we pray just as fervently for our missionaries?

How grateful and thrilled we are when a stranger shows kindness to someone we dearly love. What a blessing to know Jesus feels the same way.

Dearest heavenly Father, give us a heart to reach out to the needy, the discouraged, and those with problems within our own church family. Help us treasure our brothers and sisters in Christ. In Jesus' name, amen.

Missing in Action

I tell you the truth, whatever you did not do for one of the least of these, you did not do for me (Matthew 25:45, *New International Version*).

Scripture: **Matthew 25:41-46**
Song: **"We Are So Blessed"**

I once heard a preacher say that, in reading Scripture, we need to major on the major and minor on the minor. When certain precepts are mentioned repeatedly, we need to pay particular attention.

This passage in Matthew is major. Our Lord Jesus spends nine verses giving His Father's blessing at the judgment on those who showed compassion to "one of the least of these brothers of mine." Then He takes the next six verses to reverse the blessing. He pronounces a curse on those who did not come to the aid of "one of the least of these."

Around the world today, brothers and sisters in Christ are routinely imprisoned, tortured, and murdered for their allegiance to Christ. We must help because Jesus makes it a priority. But there's another reason. We need to be humbled by learning the depth of faith and fervor of these suffering Christians. I've read of Christians in China who rejoice when one of their number has the honor of dying for his faith.

Dear Father, we ask for Your wisdom and love for our brothers and sisters in Christ around the world. We ask for boldness to confront evil and to demand that it let Your people go. In Jesus' name, amen.

DEVOTIONS®

*F*or here have we no continuing city, but we seek one to come.

—Hebrews 13:14

AUGUST

Photo © Digital Stock

I Love You

Consecrate the fiftieth year and proclaim liberty throughout the land to all its inhabitants (Leviticus 25:10, *New International Version*).

Scripture: **Leviticus 25:8-12**
Song: **"Love Has Come"**

God established holidays that symbolized the special relationship the Israelites had with Him. Today we also celebrate special holidays.

As I write these words, it is Christmas Day. For this elementary school music teacher, it is indeed the busiest time of the year! Yet on my desk sits a box that puts things into perspective for me. The anonymous gift was wrapped in wrinkled, used wrapping paper, fastened together with at least half a roll of tape, and topped with a lopsided bow, also used. Inside, instead of tissue paper, the giver had carefully crushed black construction paper. And nestled deeply in its construction paper bed was the gift: two chocolate kisses. The message? "I love you, Mrs. Mosby."

Many years ago God sent the first Christmas gift, carefully nestled in a bed of hay inside a wooden feedbox. The message? "I love you, my children."

Heavenly Father, *we thank You for special days that we can celebrate by sharing gifts of love. May we never take our special relationship with you for granted. In Jesus' name, amen.*

August 1-7. **Mary Kay Mosby** teaches elementary music and writes children's songs and musicals. She and her husband have 3 married daughters and 4 grandchildren.

It Took a Miracle

Elijah picked up the child and carried him down from the room into the house. He gave him to his mother and said, "Look, your son is alive!" (1 Kings 17:23, *New International Version*).

Scripture: **1 Kings 17:17-24**
Song: **"'Tis So Sweet to Trust in Jesus"**

In the summer of 1999 my daughter Bethany discovered that she was expecting a baby! Everyone in the family was ecstatic! But our joy quickly turned into concern when her pregnancy began to develop new complications seemingly every day. In the process of endless testing the doctors detected a kidney abnormality in the baby, which showed up in every subsequent test, as well. The problem would demand surgical repair immediately after the baby's birth.

On March 12, 2000, tiny Noah Klay Henry was born. Our joy was bittersweet, however, because tests quickly confirmed the presence of the kidney problem. Noah was transferred to Children's Hospital in Minneapolis to await surgery. But when doctors there performed their own tests, they were baffled! The kidney problem was nowhere to be found!

Noah's health has not been perfect. Still, his family continues to trust and serve the same God of miracles who gave life to the widow's son and healing to my grandson!

O God of miracles, we thank You and praise You for Your power and compassion. Help us to remember that You still hear and answer our prayers today. In Jesus' name we pray, amen.

Whom Do You See?

Isn't this the carpenter's son? Isn't his mother's name Mary, and aren't his brothers James, Joseph, Simon and Judas? (Matthew 13:55, *New International Version*).

Scripture: **Matthew 13:54-58**
Song: **"What Child Is This?"**

The residents of Nazareth had known Jesus and His family for years. So when He returned as a famous teacher and healer, they found themselves unable to look beyond Jesus the carpenter's son and see Jesus God's Son.

Once there was an artist who wanted to paint a picture of Christ on the cross. When he had finished his first sketch, he called in his landlady's little girl. He asked her who she thought was depicted in the sketch. She replied, "It is a good man."

Knowing he had failed, the artist tore up the first sketch and began again. He held this second sketch before the little girl. The child said that it looked like a great sufferer.

Again he destroyed the sketch, and, after much prayer, made a third sketch. This time the little girl saw what the artist intended and exclaimed, "It is the Lord!"

That is what makes Christ's coming meaningful: not that He was merely a good man, not that He was a brave sufferer, but that God came! Emmanuel!

Father in Heaven, guide us in our study of Your Word, that we might be able to see You more clearly and better appreciate who You are. Please forgive us when we underestimate how You can change the lives of those who love You. In the name of Jesus I pray, amen.

The Carpenter's Son

Jesus said to them, "Only in his hometown, among his relatives and in his own house is a prophet without honor" (Mark 6:4, *New International Version*).

Scripture: **Mark 6:1-6**
Song: **"Thou Didst Leave Thy Throne"**

Jesus was doing His Father's work, teaching the multitudes who came to hear Him. But to the people of Nazareth, He was still just the son of a carpenter, and they were offended that He postured himself as something more. It seemed impossible for them to respond to Him.

When Elizabeth Barrett married Robert Browning, her parents disowned her. But because she loved them so much, she tried everything to restore her relationship with them. Every month she wrote several kind and loving letters to them. Finally, after writing letters for ten years, she received a package from her parents. But her excitement turned quickly to sorrow when she found all of her letters inside, still unopened.

Today those letters are considered to be "some of the most beautiful and expressive in all English literature." Elizabeth tried to reconcile with her parents. Jesus tried to reach out to the people of His hometown.

He's reaching out to you, today. How will you answer?

***Dear Lord,** every day we are inundated by words and thoughts, both written and spoken, that would have us doubt who You really are. Give us the wisdom, as we study Your Word, to see You and respond to You. In Jesus' name we pray, amen.*

The Custom of Worship

He went to Nazareth, where he had been brought up, and on the Sabbath day he went into the synagogue, as was his custom (Luke 4:16, *New International Version*).

Scripture: **Luke 4:14-19**
Song: **"Blest Be the Tie that Binds"**

Synagogues were used for worship on the Sabbath and as boys' schools during the week. Synagogues were established during the exile, when the Jews no longer had the temple, but they continued to exist even after the temple had been rebuilt. Our verse says that Jesus went to the synagogue, "as was his custom." The Son of God knew the importance of regularly attending worship services.

One day a church member and his minister were relaxing in front of a fireplace. The church member said, "I can worship just as easily in my garden as I can in a church pew." The minister thought for a moment and then stepped closer to the fire. He picked up the long fireplace tongs and removed one single glowing ember from the fire. Then he carefully placed it on the hearth. They watched as the ember became nothing but black ash. After a few moments of silence the church member said, "You don't have to say a word. I understand. I can't worship alone any more than I can live alone. I'll be in church next Sunday!"

The environment of worship is basic to Christian growth. We'll see you in church next Sunday!

Mighty God, *thank You for the privilege of worship. May it be said that we, like Christ, worship regularly, as is our custom. In Jesus' name, amen.*

Good News!

And he began by saying to them, "Today this scripture is fulfilled in your hearing" (Luke 4:21, *New International Version*).

Scripture: **Luke 4:20-24**
Song: **"O Come, O Come, Emmanuel"**

The story is told of two unbelievers who were on a train and began to discuss Christ's life. One man said, "I think an interesting romance could be written about Him."

The other man replied, "And you are just the man to write it. Set forth the correct view of His life and character. Tear down the prevailing sentiment as to His divinity, and paint Him as He was—a man among men."

And so the decision was made, and the romance was written. The author of the resulting novel was General Lew Wallace, and the name of his book was *Ben Hur*.

But in the process of writing *Ben Hur*, something very interesting happened. The more that Wallace studied Christ's life and character, the more convinced he became that Jesus was more than just a man among men. Wallace came to declare, "Verily, this was the Son of God."

Truly, Christ was and is God's Son! When we accept this fact, we have no difficulty in understanding and accepting Christ's declaration in today's verse: "Today this scripture is fulfilled in your hearing."

Who among your friends needs to meet Jesus today?

Lord, as Your children, we recognize You as the Son of God. Let us take this good news to the world, especially to those who believe that You were merely a man among men. In Jesus' name we pray, amen.

It Can't Be True!

"I tell you the truth," he continued, "no prophet is accepted in his hometown" (Luke 4:24, *New International Version*).

Scripture: **Luke 4:25-30**
Song: **"Shine!"**

The people of Nazareth were enraged by Jesus' remarks. Among other things, Jesus dared to say that God sometimes reached out to the Gentiles. But God did, and now what a responsibility is ours!

By the Amazon River a missionary was teaching a group of children about Jesus. An old man with stooped shoulders and gray hair joined them. He listened closely as the woman told the story of God's grace, as revealed in Christ. When the children were gone, the old man spoke to the missionary: "May I ask if this story is true?"

"Of course," she replied. "It's in the Word of God!"

The old man said, "This is the first time in my life that I have heard that a person must give his life to Jesus to have forgiveness from sin and eternal life. If this story were true, someone would have come before now to tell it. I am old. My parents lived and died without having heard it. It can't be true, or someone would have come sooner." Although the missionary tried, she could not convince the old man. Turning back into the darkness, he just kept repeating, "It can't be true, or someone would have come sooner."

Our dear Lord and heavenly Father, we are so thankful that it was Your plan that Christ would come to die for all people. May we be missionaries of salvation to everyone we meet. In Jesus' name we pray, amen.

Just Say the Word

But say the word, and my servant will be healed (Luke 7:7, *New International Version*).

Scripture: Luke 7:1-10
Song: "Just When I Need Him Most"

We have a friend who owns a fair amount of stock. He's unselfish and often sells some to give something to the needy. Occasionally, a particular charity will contact him, asking for his help with special concerns.

When this happens, does our friend hop a plane to New York City, take a taxi to Wall Street, and enter the stock exchange to transact business? Of course not! He simply picks up his telephone, calls his broker, and says, "Sell." Within days, the charity has its money.

A Roman centurion in Jesus' day had a servant who was ill. The official was so concerned that he sent some Jews to find Jesus. Yet, as this man thought on the situation, he realized that Jesus' physical presence wasn't necessary. For if Jesus was indeed the Son of God, He had only to speak for His power to be released.

When Jesus heard of this Gentile's faith, He did speak—and the servant immediately was healed.

Lord God, thank You for Your powerful Word—so that Jesus had only to speak to bring healing to a centurion's servant. Thank You that the same power is available to cleanse us from sin today. In Jesus' name, amen.

August 8-14. **Chris Ahlemann** is a writer, minister's wife, teacher, and church missions director. She and her husband have two grown children and one grandson.

Enough for All

Whoever comes to me I will never drive away (John 6:37, *New International Version*).

Scripture: Matthew 9:18-26
Song: "Room at the Cross for You"

I once knew a woman who had ten children. And she always seemed to have time for each of them. There was John, who needed money for camp, and Mary, who wanted help making doll clothes. Philip was having trouble in college.

Jesus was like that woman. One day a ruler came to Him, grieving over the death of his daughter. Would Jesus come and make her live again? Of course, Jesus went. But on the way, He encountered a woman who'd been bleeding for twelve years. Did Jesus ignore her so He could hurry on to the ruler's home? No. He seemed, in fact, to understand her sensitive nature and took time to speak to her kindly. "You are healed," He said. But wait! What about the ruler's family? Was his family to continue grieving with no hope? Again, the answer is no. Jesus took time to enter the home and bid the child rise.

Perhaps today you have a need. But so does your neighbor, your boss, or your cousin. Don't worry. Jesus has enough time, enough power, and enough love to meet the needs of all His children.

Precious Father, thank You for seeing each of Your children as someone special. We praise You for using Your vast resources to meet the unique needs of each one. In Jesus' name, amen.

Seeing the Christ

You are the Christ, the Son of the living God (Matthew 16:16, *New International Version*).

Scripture: **Matthew 9:27-31**
Song: **"No Other Plea"**

How precious is the gift of sight! Isn't it wonderful to marvel at emerald grass or turquoise skies, or to view the path ahead. The two men in our Scripture for today had experienced none of these things. They could not see the fruit in the market or view the faces of those milling about. Yet they recognized one man who stood out among the crowd. He spoke with love, compassion, and authority. And something about His presence brought to mind prophecies concerning the Messiah.

"Son of David!" they cried.

Jesus went on by. But the men would not be deterred. They had recognized Him as the one God had promised, and they wouldn't let Him go. Following Jesus into a nearby house, they approached Him. Jesus asked them if they believed He could heal their eyes.

"Oh, yes, " they replied. "You are the Lord. You are the promised one. You can do anything."

Jesus touched their eyes then and gave them physical sight. And all because, through their blindness, they recognized that He was the Christ.

Dear Father, thank You for Jesus, the redeemer promised to humankind. And thank You that, when we recognize Him, You give us a whole new perspective on life. In Jesus' name, amen.

Life Restored

Immediately her bleeding stopped and she felt in her body that she was freed from her suffering (Mark 5:29, *New International Version*).

Scripture: **Mark 5:24-34**
Song: **"Since Jesus Passed By"**

Forty-eight years ago I nearly lost my parents in an automobile accident. Those first on the scene said that my father nearly bled to death. In those days before seat belts, he'd been thrown through the windshield. Only the quick action of ambulance attendants and doctors—and the grace of God—saved his life.

There was a woman in the Bible who had also lost a lot of blood—slowly, over a period of twelve years. She'd spent all her money on doctors and still was not well. Then one day, in the midst of a crowd, she saw Jesus. If only she could touch Him! She did, and immediately her bleeding stopped. The pain that had plagued her was gone. Now she was free to live.

So many of us in modern society bleed on the inside. Shattered dreams, broken promises, and bitter disappointments cause the essence of life to drain away. Yet, in the midst of all this, Jesus still stands. And if we'll stretch out a hand of faith, He will stop our bleeding and give hope for the future.

Loving Father, how good it is to know that when our broken hearts have bled until we're too weak to go on, You have the power to make the bleeding cease and to quicken our lives. Thank You. In Jesus' name, amen.

Believing Brings Hope

But the righteous hath hope in his death (Proverbs 14:32).

Scripture: **Mark 5:35-43**
Song: **"The Promise"**

I recently attended the funeral of a neighbor. Following the service, the widow wailed and struck at the casket in her grief. I found the scene especially unsettling because I knew several people had tried to share Jesus with her prior to her husband's death.

Later, I spoke to the funeral director of my concern. He shook his head and said, "I've been conducting funerals for over twenty years, and I can always tell if members of the family are believers or not. Those who aren't come completely unglued. But those who do believe, even though they cry, are filled with hope. They know that Jesus will raise their loved ones to new life."

All the neighbors and friends who had crowded into the home of Jairus that day were like the widow of my neighbor. They wept and wailed because they thought death was the end of everything. But Jairus and his wife had hope. They believed that Jesus could overcome this final threat. And because of their belief, Jesus allowed them to see firsthand that He was indeed more powerful than death.

"Arise," He said, and their hope became sight.

Almighty God, *thank You for sending Jesus to show us that You have power over death. Help us to believe in that power until it fills our hearts with hope. In Jesus' powerful name, amen.*

Releasing God's Power

"Who touched me?" Jesus asked. . . . "Someone touched me; I know that power has gone out from me" (Luke 8:45, 46, *New International Version*).

Scripture: **Luke 8:40-48**
Song: **"He Is Able to Deliver Thee"**

I once knew a woman who suffered from feelings of inferiority. Day after day she moved through life, fearing she didn't count. Why did others have confidence when she had none? She talked to friends, but they dismissed her as a worrier. She married well, thinking a husband would help. But he, too, failed her.

And then one day someone told her about Jesus. He sounded so wonderful that she decided to attend church. Quietly she slipped into the back pew. Sometime during the service she began to sense that He was real—and not only real *somewhere* but present with her. Dare she claim Him for her own? She reached out to Him that day and felt His life-changing power. By faith she had found His saving power.

Another woman once suffered with no one to help her. But when she heard about Jesus, she dared to reach out and touch His cloak. Instantly, she felt a power. A power so incredible that Jesus felt it leave Him. And when He saw the woman, He told her that she was healed. Her act of faith had made her whole.

Precious Lord, *thank You for the power of Your presence which You freely give to anyone who will stretch forth the hand of faith. In Jesus' name, amen.*

A Child Lives

Then a man named Jairus, a ruler of the synagogue, came and fell at Jesus' feet, pleading with him to come to his house because his only daughter, a girl of about twelve, was dying (Luke 8:41, 42, *New International Version*).

Scripture: **Luke 8:49-56**
Song: **"He Touched Me"**

A Christian couple lost their only daughter. Oh, she did not die. Without telling them where she was going, she just disappeared into a life of sin. Day after day they feared for her safety. In desperation, they turned to Jesus. Falling on their faces, they pleaded with Him to restore their child to an honorable, decent life. Their friends told them to stop wasting their time. The girl was gone forever, they said.

But the parents believed in the power of God and continued to pray. And then one day, their daughter returned. Jesus had touched her, she said, and had given her real life.

A man named Jairus was losing his only daughter to death. He was so broken up that he came and fell at Jesus' feet. This ruler of the Jews recognized the awesome power of God and pleaded for the life of his child. Friends and family told him to stop bothering Jesus. They said the girl was dead and nothing could be done. But Jairus and his wife clung to the belief that Jesus had power over death.

And He rewarded their faith. Isn't Jesus wonderful?

Dear God, *thank You for the power You have to restore life. Thank You for hearing the cries of broken parents everywhere and for rewarding their faith. In Jesus' name, amen.*

Training and Toothpicks

And thou shalt teach them diligently unto thy children, and shalt talk of them when thou sittest in thine house (Deuteronomy 6:7).

Scripture: **Deuteronomy 6:1-9**
Song: **"Love at Home"**

Supper time was family time at our farm home. After we had eaten, Papa brought out his well-worn Bible. Sitting next to Papa, I begged for stories like David and Goliath or Daniel in the lions' den—never tiring of hearing them. Sometimes I became so intrigued that I would lean closer and closer to the big Bible until Papa gently pushed my head away so he could see the text.

After reading the Bible, though he was tired from a hard day's work, Papa said a long prayer, pleading for God's blessing and mercy for each of us.

Afterward he went around the table to reach for a toothpick in the cupboard. Then he planted a kiss on Mama's forehead, and Mama said, "Oh, Papa," pushing him away. We all giggled each time, anticipating this little ritual.

The Word of God, the prayer, and the love shown all gave our young lives the security needed in a family.

Dear Father, *thank You for the example of Christian parents. Help us be faithful to Your Word, remembering that others may be following in our steps. In Jesus' name, amen.*

August 15-21. **Mary Ellen Gudeman** was a missionary in Japan for 26 years. She now writes and works with international students and refugees.

Sharing and Caring

Thou shalt not defraud thy neighbor, neither rob him (Leviticus 19:13).

Scripture: **Leviticus 19:11-18**
Song: **"Living for Jesus"**

Farming during the Depression could be risky. Bad weather could wipe out a whole year's work. Pests were a problem, too. One summer chinch bugs destroyed many fields of corn. Papa joined anxious neighbors as they helped each other. Standing like sentinels, they took turns pouring huge buckets of creosote across dusty country roads to keep the invaders from destroying the next farmer's crop. I watched Papa's sad face as he stared at the black insect army crawling across the fields, wiping out days of hard labor—and a whole year's income.

Strong ties among neighbors seemed essential to economic survival. Papa and Eli, a neighboring farmer, owned an old threshing machine, which was shared among ten other farmers as well. Community spirit ran deep; the farmers combined their efforts in harvesting the grain and took pride in helping each other.

At the end of a season, Papa and Eli had an ice cream social for all the families. The books were balanced, and adjustments made for the farmers who suffered more loss than others.

Dear Father, *thank You for the godly example of an earthly father. Help me be generous, as he was, and share what I have with someone more needy than I am. In Jesus' name, amen.*

The Price

He is despised and rejected of men . . . yet he opened not his mouth (Isaiah 53:3, 7).

Scripture: **Matthew 22:34-40**
Song: **"Wounded for Me"**

Isaiah seems to use every possible definition he can to portray the suffering of the Messiah prophesied to come. His rejection by His own people sounds overwhelmingly harsh. In stark contrast is the love of Jesus, who perfectly demonstrates the love He taught.

When I was in Japan, I visited Mikimoto Pearl Island. I watched the divers gather oysters. Later, in the processing room, I noted a shallow pan of water with some oysters afloat. A sign advertised a 500-yen fee for mounting any pearl found. After gazing at these unattractive creatures, I finally decided to purchase one. When the clerk reached for a knife, I objected. "What happens to the oyster?"

"It dies, of course," an irritated voice replied.

I shuddered and paused. She turned to other customers. "It'll die anyway," I thought. "Someone else will buy it." Finally I summoned the clerk, turning my back on the oyster. I thought of the cross and the price our Savior paid. The world finds no beauty in Him and turns its back. Yet He loves me more than himself, and He gives me beauty and value when I love Him with all my heart, soul, and mind.

Dear Father, *thank You for the cross where my Savior bore all my sin debt. Because of this price, I am not only forgiven, I have that glorious hope to spend eternity with Him. In Jesus' name, amen.*

Grace Exemplified

And thou shalt love the Lord thy God with all thy heart, and with all thy soul, and with all thy mind, and with all thy strength: this is the first commandment (Mark 12:30).

Scripture: **Mark 12:28-34**
Song: **"I Love You, Lord"**

While on a missionary furlough, I was given the painting of *Grace* by Eric Enstrom. It reminded me of my father when he said grace for our meals. When I returned to Japan, I hung the painting in the entrance of my apartment, where my friend, Dote-san, often admired it.

Dote-san exemplified another kind of grace. She helped me with neighborhood outreach. Whenever she came to visit, she brought a bouquet of flowers or some fresh fish or sweet cakes. Once I had to be hospitalized for a long period of time. Dote-san made many trips to see me, bringing my mail and always some gift.

Upon my retirement, I felt sorrowful to leave this devoted friend. In quiet unassuming ways, she had filled a need in my life. How could I thank her? *Grace*, of course! She clasped the painting to her bosom and bowed deeply as we said our *sayonaras.*

My father and Dote-san understood grace. They lived the Lord's first commandment. Their lives reflected their commitment to the Lord, whom they loved with all their heart, soul, mind, and strength.

Dear Father, *thank You for the gracious lives of people who literally live Your first commandment. Help me go and do likewise. In Jesus' name, amen.*

Knitted Together

Holding the Head, from which all the body by joints and bands having nourishment ministered, and knit together, increaseth with the increase of God (Colossians 2:19).

Scripture: Luke 10:25-29
Song: "Freely, Freely"

Many years ago a friend who lived in the same boarding house as I volunteered to teach me how to knit.

"For now, just make small squares," she explained. "I'll only teach you the knitting stitch at first because your stitches will change. Later I'll teach you how to purl."

Periodically, my friend dropped in to evaluate my progress. "Make a few more," she prodded as she looked over my handiwork. Then one day she moved away.

Hoping someone would come along who could teach me how to purl, I bought more yarn and continued making squares. I improved with the practice, but I could not go on to anything new. Eventually, with no hope of an instructor in sight, I decided to make an afghan from all the squares. Amazingly, the most recent, well-knit squares stretched to accommodate the poor ones made earlier.

Our lives are daily blended with the lives of others. As we yield ourselves to our Creator, the weaker ones are made stronger, and the strong share in the joy of this fellowship.

Dear Creator God, help me yield to Your pattern for my life and be an example, as well, to those around me who need my encouragement, my love, and my time. In Jesus' name, amen.

Open My Eyes

But a certain Samaritan, as he journeyed, came where he was; and when he saw him, he had compassion on him (Luke 10:33).

Scripture: **Luke 10:30-37**
Song: **"Close to Thee"**

I gasped when I saw a girl stumble and fall face down on the sandy, graveled surface at the train station in Japan where I served as a missionary. "Somebody help her!" I gasped frantically as the crowd swept me into the waiting train car. The girl recovered and jumped on the train just before the door closed.

My head ached from fatigue, the heat, and hunger after a busy day on campuses teaching Bible classes. The cars swayed and jostled the poor girl in front of me. Grit and sand clung to her. She bled from her mouth, hands, elbows, and knees. Other passengers looked away.

I struggled to open my handbag for some tissues, but overwhelmed from the stifling air, the packed bodies, the pathetic sight, and my own tiredness, I began to faint. The train jerked to a stop, and I fell into an empty seat as passengers vacated. After a few more stops, I spotted the girl getting off—and felt sad about my own helplessness.

As I stumbled out at my station, I prayed for the unknown passenger whom I could not help. Sometimes praying is all a "good Samaritan" can do for someone in need.

Dear Father, *open my eyes to see and my heart to feel the needs of so many around me. Help me reach out to them with the touch of a good Samaritan. In Jesus' name, amen.*

My Love Debt

Owe no man any thing, but to love one another: for he that loveth another hath fulfilled the law (Romans 13:8).

Scripture: **Romans 13:8-14**
Song: **"In Christ There Is No East or West"**

Paul seems to be saying the debt to love others can never be paid in full. While serving as a missionary, I learned one day how difficult it can be to try to pay it.

A young working girl saw a leaflet about our Saturday youth meetings and decided to attend. While getting acquainted, I noted she lived near my apartment. She seemed lonely so, despite my overloaded schedule, I invited her for a visit.

I watched her as we talked—her sallow face, the bony hands grasping her stomach, the nervous cough. She shared about her lifestyle of drinking and her suicidal thoughts. This visit led to innumerable visits and countless hours of counseling as I shared God's Word with her.

I noticed that the young people avoided her when she came to our Saturday meetings, intensifying her loneliness. Her brother's illness and subsequent death added to her bitterness. I often became weary hearing about her many problems. But one day the message of the Bible entered her heart, and she trusted in Christ. Then gradually she learned how to get along better with others and found friends in the church.

Dear Father, lead me to hungry, lonely hearts and help me take the time to share Your Word with them. In Jesus' name, amen.

Christians Are Equals

Make every effort to keep the unity of the Spirit through the bond of peace (Ephesians 4:3, *New International Version*).

Scripture: **Ephesians 4:1-6**
Song: **"The Bond of Love"**

Oliver Cromwell had replaced the king of England, and by 1653 he went by the title of Lord Protector of England. When he received a letter from the king of France, he refused to accept it until the king referred to him as brother. Cromwell saw himself as an equal.

Christians are equal. In today's text the apostle Paul tells us to be humble, be gentle, be patient. When we place ourselves first, we lose sight of the Lord Jesus. However, when we allow the Lord into our lives and give Him first place, there's a strong sense of being one with other Christians.

Unity requires effort. When we all focus on the Lord Jesus, there is unity and, above all, peace. When self rules, peace departs. When we are at war with others, we are at war with ourselves. But when Christ enters our lives, the warring part of us departs and we are at peace. It takes effort, nevertheless, to stay at peace. That's the reason Paul encourages us to work hard at keeping the unity of the Spirit through the bond of peace.

Gracious Lord, help us to keep our eyes on You and to receive Your strength so that we can live at peace with others. In Jesus' name, amen.

August 22-28. **David R. Nicholas** is a minister and writer who lives with his wife, Judith, in New South Wales, Australia.

Imitating Christ

Your attitude should be the same as that of Christ Jesus: . . . taking the very nature of a servant, being made in human likeness. . . . he humbled himself (Philippians 2:5-8, *New International Version*).

Scripture: **Philippians 2:1-8**
Song: **"Just a Closer Walk with Thee"**

James Thurber wrote *The Secret Life of Walter Mitty*. Mitty was a daydreamer. He often sat in an old chair and dreamed: one moment he was a sea captain, in the next moment a great surgeon, and then a brave army captain. Mitty was comparing himself with others. Christians need only compare themselves with Christ. When we do this, there is no place for pride. We are always humbled when we look at the Lord.

Believers are called to imitate the life of Jesus. Our example is clearly set out in the New Testament, where we can follow the life and times of Jesus, the Messiah. It was a Japanese Christian, Toyohiko Kagawa, who said: "I read somewhere that this young man, Jesus Christ, went about doing good. But I just go about."

The exciting thing about the Christian life is that, if we keep our eyes on Jesus Christ, we'll automatically discover that we go about doing good—because we'll be imitating the life of our Lord and Master.

Almighty God, please help us to keep focusing on the life of Your Son. We know that, if we do this, we'll become more and more like Him. This we pray in the name of Jesus, amen.

The Door Is Low

Humble yourselves, therefore, under God's mighty hand, that he may lift you up in due time (1 Peter 5:6, *New International Version*).

Scripture: **1 Peter 5:3-10**
Song: **"Humble Thyself in the Sight of the Lord"**

An unknown writer wrote: "Humble we must be if to Heaven we go. High is the roof there but the door is low."

The early disciples had the advantage of living with Jesus in person. They saw how He lived and how He spoke. Perhaps most significant of all, they saw how He acted in various situations. They saw His humility. When we become Christians, we are called to live a life based on the life of Jesus.

While we do not have the advantage of having lived with Jesus while He was on earth, we do have the advantage of all the writings His disciples left behind. We also have the presence of the Holy Spirit to guide and direct us. Following Jesus would be extremely difficult on our own. So Jesus promised us the Holy Spirit. Paul explains, "The Spirit helps us in our weakness" (Romans 8:26, *New International Version*).

One Christian writer observed that many of us are "too talented." With our own talents we may fail to depend on the power of the Spirit. When we humble ourselves and lean on Him, then we find true power.

Lord, *thank You so much for providing the way for us to humble ourselves through the guidance of Your Holy Spirit. In Jesus' name, amen.*

Christ Invites Everyone

He sent his servants to those who had been invited to the banquet to tell them to come, but they refused to come (Matthew 22:3, *New International Version*).

Scripture: **Matthew 22:1-10**
Song: **"Bring Them In"**

Some years ago I was chaplain on a Greek ship, the *Ellinis*, a vessel that was taking immigrants to Australia. One evening Captain Kaliviotis invited my wife and me to dine at his table. As a chaplain it was my duty to attend. I could not refuse. The captain invited. I accepted. Many people would have liked an invitation for the captain's table. But invitations were restricted, so few among the many on the ship were ever invited.

How different is the Lord's invitation—offered to everyone. The story recorded in today's reading tells of people invited to a banquet but refusing the invitation. Our Lord offers the gift of salvation, but many refuse His gift. Many invitations, myriads in fact, have been issued by the Lord, for all are invited to accept His invitation.

God has been most patient. Through the centuries He has sent various invitations encouraging people to accept the offer of His love. The greatest of these invitations came when God sent His Son into the world. The cross is God's greatest invitation.

Thank You, Lord, *for giving us an invitation to share life with You throughout eternity. Please help us to tell as many others as possible about Your wonderful invitation. In Jesus' name, amen.*

The Wisdom of Jesus

But they remained silent. So taking hold of the man, he healed him and sent him away (Luke 14:4, *New International Version*).

Scripture: **Luke 14:1-6**
Song: **"God Will Take Care of You"**

God has placed some wonderful doctors on earth. God heals in many different ways, but we often overlook the fact that doctors have been given skill from on high.

The incident in our reading is recorded by Dr. Luke. Being a medical man, Luke must have been most interested in the healing methods of the great physician. In this case a man with dropsy was healed. Dropsy has been described as "an unnatural collection of water in any part of the body."

Some suggest the religious leaders (the Pharisees) had deliberately placed the sick man there to try and trap Jesus. Would He heal on the Sabbath, in violation of their interpretation of the Jewish law? However, Jesus was not to be trapped—for He was aware of their traps and tricks.

We see in this story the wonderful power of Jesus to heal. We see also His incredible understanding. If He knew the scheming of the Pharisees, then He knows my heart as well. And, wonder of wonders, He does not turn away. He offers to cleanse my heart as surely as He healed the man with dropsy.

Heavenly Father, *help us to believe in Your healing powers and to trust You to select the way You may choose to heal us. We ask this in the name of Jesus, the great physician, amen.*

You Go First; I Follow

But when you are invited, take the lowest place, so that when your host comes, he will say to you, "Friend, move up to a better place." Then you will be honored in the presence of all your fellow guests (Luke 14:10, *New International Version*).

Scripture: **Luke 14:7-14**
Song: **"I'll Put Jesus First in My Life"**

Principal Cairns, a Scot, was well known for being humble. One day when he arrived at a platform, there was a burst of applause. Cairns stood aside and let the man after him go first and began himself to applaud. He never dreamt the applause could possibly be for him—it had to be for the other man.

Pride and conceit can cut us off from God and from His grace. Benjamin Whichcote went so far as to say, "A proud man has no God."

Jesus accepted an invitation to a Sabbath meal to be held in a house owned by one of the Jewish rulers of the Pharisees. Perhaps it was a ruler of the synagogue where Jesus had taught. As we saw yesterday, the Jewish leaders were persistently trying to trap Jesus. Proud of their so-called spirituality, these leaders were bounded on the north, south, east, and west by Self.

But Jesus said, "He who humbles himself will be exalted" (v. 11, *New International Version*).

Dear Lord, *help us, please, to put others first and not always to seek first place for ourselves. Please fill us with Your grace, for Jesus' sake. In His name we pray, amen.*

God Invites

For he says, "In the time of my favor I heard you, and in the day of salvation I helped you." I tell you, now is the time of God's favor, now is the day of salvation (2 Corinthians 6:2, *New International Version*).

Scripture: **Luke 14:15-24**
Song: **"Jesus Shall Reign"**

An old woman lived in a small cottage not far from Queen Victoria's castle in Scotland. One day, the woman quarreled with her neighbor. In anger she shut her door, locked it, and determined not to answer it. A little while later there was a gentle tap, tap at the door. The woman said, "Go away. I won't let you in." Imagine how she felt next day when she was told that the Queen had stopped outside her door and had been refused entry. The Queen never called again.

In our passage today, we find the story of an invitation that was given for a feast; but those invited would not come. God has constantly sent out His messengers to tell the world of His endless love. The efforts of these messengers go all the way back to the Old Testament.

Finally God sent His only Son. Jesus told people about God's goodness and longsuffering. He taught that God loves us in spite of all the wrongs we have done. Surely we cannot refuse the invitations of God.

Heavenly Father, *thank You for Your invitation to become Your children. Please help us to tell others of Your wonderful invitation. In the name of Jesus, we pray, amen.*

The Spirit of God

Even on my servants, both men and women, I will pour out my Spirit in those days (Joel 2:29, *New International Version*).

Scripture: Joel 2:23-29
Song: "Sweet, Sweet Spirit"

As a kid, I had a very worldly understanding of the Holy Spirit. He was always called the Holy "Ghost" then, and I envisioned Him as a sort of white wispy something that hovered around. I never was sure what He did! Fortunately, as I got older, I understood more about the importance of the Holy Spirit.

In this passage from Joel, God is promising to send the Holy Spirit to all of His followers, regardless of sex, age, or rank. Peter quoted this passage from Joel in his Pentecost sermon (Acts 2:16-21), where it specifically referred to the divinely empowered apostles. Peter went on to say the gift of the Holy Spirit would be given to all who responded to the gospel message (Acts 2:38, 39).

What does that mean for us today? The Holy Spirit is for all of us. Contrary to my childish concepts, He doesn't hover around us; this Spirit of God lives within us. Through the Holy Spirit we can live in a God-pleasing way.

Loving Father, we are grateful that You pour the Spirit on us and that the Holy Spirit lives within each of us. Help us to make your Spirit welcome in our lives as we follow and obey You. In Jesus' name I ask this. Amen.

August 29-31. **Jeanette Dall** is a freelance writer and day care provider living in Carol Stream, Illinois. She has a background that includes teaching and editorial work.

True Joy

Heart, body, and soul are filled with joy. (Psalm 16:9, *The Living Bible*).

Scripture: **Psalm 16:5-11**
Song: **"The Joy of the Lord"**

Many of our Christian hymns are about joy or being joyful. Joyfulness is also frequently used as a sermon topic. I often became upset with all this talk about joyfulness. How could I be filled with joy when my mother was dying of a heart condition? Joyfulness seemed to be out of reach when there was very little money and lots of bills. I felt more like crying than smiling or singing "joy" songs.

Then I talked about this with a friend. "How can I be filled with joy?" I asked. "I just can't laugh and shout with joy all the time."

My friend pointed out that I was confusing joy with happiness. Happiness is temporary because it is based on outward circumstances. We are happy to have a nice car. But we quickly become unhappy when it breaks down.

True joy is far deeper than happiness. We can be joyful even in the middle of deep troubles. Joy is lasting because it is based on God's presence in our lives. God always lives within us—through the great, not-so-great, and absolutely terrible times. When we remember God's daily presence, we can find contentment. And that is true joy.

Dear God, thank You for living within us. Help us to remember that You are always with us in all our circumstances. Let us know contentment and true joy in our lives as we think of all that You do for us. In Jesus' name, amen.

I Don't Speak Bird

Now when this was noised abroad, the multitude came together, and were confounded, because that every man heard them speak in his own language (Acts 2:6).

Scripture: **Acts 2:1-13**
Song: **"Lift High the Cross"**

My young grandson and I were outdoors enjoying a warm spring day. Lots of birds were visiting my bird feeders. Singing, chirping, and squawking could be heard all around us. "Boy, the birds sure are noisy," Matthew said.

"What do you think they're saying," I asked.

Matthew replied, "Grammy, I don't speak bird!"

Well, I don't speak or understand "bird" either. So I could only guess what they were chattering about.

That may have been how the visitors to Jerusalem felt on Pentecost. They followed the sound of a mighty wind to a house where the disciples were preaching. At first it must have sounded like gibberish

But as the crowd gathered, each person soon realized that one of the disciples was speaking his or her own language. God wanted the good news of Jesus' death and resurrection to be spread to all parts of the world. And for that to happen, these people had to hear and understand what was being said. Then they could carry the message home.

Isn't it great that God can understand all of us?

Heavenly Father, help us to spread the good news to people all over the world by supporting missionaries. Be with those who translate the Bible into many languages and bless their work. In Jesus' name I pray. Amen.

DEVOTIONS®

I will remember the deeds of the LORD; yes, I will remember your miracles of long ago.

—Psalm 77; 11, *NIV*

SEPTEMBER

Photo © Digital Stock

Gary Allen, editor

Who Will You Call?

Everyone who calls on the name of the Lord will be saved (Acts 2:21, *New International Version*).

Scripture: **Acts 2:14-21**
Song: **"Amazing Grace"**

A woman prepared dinner for her family. As it cooked, she made a phone call and checked her e-mail. Suddenly the smoke alarm startled her. Hardly able to see the stove through the choking smoke, she frantically poured water on the blaze . . . but that only spread the fire. Finally, she ran to a neighbor's and called the fire department. No one was hurt, but the house soon lay in smoldering ruins. If only she had called for help immediately, instead of taking matters into her own hands!

Peter reminded his hearers that God would pour out His Spirit on all people in "the last days." No doubt those days include the entire period between Christ's first and second coming, and thus we live in those days.

We do know that many troubling and scary things are happening in our world today, and sometimes we feel overwhelmed. But remember that the Spirit is here, too. And one thing always remains certain: We can't save ourselves. That always takes a call to the Lord.

Let me run to You first, Dear Lord, rather than trying all my other ingenious plans when I need Your saving help. Remind me of the power of Your name, through which I pray. Amen.

September 1-4. **Jeanette Dall** is a freelance writer and daycare provider living in Carol Stream, Illinois. Her background includes teaching and editorial work.

Solid Proof

God proved that he sent Jesus to you by having him work miracles, wonders, and signs (Acts 2:22, *Contemporary English Version*).

Scripture: **Acts 2:22-28**
Song: **"Lord of Miracles"**

My washer sounded as though it was on its last leg—or spin. It really needed repairs, so I called a company that advertised "fast service." Later, a man appeared at my door and said: "I'm the guy who's supposed to fix that washing machine for you." He showed me his ID tag and all the information I'd given the repair company over the phone. The company's name was also on his truck. But my best proof that he was the repairman? That came when my old, noisy washer began working ever-so-smoothly—and quietly too!

Often we need to prove that we really are who we claim to be. Even Jesus had to do that, since many people didn't believe He was the Messiah. Even today, people might think Jesus was a good man and a great teacher. But God in the flesh? Don't push it, right?

But the undeniable truth flowed from the works Jesus did—all the miracles, wonders, and signs that only true deity can manage. If He has worked a miracle in your heart, as well, then why not pause for a moment and offer your heartfelt thanks?

Father, thank You for sending Jesus into the world and into my life. Move me to tell the truth about Him to any who are skeptical. In His name, amen.

We Saw: He Lives!

God has raised this Jesus to life, and we are all witnesses of the fact (Acts 2:32, *New International Version*).

Scripture: **Acts 2:29-36**
Song: **"I Know that My Redeemer Lives"**

My husband enjoys watching baseball games on TV or listening to them on the radio. He's a big fan of the local teams—cheering their wins and bemoaning their losses. He also reads the game coverages in the sport pages of the newspaper. But nothing beats being at the game in person. Then he can hear the crack of the bat or see the dust fly when someone slides into home. And the best part is being able to say, "I saw it happen!"

Many of the people in Peter's audience may have heard about Jesus before this day of preaching. They may even have heard how Jesus had been crucified a few months earlier. But now they were hearing all the details and how the prophets had foretold all that had happened. And then came the shocker—Jesus was alive!

Just hearsay? No. Peter and the other disciples had seen Jesus alive many times after He rose from the dead. They were spectators of the real thing; no need to read about it in the morning's *Jerusalem Times*. What wonderful news for all believers!

Almighty God, thank You for sending Jesus to die for the sins of all people. Thanks also for raising Jesus from the dead. Now we know that we will also be resurrected on the last day. Help us to be witnesses and spread this news to others. In the name of our Savior, Jesus Christ, amen.

The Rest of the Story

They spent their time learning from the apostles, and they were like family to each other. They also broke bread and prayed together (Acts 2:42, *Contemporary English Version*).

Scripture: **Acts 2:1-8, 37-42**
Song: **"Blest Be the Tie that Binds"**

Paul Harvey, radio news commentator in Chicago, uses an interesting format to deliver one of his special programs. He selects an obscure story of history, with many details, and tells it in such a way that listeners can't wait to find out how it ends. Just when the story reaches its most intriguing point . . . there will be a commercial. After the commercial, Mr. Harvey says, "And now for the rest of the story." He then proceeds to tell the conclusion of the story and reveal the true identity of its hero.

Peter and the disciples had told the story of Jesus. They had given a summary of all He'd taught and then focused on His death, burial, and resurrection. Three thousand of the listeners believed what Peter said, repented of their sins that very day, and were baptized.

Now for the rest of the story. The believers worshiped together, learned more about Jesus at the apostles' teaching sessions, shared in the Lord's Supper, and prayed. This first church is a model for us. Hopefully, the rest of our life story will be one of fellowship and worship.

Holy God, help us always be excited and awed by the truth of the gospel. Forgive us when we take Christ's death and resurrection for granted. In Your holy name we pray. Amen.

Hold On—or Not?

Do not be hardhearted or tightfisted toward your poor brother (Deuteronomy 15:7, *New International Version*).

Scripture: **Deuteronomy 15:4-8**
Song: **"My Gratitude Now Accept, O God"**

I rushed past a woman standing near the grocery entrance and heard her say: "That's a beautiful cross." Gently, I touched the blue sapphire cross that hung at my neck on a silver chain. I rarely took it off.

While checking out, I sensed the inaudible words, "Give her the cross." I shook my head. Was I imagining things? I avoided the woman when I exited. Clutching my cross tightly, I turned the ignition key. Again I sensed, "Give her the cross."

Sighing deeply, I unfastened the clasp, pulled up beside the woman, and reached out the window. I dropped the cross and a church calling card into her hand. "I believe God wants you to have this," I said and drove away as she stood looking at the cross in her hand.

Did I do the right thing? I honestly don't know. But I do know I wasn't tightfisted or hardhearted in those few moments. For me, at least, that was beneficial, a practical opportunity for spiritual growth.

Dear Father, *thank You for sending Your Son, Jesus, as a living example of a generous spirit. Thank You for convicting and forgiving us when we so often fall short of His will. In His precious name we pray. Amen.*

September 5-11. **SanDee Hardwig** is a writer, high-school tutor, and prison minister. She lives in Brown Deer, Wisconsin, along with her three perky cats.

Whom Will We Summon?

Surely you will summon nations you know not, and nations that do not know you will hasten to you, because of the Lord your God (Isaiah 55:5, *New International Version*).

Scripture: **Isaiah 55:1-7**
Song: **"Shout to the North"**

He left my condo half painted, having been sent to jail before he could finish the job. I felt sorry for him, and I did want to pay him for the hours he'd put in. So I went to the jail planning only to deposit my unhappy painter's wages at the front desk.

But I was "out and about" that day—so why not pay a visit to some of the inmates? I found my painter, and we prayed together. That very day, he accepted Christ and expressed a desire for baptism.

A few months later, I heard he was leading Bible studies among the men—and I had become a clergy visitor to prisons. I established Internet prayer partners for the men, and kind people worldwide began writing and sending Christian literature to those I visited. Chaplains and officers got study Bibles into their hands. Transferred inmates started study groups in other dorms and prisons.

Did my half-job painter and I do this on our own? No. Surely, those of us who did not know each other were summoned to serve together because of our Lord God.

Precious Lord, I am amazed at the way You bring Your people together for ministry. Let me continue to witness to Your greatness that You might summon to Your grace each person I meet. In Christ's name, amen.

No U-hauls

This is how it will be with anyone who stores up things for himself but is not rich toward God (Luke 12:21, *New International Version*).

Scripture: **Luke 12:13-21**
Song: **"Laying It Down"**

A rich zinc and copper vein was discovered bordering Mole Lake Indian Reservation in 1968. In 1975, Exxon Corporation proposed mining there, and cash-poor county residents anticipated a huge economic boost.

The Chippewa tribe on the reservation feared toxic waste would poison their lake, however. So the tribe purchased the proposed mine site in 2003. Thus ended a twenty-eight year legal battle between economic hopefuls and environmental guardians. The minerals remained in the ground.

When we "count our chickens before they hatch," we often end up with broken eggs . . . and shattered dreams. The rich man harvested more than he could store in his barns, so he planned to build bigger barns. But God asked, "Who will get what you prepared for yourself?" (v. 19). Someone else would get it all, since no U-haul followed his funeral procession.

Storing things for yourself today? Perhaps the better perspective comes from church father Ambrose, who said: "Bosoms of the poor, houses of widows, mouths of children, these are the barns that last forever."

Oh God, forgive our selfishly clenched eyes, ears, and fists. Teach us to be good stewards of Your gifts. For we pray in Your loving name. Amen.

Resting in Jesus?

Who of you by worrying can add a single hour to life? Since you cannot do this very little thing, why do you worry about the rest? (Luke 12:25, 26, *New International Version*).

Scripture: **Luke 12:22-34**
Song: **"Favorite Place"**

LaVerne decorates cakes like an artist. But when it came time to create her own son's wedding cake, she worried herself sick.

"What if I botch the job?"

"What if he doesn't like it?"

"What if . . ."

But she knew the words of Jesus, too, calling her to let go of her worries. She baked the cake and made the flowers beforehand. She planned to do the finishing touches before the rehearsal, but ended up with a violent migraine headache. She spent hours in a darkened hotel room juggling ice packs.

Still she clung to the words of Jesus: "Why do you worry?" In spite of her searing pain, she completed the cake for the wedding . . . and it was beautiful (not to mention delicious)!

Yet poor LaVerne missed the rehearsal and dinner and was too exhausted to enjoy the wedding. When we worry, don't we miss out on the peace and joy God offers us?

Faithful God, we praise You. As we gather around Your table, You nurture us. Forgive us when we worry and forget Your comforting words. And thank You for Your patience. In Jesus' name we pray. Amen.

Unconditional Devotion

They devoted themselves to the apostles' teaching and to the fellowship, to the breaking of bread and to prayer. . . . All the believers were together and had everything in common (Acts 2:42, 44, *New International Version*).

Scripture: **Acts 2:42-47**
Song: **"Thank You for the Blood"**

How we long to be loved—just as we are, with all our quirks! In the film *Unconditional Love* a snippet of dialogue goes like this: "Cut off my ears, steal my money, and I'll love you anyway . . . you don't have to love me back."

But is it really possible to love each other like that, without expecting love in return? What about that kind of devotion among church members, where we might even give our possessions for the common good, without expecting a return on our "investment"?

Jesus was a living example of how to do it. He suffered greatly, and died, to bring us into fellowship with the Father, investing not merely in our potential but in our actual sinnerhood. He asks us, in return, to open our hearts and love Him and love each other. But He certainly allows us the freedom *not* to love back.

One of my dictionaries defines *unconditional* as "without reservation or condition; absolute." That is the way God loves us. He holds us close, no matter what.

Lord God, *thank You for loving us more than we can imagine. Without You, we are nothing. May we take the freedom You allow and use it to love You back. We pray these things in Jesus' precious name. Amen.*

Planning to Share?

All the believers were one in heart and mind; . . . they shared everything they had (Acts 4:32, *New International Version*).

Scripture: **Acts 4:32-37**
Song: **"Lord, You Have Come to the Lakeshore"**

Todd is a paraplegic, a single parent and a college student. That hasn't stopped him from giving. He teaches children's church twice a week. Before that, he sang in the choir. And he painted a beautiful mural of Jesus' baptism—no small task from a wheelchair!

Last winter a fire destroyed all of Todd's bedroom furniture, clothing, bedding, computer, and medical supplies. The smoke and filth made it impossible for him and his twelve-year-old son to live at home until it had been thoroughly cleaned. Having very little money, the two needed help.

A few church members came together to meet the need: they gave money, furniture, clothing, and food. The Red Cross provided a place to sleep until Todd and his son could move back home. And Todd continues to teach his class twice a week.

With great power the apostles testified to Jesus' resurrection. When we share, we too testify to His living presence among us. But are there any around you who are needy at the moment? What are you planning to do?

Jesus, give me the eyes to see others' needs today. Help me realize that each instance of need is a call to me—to loosen my grip on the things You've entrusted to me for my use. In Your holy name, amen.

A Sound Unheard

More and more men and women believed in the Lord and were added to their numbers (Acts 5:14, *New International Version*).

Scripture: **Acts 5:12-16**
Song: **"Lord Reign in Me"**

Three thousand folks earnestly worshiped, prayed, repented, and sought God during the three-day conference led by a well-known speaker. "The Seeds of Selfishness" was the topic, and some of the lessons weren't easy to take. I know; I was there.

But I learned. I learned that when we seek God with our whole heart, He lifts away the shame and blame from our lives, one layer at a time. During the final session we experienced a powerful, but comforting presence. No one spoke, not even our speaker, for quite a while. And into my mind flowed the words from David Baroni's song: "There's a Holy Wind, a force unseen, a sound unheard. It's the power that flows from the living Word."

We sensed a cleansing and healing taking place. One called out, "Thank You, God." Some sobbed. Some wept quietly. That is the sight and sound of men and women believing in the Lord. The means of change hasn't changed through the centuries, but countless lives continue to change. As Joyce Meyer says, "I'm not where I'm *supposed* to be, but thank God I'm not where I *used to* be."

Mighty God, in repentance and in faith we cry out for Your presence. In the name of Your Son, our Savior, we pray. Amen.

Proof in the Pudding

Go your way, and tell John what things ye have seen and heard (Luke 7:22).

Scripture: **Luke 7:18-23**
Song: **"I Would Be True"**

Woman number one rebounds from sin. She becomes serious about her Christian faith, and you see it in her ministry involvement. You witness it in the Bible teaching she gives her child. You note that she takes a mission trip to Africa. She makes increasingly healthy moral decisions.

Woman number two also professes faith. She leaves the church for years. She is diagnosed as an alcoholic and has a mental breakdown. Later, she heads off to an exotic island for a vacation and tells about all the night spots. She meets a man there and discusses "spirituality," though he later tells her he has a problem with drugs.

Which woman is more credible as a representative of Christ? Of course, we are not saved by our conduct. But when John asked Jesus how to recognize whether He was the Messiah, Jesus responded by saying, essentially: Check out the pudding. Inventory My behavior. Verify My claims by My conduct. What say you, jury?

And . . . like Christ, so Christ's.

Lord, by grace I am saved, but saved for a purpose: to show my gratitude in good works that bring You glory. May the things people see in me point to Your great goodness in my life. In Christ's name, amen.

September 12-18. **Jim Townsend,** college teacher and freelance editor, presently ministers at a place called Park Place (he figures Boardwalk is next for him).

Stuff: Just Nonsense?

He told them: "Take nothing for the journey—no staff, no bag, no bread, no money, no extra tunic" (Luke 9:3, *New International Version*).

Scripture: **Luke 9:1-6**
Song: **"Take My Life and Let It Be"**

"Necessities and Niceties" is a fitting title for Luke 9:3. Five times Jesus used the negative modifier "no," not wanting His disciples encumbered by any extras.

Admittedly here, Jesus wasn't laying out long-term, all-time absolutes for His followers on every occasion. (These prohibitions probably wouldn't work for your next trip, even if it were a short-term campout.) Yet shouldn't those who don't regard this present earth as their final destination think a bit more like minimalists when it comes to material matters? After all, how much of our household stuff qualifies as "necessity" and how much as "nicety"? When so many are starving to death, do we really need to eat out at restaurants so much? Do we really need that expensive gym equipment, so soon abandoned, in order to get our necessary exercise?

Yes, these early followers of Jesus had power (see verse 1) and had a message (see verses 2 and 6). But they didn't have a ton of stuff. Maybe we should say, not "stuff and nonsense," but stuff *is* nonsense.

O Lord, help me to be balanced when it comes to eternity and earth in the matter of my material matters—as to what matters most. In the name of Your sacrificial Son, I pray. Amen.

Air-Hammer Authority

They were amazed at his teaching, because his message had authority (Luke 4:32, *New International Version*).

Scripture: **Luke 4:31-37**
Song: **"Jesus Almighty Savior"**

On our cross-country car trip from Tennessee to California, we stopped to see the monumental Hoover Dam. I remember the vastness of the cliff-like, man made structure. However, what really caught my eye were the teensy-weensy chipmunk-like creatures that were running up and down the sides of that huge architectural wonder. The largeness of the structure was offset by the littleness of those scampering animals, creating a unique memory.

Jesus' uniqueness was dramatically demonstrated in His authority. Twice in this passage His audience was amazed at it. He wasn't one of the stereotypical scribes of New Testament times. He didn't just parrot the past and ditto others' teachings. His teaching was one facet of the fact that He is the Unique One of our universe.

A second feature of His air-hammer authority was His activism. His teaching wasn't mere talk. He backed up all He said with blockbuster action that was (literally) daredevil confrontation. Even His exorcisms were the exercise of divine authority.

Jesus, by Your authority, You change us into Your sons and daughters. So please let some of Your changes in me be apparent to those around me, that they may want to experience Your authority, too. In Your great name, amen.

Beauty and Begging

Now a man crippled from birth was being carried to the temple gate called Beautiful, where he was put every day to beg from those going into the temple courts (Acts 3:2, *New International Version*).

Scripture: **Acts 3:1-5**
Song: **"For the Beauty of the Earth"**

A teacher played a recording of an orchestral masterpiece to enhance her class's musical appreciation. As the symphony rose to a crescendo, the noise of scraping interrupted the beautiful sounds. It was a student maneuvering down the hall on his crutches. On another occasion, a speaker was describing the beautiful order God employed on our planet—when his speech was interrupted by the blare of police-car sirens in the background.

In our Scripture today there seems to be a contrasting clash between the beauty of the temple and the beggar of the text. Of course, both are beautiful in God's eyes, though the man's disability seems to strike an unharmonious note against the architecture rising behind him. Those stones were very much in alignment while his bones were, in some sense, misplaced.

It's true that God originally pronounced our world very good. Now we live on a planet filled with squeaks and sins and sicknesses and sorrows. Yet when Jesus enters the picture, He restores its original beauty.

Master Artist, thank You for the beauty that You paint on the canvass of our lives, when we are well and when we suffer. In Christ, amen.

Power of Positive Power

Then Peter said, Silver and gold have I none; but such as I have give I thee: In the name of Jesus Christ of Nazareth rise up and walk (Acts 3:6).

Scripture: **Acts 3:6-10**
Song: **"It Is No Secret What God Can Do"**

Jesus once (in Mark 14:8) spoke of a woman who had done *what she could.* In similar fashion, Peter focused not on what he did *not* have (silver and gold), but upon what he *did* have to give though Christ's power. In contrast, the world is filled with people who major on what they don't have and can't give.

I once knew a man who was almost totally blind. He seemed to mope a lot, even though he could have, for instance, used his five-room basement—filled with unbelievable technical equipment—to rent out to another machinist. He could explain such mechanical equipment to a young teen (or several trainees) and prepare him (or them) for a career in carpentry, mechanical work, etc.

But he seemed to focus mostly on what he couldn't do. I felt sorry for his near-blindness, but I knew he could do a whole lot more than he seemed to be doing.

Paul said he could do all things (including being poor or being prosperous) through Christ's strengthening. Let me ask you: are you part of the whine-and-dine club, or are you a card-carrying member of the can-do's?

Lord, help me at least to do what I can do for You, trusting You for added strength and enablement to do what is beyond me. In Jesus' name, amen.

Deicide

You killed the author of life, but God raised him from the dead
(Acts 3:15, *New International Version*).

Scripture: **Acts 3:11-16**
Song: **"Wonderful Grace of Jesus"**

Herman Melville told the story of an Italian inventor, architect, and sculptor. This genius built a bell tower. On it he placed huge sculpted figures that were primed mechanically to strike the clock at prearranged times. However, the maker failed to observe the clockwork's regularity, and the figures ended up striking and killing their inventor. The creation killed its own creator!

Peter virtually accuses his audience of performing this same feat: they took the life of the inventor of life. This might be called deicide. Regicide is king killing, and patricide is father killing, but deicide involves the killers killing the very one who is called life itself (see John 1:4; 14:6). Do you hear the weirdness involved in this act—putting life to death? It would be like some astronaut in outer space pulling the plug, so to speak, on all the astronauts' oxygen supplies.

What grace it must take God sometimes to put up with the disgrace of our sinful shenanigans on this planet! We shut out the life of His Son, yet He proceeds to offer us the sunlit generosity of His grace.

Father, Your grace can only be met properly by our gracias, *our gratitude for all You have done,* gratis, *for the likes of us who have been disgraceful again and again. So, thank You, thank You, thank You! In Jesus' name, amen.*

Profit from the Prophets

Yea, and all the prophets from Samuel and those that follow after, as many as have spoken, have likewise foretold these days (Acts 3:24).

Scripture: **Acts 3:17-26**
Song: **"How Firm a Foundation"**

I had a friend who worked years ago as an announcer at a small radio station. Hourly, she would call the weather service for the most recent official forecast to mention on-air between songs. However, once when she couldn't secure the weather forecast, she looked outside her studio window, tabulated the ratio of clouds to sunny skies, and forecasted (off the top of her head) a thirty per cent chance of rain. Not precisely perfect prophecy there!

Five times in Acts 3:17-26 the "prophets" or a "prophet" are mentioned. However, Peter's audience failed to profit from their prophets. They were supposed to be heirs of the prophets, yet most of the nation actively excommunicated itself from God (see verse 23).

Has God been trying to communicate to you about something specific in Scripture? Have you been tuning down your hearing aid, so to speak? There's nothing wrong with God's transmitter, but is there any interceptive static crackling between God's transmission and your receiver? His prophetic speech is perfect, but we may occasionally need to check our ears.

Dear God, *help me do regular checkups on my spiritual hearing. In the name of Your Son, my Savior, I pray. Amen.*

Putting on His Armor

Put on the full armor of God so that you can take your stand against the devil's schemes (Ephesians 6:11, *New International Version*).

Scripture: **Ephesians 6:10-20**
Song: **"Onward Christian Soldiers"**

A friend of mine once described how he imagined putting on the armor of God each morning as he dressed. Bob's gentle spirit and life of faith showed that his daily preparation was not in vain.

Bob called one day and invited me to his house. I immediately left the office, wondering if there was some problem that required my help. When I arrived, he invited me to sit in a shady spot by the stream and told me he was so impressed with his Bible reading that morning that he wanted to share it with me. It turned out to be a refreshing break in an otherwise tedious day. I left Bob's house invigorated in my walk with the Lord.

We are not alone in the struggle we have against the spiritual forces of evil. Precious moments with a fellow warrior can make a lasting impression and supply us much-needed ammunition.

Lord, as others have encouraged me, help me to be of encouragement to others. We are not alone in this struggle, and I thank You for those who have helped me along the way. In the name of Jesus, my shield and sword in the battle, I pray. Amen.

September 19-25. **Dan Nicksich** is senior minister of First Christian Church, Somerset, Pennsylvania. He also writes for numerous Christian publishers.

Gentle and Caring

We were gentle among you, like a mother caring for her little children (1 Thessalonians 2:7, *New International Version*).

Scripture: 1 Thessalonians 2:1-8
Song: "The Family of God"

A wonderful Christian couple decided to try being foster-care parents. It was to be temporary, caring for three sisters of a different race until a suitable adoptive family could be found. When a potential family came to their attention, Dave and Debbie realized their powerful feelings as care providers; they couldn't bear the thought of "losing" the girls. Their family of four has now grown to eight after they adopted the three along with Matthew (their youngest, and the only boy among the six children).

The apostle Paul describes his relationship with the Thessalonians as that of a mother taking care of her children. We tend to view the apostles as the ultimate authorities within the church, yet Paul saw himself as a caring parent. It wasn't power that defined his role, but benevolent love.

Those we seek to influence for Christ have a right to examine our motives. For example, do we witness only because we enjoy giving advice or explaining concepts? Or we could put it like this: they'll never care how much you know until they know how much you care.

Help us, Father, to share Your love with others. We count it a privilege to be part of Your family and would like to see others also come to know the joy that is in Christ, through whom we pray. Amen.

Disturbed by the Message

They were greatly disturbed because the apostles were teaching the people and proclaiming in Jesus the resurrection of the dead (Acts 4:2, *New International Version*).

Scripture: **Acts 4:1-4**
Song: **"We've a Story to Tell to the Nations"**

Five men were determined to reach a war-like tribe for Jesus Christ. They had decided, in advance, that they would not defend themselves if attacked. That determination proved prophetic as the five were killed in an attack by the very tribe they sought to love.

Elizabeth Elliot captures the story in her book *Shadow of the Almighty*. Her husband, Jim Elliot, was one of the five killed in January, 1956. Later, Elizabeth was invited to live with and teach the same people who had killed her husband, the tribe once known as the Aucas.

Some of that same war party that had killed men preaching Christ would later accept Jesus. They would admit that these white men who had fired warning shots without turning guns on them had ignited their curiosity about what brought them. They wanted to learn more—and they *did* learn. Much more!

We seek to share a message that disturbs some people. Yet we can praise God because faithful proclamation, in spite of persecution, produces results.

Lord, *why do we struggle to share the good news? Do we worry about rejection? Do we fear the response we may receive? Help us, Lord, to share faithfully what others have yet to hear. In Christ we pray. Amen.*

Healing for the Soul

Without faith it is impossible to please God, because anyone who comes to him must believe that he exists and that he rewards those who earnestly seek him (Hebrews 11:6, *New International Version*).

Scripture: **Acts 4:5-12**
Song: **"It Is Well with My Soul"**

An athlete was severely injured in a trampoline accident. He had been an Olympic hopeful in his sport, pole-vaulting, but now he was paralyzed and unable ever to compete again. He would later say that faith prepares you for one of two things: "Healing is one. Peace of mind, if healing doesn't come, is the other." Just as I am drawn to stories of healing, I find myself enthralled with those who exhibit great faith despite its absence.

In the book of Acts we see the apostles consistently using a healing event as the forum in which to proclaim the gospel. Miraculous power was displayed that on-lookers might grasp hold of something far more significant: spiritual healing for the soul. Sadly, the ruling body of the Jewish people often expressed outrage about this.

But the point is, we can go through life physically whole yet spiritually dead. And we can be physically afflicted yet spiritually whole. We can't always control our physical state, but our spiritual condition is largely a matter of choice.

In sickness or in health, in distress or in peace, **help us, Lord,** *to pursue the blessings of the gospel in faith. In Jesus' name we pray. Amen.*

The Most Ordinary of Men

When they saw the courage of Peter and John and realized that they were unschooled, ordinary men, they were astonished and they took note that these men had been with Jesus (Acts 4:13, *New International Version*).

Scripture: **Acts 4:13-17**
Song: **"Revive Us Again"**

The church's revival meetings didn't bring overflowing crowds. There wasn't a flood of responses to the preaching. There were, however, two women who came forward and committed their lives to Christ. Following their baptism, they expressed thanks to their friend John, who had invited them to the meetings.

You could have heard a pin drop in the sanctuary. John was a mildly retarded man who pedaled his bicycle all over town while delivering newspapers. He was, by all accounts, the most ordinary of persons. Most assumed there was little he could do in the Lord's service, but he did invite his customers to church services. Some of those customers were probably amused, others irritated. But two names were added to the Lamb's book of life as a result of John's sincere efforts.

The work of the kingdom of Heaven isn't limited to the highly educated. Jesus did not select His apostles from either the religious elite nor society's celebrities. Thank God!

Lord, *Your kingdom continues to expand through the efforts of humble men and women. Use us all in Your service today. In Jesus' name, amen.*

Reverse Psychology

They called them in again and commanded them not to speak or teach at all in the name of Jesus (Acts 4:18, *New International Version*).

Scripture: **Acts 4:18-22**
Song: **"Who Is on the Lord's Side?"**

Tom Sawyer once convinced a group of his friends that whitewashing a fence was great fun, an event not to be missed. He then sat back and watched others enthusiastically tackle his dreaded chore.

We call it reverse psychology. It's the art of acting as if what you want is what you *don't* want (or vice versa). Parents sometimes joke that it's a great childrearing method, since the kids already excel at contrary behavior.

It wasn't reverse psychology, however, when the Sanhedrin leaders ordered Peter and John not to proclaim Jesus. It was more on the order of a threat.

What if we were faced with a similar situation? What if we were threatened with imprisonment and/or beatings if we dared proclaim the gospel? Would we express the same defiant spirit? Would we, too, spark a revival of evangelistic fervor within the church?

As I ponder my own response, I wonder whether a little dose of reverse psychology might be a good thing here. Listen, Satan says don't bother sharing the good news of the gospel with others. Now what will you do?

Lord, *stir within me an evangelistic spark today. Inspire me, that I might take the gospel to someone in need. In Jesus' name, amen.*

Nothing More, Nothing Less

Now, Lord, consider their threats and enable your servants to speak your word with great boldness (Acts 4:29, *New International Version*).

Scripture: **Acts 4:23-31**
Song: **"Have Thine Own Way, Lord"**

For such a brief prayer, it was packed with tremendous meaning. Bobby Richardson, former second baseman, delivered it for the New York Yankees at a Fellowship of Christian Athletes gathering. "Your will, Lord—nothing more, nothing less, and nothing else."

How often do our prayers stray from God's will to our wants? Jesus Himself demonstrated in the Garden of Gethsemane that anyone can face this same struggle. Yet even though he knew God's will involved terrible suffering, Jesus' prayerful struggle concluded with: "Not my will but yours be done."

The believers in Acts faced constant persecution if they continued proclaiming the gospel. To their credit, they understood God's will and prayed for enablement to keep speaking with boldness. And such a prayer unleashes the power of God. Not only was their meeting place shaken; their request was granted as they courageously proclaimed the Word of God.

Father, it's so easy for us to place our will, our desires, and our wants ahead of Your own. Help us to be the obedient children You call us to be. Help us to humbly accept Your plan and then carry it out in Your strength. In Christ's name we pray. Amen.

Good Pie!

Blessed are you when people insult you, persecute you and falsely say all kinds of evil against you because of me (Matthew 5:11, *New International Version*).

Scripture: **Acts 6:8-15**
Song: **"Shine"**

Take a gallon of vanilla soft-serve ice cream, stir in a jar of creamy peanut butter, then spoon it all into a pie shell. Add a layer of chocolate syrup and whipped cream, and top with chopped nuts. Freeze for at least one hour, and you have our family's favorite dessert.

One evening we served it to our new neighbors after dinner, leaving only a slice left in the pan. The following day, after the early news, I heard my beloved husband rummaging through the freezer. With a slam of the door and a great big huff, he pointed a sure-of-the-facts finger in my direction. "You ate the last of it didn't you?"

"Never touched it." Persecuted, I did *not* feel blessed. Then, as if on cue, our three- and six-year-olds skipped in from the back yard and tossed a couple of forks into the sink. The three-year-old eagerly said, "Good pie."

Stephen endured false accusations of blasphemy, something much more serious than family squabbles over food. But I'm so impressed: he just kept speaking the truth.

Dear Lord, *next time I face false accusations, please help me to remain focused on You, as Stephen was. In Jesus' name I pray. Amen.*

September 26-October 2. **Rhonda DeYoung** is a freelance writer from Denver. She is married to Randy and has two children, Richelle and Riggs.

It's How You Look at It

They are from the world and therefore speak from the viewpoint of the world, and the world listens to them (1 John 4:5, *New International Version*).

Scripture: **Acts 7:1-8**
Song: **"Live Out Loud"**

The smooth flow of traffic came to an abrupt halt. Rows of red brake lights were all I could see, yet the light blazed a bright green. Cheated out of his turn to leave the intersection, the driver of the Jeep Wrangler behind me anxiously stood on his horn. The light now glowed red as 30 of us waited for another round of stop and go. I almost rolled up my window to escape the incessant honking when, over the noise, a different honk rang in my ear.

On the grassy shoulder of the road, a mother goose waddled forward, followed by six fuzzy goslings. They climbed the embankment and headed to the lake on the other side. Only the first couple of drivers were able to view this tiny fury parade cross from one side of the street to the other while the rest of us sat fuming at our delay.

Stephen proclaimed a unique view of history as he recounted how salvation revolved around the Law of Moses and the temple at Jerusalem. His words cause me to ask: "From my viewpoint, what is the center of my universe? When I look, am I seeing only the next delay in my plans? Or do I view the Lord of all my journeys?

Heavenly Father, *allow us to see the world through Your eyes this day. Show us Your truth in every situation. In the name of Jesus, amen.*

Good to Remember

I will remember the deeds of the Lord; yes, I will remember your miracles of long ago (Psalm 77:11, *New International Version*).

Scripture: **Acts 7:9-16**
Song: **"Ancient of Days"**

When I awoke, there was a small pool of blood on the sheets, and I winced with excruciating cramps. My husband and I rushed to the hospital and endured an hour-long wait, followed by a painful ultrasound. The doctor said, "You are having a miscarriage." I began crying as he left us pondering the future. Several years of uncomfortable, clinical tests slowly deflated our bubble of hope. How could we ever have a child? My obstetrician said I would never even be able to become pregnant.

But the tiny life that had so quickly left me years ago reminded me that, at least once, I had indeed become pregnant. That painful experience seemed to keep my hope alive. Since then—what a miracle!—we've been blessed with two healthy children.

Remembering God's goodness of the past works wonders. Stephen remembered Joseph's struggles and recalled how God blessed that man's life. Is there something God successfully brought you through long ago? Something that can support your progress in a current struggle?

Thank You, Lord, *for all You've done in the past. I gratefully thank You for all that I can overcome in the future as I draw upon Your strength and peace. In Jesus' precious name I pray. Amen.*

Misunderstood?

Good understanding wins favor, but the way of the unfaithful is hard (Proverbs 13:15, *New International Version*).

Scripture: **Acts 7:17-29**
Song: **Trust and Obey**

"Good afternoon, may I help you?"

"I need a replacement cup-holder for my computer. It's under warranty, and the cup-holder recently snapped off," said the customer to the technician on the other line.

"Cup-holder?" questioned the confused tech.

"You know—where you push the button and the tray slides open. I had my coffee cup on it, and it just broke."

"Ma'am, that was not a cup holder, it was a CD drive. You are supposed to put compact disks in that tray to run your software. I'm sorry, but the warranty doesn't cover negligence." Embarrassed by her own ignorance, the coffee drinker quickly hung up the phone.

Stephen recalled a time when Moses fled to the desert because his own people misunderstood his motive for killing a cruel Egyptian overseer. Moses intended to show that he would free his people, but the next day when Moses intervened in a fight between two of his fellow Hebrews, they accused him of wanting to rule over them.

Have you ever left a situation or relationship because of a great misunderstanding like that? Looking back, what have you learned from the experience?

Lord, today let me forgive anyone who has misunderstood my intentions. May Your Word show the way, as I pray in Your holy name. Amen.

Pomegranate to Praline

The mountains may be removed and the hills may shake, but my lovingkindness will not be removed from you (Isaiah 54:10, *New American Standard Bible*).

Scripture: **Acts 7:30-43**
Song: **"There's a Light upon the Mountains"**

I decided on a new hair color. Noticing how nice the woman on the box looked, I brought the coloring kit home and endured a messy half hour with gloves, followed by a brightly colored rinse. Then I removed the towel from my hair, looked in the mirror . . . and cried. I scrambled through the trash for the box and finally noticed its label: "Pomegranate." Note-to-self: *Not my color!*

I grew my hair for six weeks and then tried again. This time I read the entire box, including the name of the color, making sure there was no reference to purple. Just as before, I applied, waited, and rinsed. I raced to the mirror; my new color glistened with lovely highlights—"Praline."

The people that Moses led out of the desert encountered many "pomegranate" experiences, often thinking God had removed himself. They complained of hunger, thirst, and sand in their shoes. However, without these pomegranates, the "pralines" of their clothes not wearing out, of getting water from a rock, and of gathering manna would never have seemed such blessings. But what are your pralines?

Lord, *help us not to complain at the first sign of disappointment. Show us our blessings during the times of struggle, too! In Christ's name, amen.*

My Prayer Notes

DEVOTIONS

*I*n keeping with his promise we are looking forward to a new heaven and a new earth, the home of righteousness

—2 Peter 3:13, *NIV*

OCTOBER

Photo © Stockbyte

Gary Allen, editor

© 2004 STANDARD PUBLISHING, 8121 Hamilton Avenue, Cincinnati, Ohio, 45231, a division of STANDEX INTERNATIONAL Corporation. Topics based on the Home Daily Bible Readings, International Sunday School Lessons. © 2002 by the Committee on the Uniform Series. Printed in the U.S.A. Scripture taken from the King James Version unless otherwise identified. Scripture taken from the HOLY BIBLE, NEW INTERNATIONAL VERSION®. NIV®. COPYRIGHT © 1973, 1978, 1984 by International Bible Society. Used by permission of Zondervan Publishing House. All rights reserved. Scripture taken from the *New American Standard Bible* (NASB), © The Lockman Foundation, 1960, 1962, 1963, 1968, 1971, 1972, 1973, 1975, 1977. Used by permission. Scripture taken from the *New King James Version.* Copyright © 1982 by Thomas Nelson, Inc. Used by permission. All rights reserved.

God's Real Home

In keeping with his promise we are looking forward to a new heaven and a new earth, the home of righteousness (2 Peter 3:13, *New International Version*).

Scripture: **Acts 7:44-53**
Song: **"I Am the Way"**

Even though the gorgeous orange and purple sunset took my breath away, as it had the three previous evenings of our camping trip, dread came upon me as I walked back to our tent. Inside were all the comforts of home—a cot with a foam pad, a down sleeping bag, and an extra soft pillow. A cooler kept eggs and drinks cold, and a miniature gas range cooked the daily catch. We even had a portable shower with solar-heated water.

Yet even with all the amenities, I missed my home. I longed for my comfy furniture, my shady patio, my kitchen with room to stretch, an ice machine, and the ability to sip my coffee at leisure.

In a word, I felt homesick. Nevertheless, knowing this tent was only our temporary home, I enjoyed one last night in the woods.

Stephen reminds us in Acts that our places of worship here on earth are only temporary tabernacles for the Lord. Heaven is God's throne, the earth is His footstool, and our bodies are His temple. How well kept is God's dwelling place in you these days? Is it a home of righteousness?

Father, throw out the any attitudes that no longer fit in Your dwelling place. Move in and take over as head of this temple. In Your name, amen.

Goggles of Hope

You said, "Behold, the Lord our God has shown us His glory and His greatness, and we have heard His voice from the midst of the fire; we have seen today that God speaks with man, yet he lives" (Deuteronomy 5:24, *New American Standard Bible*).

Scripture: **Acts 7:54-60**
Song: **"I See the Lord"**

Even if a Navy Seal team arrived on shore as planned, they might be visually impaired by a darkness that seamlessly merges a moonless sky with a formless landscape. They could hear their enemy's talk, smell the smoke of their campfires, and even feel a trip-wire run across their legs. However, equipped with night-vision goggles, they could actually see the enemy before having to hear them.

Right before Stephen was stoned to death by an angry mob of accusers, he looked up to see God in all His glory, with the Son at His right hand. No one else could see this sight, only Stephen. Even as he lay dying, he asked that God forgive his killers. His perspective of hope brought peace even during his brutal killing.

If you've ever had to face undeserved accusation and persecution, like Stephen you may have experienced a brief glimpse of Heaven that helped you endure. Even in the midst of the fire, it is possible to see and know our glorious Lord.

Dear Lord, *show me what good plans You have in mind for my life, and help me to stay true to those plans. Keep me focused on You, using the night vision of hope that You graciously provide. In Jesus' name I pray. Amen.*

Hard Hearts

For this reason a man will leave his father and mother and be united to his wife, and the two will become one flesh (Matthew 19:5, *New International Version*).

Scripture: **Matthew 19:1-12**
Song: **"I Surrender All"**

How to have a successful marriage? Our radio and TV programs, our bookstores and magazines—all are loaded with how to's for making difficult marriages into healthy relationships. Our text shows this is not a new problem, as Jesus had to teach on marriage, too. In verse 8 Jesus said people divorce because they have hard hearts. And hard-heartedness is involved in any problem relationship, not just a bad marriage.

Janet's son lived with his father after their divorce 26 years ago. At age 38, the son still carries grudges against his mother because the father taught him she is "a bad woman." We could call it rebellion. Or sin. Maybe unforgiveness? Regardless, in every problem relationship the troubles remain until the hard-hearted one softens his or her heart.

Isn't God good? He's given the complete "how to" on living without hard-heartedness in a marriage: "Submit to one another out of reverence for Christ" (Ephesians 5:19)

Lord, search my heart for hard-heartedness, and remind me of any unforgiveness. You are my best friend, God. In Your name I pray. Amen.

October 3-9. **Audrey Hebbert** lives in Omaha, Nebraska, where she works as a writer, intercessor, and mentor in her congregation.

Whether Healed or Not

Two blind men were sitting by the roadside, and when they heard that Jesus was going by, they shouted, "Lord, Son of David, have mercy on us!" (Matthew 20:30, *New International Version*).

Scripture: **Matthew 20:29-34**
Song: **"Jesus Loves Me"**

Did Jesus hear these two desperate men the first time they called out to Him? Yes. But the blind men didn't know that. They disregarded the shushing crowd (see verse 30) and kept shouting for Jesus' attention.

I often pray for people to be healed. Jeannie asked me to pray for healing for her back. Before the prayer ended, she announced that she'd had this condition for a long time, and the doctor didn't think it could be healed. Faith? Little to none. Proclamations of disbelief? Constant. But I continue to hold Jeannie in my prayers.

Like the blind men, we may often need to persevere in seeking God's will. My friend Dan needed inner healing from childhood abuse. He persevered for several months, day in day out, praying, "Show me Your truth, Lord." He is finding more and more peace in his days.

What do you need at the moment? Cry out and believe. Jesus has heard you. But are you ready to trust His best for you, whether healed or not?

Lord, I ask You to gather up everything about this problem and hold it close to Your heart. Pour in Your truth, Lord, and give me the courage to accept Your will in all things. In Your name I pray. Amen.

He Still Seeks

The Son of Man has come to seek and to save that which was lost (Luke 19:10, *New King James Version*).

Scripture: **Luke 19:1-10**
Song: **"Zaccheus Was a Wee Little Man"**

Jesus met Zaccheus in Jericho, a city hardly considered the center of theological thought or godly conduct. What was Zaccheus doing there? Getting rich. Why did he want to see Jesus? Curiosity.

In verse 5, Jesus said, "I must stay at your house." He knew what the Father planned. Zaccheus still had a choice. He could have said, "Jesus, I'm too busy to serve Your needs." Instead, he opened his heart and house to the Son of God.

Sometimes we feel called to be in a certain place, for a certain unknown reason, and then a "chance encounter" occurs. Then our excitement rises as a new Zaccheus-like story unfolds before our eyes, and conviction, conversion, or healing takes place. Sometimes the transformation occurs without our knowledge, and we hear the story later. Regardless, a soul is nurtured or a life changed for God's glory because we acted upon the gentle nudging of God's Spirit. The key is to know for certain that Jesus came to seek needful people—then to look around us for the people in our world who are prime candidates for His loving invitation.

Lord, You're welcome to work a Zaccheus story in my life at any time. Let me always be ready to help someone know You better. In Jesus' name, amen.

Needing Water?

If you knew the gift of God, and who it is who says to you, "Give me a drink," you would have asked Him, and He would have given you living water (John 4:10, *New King James Version*).

Scripture: **John 4:1-10**
Song: **"Let the River Flow"**

Jesus knew the Samaritan woman's self-talk as she hurried to the well. It may have gone something like this: "I'm no good. Why was I born, anyway? I've married five husbands looking for true love, and now I'm living with this new lout. . . . I'll get water early and avoid those uppity married women with their darling children."

Now Jesus could have slumped close-mouthed by the well, pondering His weariness and hunger. He deserved a rest, having walked many miles that day. Instead, He did His Father's will and broke two cultural rules: He spoke with a Samaritan, and He spoke with a "married" woman.

Jesus used terms the woman understood, and she believed. Her life and self-talk changed forever.

Thankfully, Jesus still obeys the Father's will. He talks to any of us who truly listens, in terms we understand. He reads and heals destructive self-talk. He offers acceptance when all around us we meet with disapproval. Will you take some time today to listen, open your heart, and ask for a drink of His living water?

Lord, I'm listening for Your tender, irresistible voice. Thank You for desiring fellowship with me. I want to know You so much better. In Jesus' name I pray. Amen.

No Flip of the Switch

The water that I shall give him will become in him a fountain of water springing up into everlasting life (John 4:14, *New King James Version*).

Scripture: **John 4:11-15**
Song: **"There Is a Fountain Filled With Blood"**

People ooh and ahh over the fountain I created, with its marble rolling pin (handles removed), a submersible pump, and decorative rocks. I flip the switch, and water flows up through the rolling pin and splashes onto the stones in the container.

The Samaritan woman asked the eternal question, "Where do you get your living water?" In response, Jesus drew a word picture (in verse 14) that describes the Holy Spirit as water that bubbles up and overflows from Christians onto the lives around us.

After a while the water in my fountain became murky, and I had to dump everything out and clean it. I put it back together, but the stream didn't flow. I took the whole thing apart again and found a rock lodged in the pin.

We may feel as if our lives aren't flowing well. When something like fear or lust clogs our lives, we can ask God to fix this sad state of our hearts, to forgive us . . . and He does. You see, I turn off the switch every evening and stop my fountain. Our God never flips the switch.

Father, help me remember that Your Spirit witnesses to the living Christ in me. Please help me get rid of anything that clogs the outflow of His love in my world. In Christ's holy name I pray. Amen.

Needing More Joy?

There was great joy in that city (Acts 8:8, *New King James Version*).

Scripture: Acts 8:4-13
Song: "Joy, Joy Down in My Heart"

Norman endured dreary days, consumed with guilt over past sins. "I know the Bible says I'm forgiven, but I can't seem to forgive myself," he moaned. We prayed together, and Norman asked for joy. On my next visit, his face was radiant. "I've finally learned to let God love me," he said. What joy, no matter the circumstances!

Jesus laid the groundwork for the Samaritans' joy after His encounter with the woman at the well, when He stayed two days more, and many believed on Him (see John 4:40, 41). The Bible doesn't tell us, but possibly those believers gathered regularly and studied the Scriptures. Regardless, the Samaritans experienced joy after Philip ministered among them. Can you imagine the multitudes, ecstatic with their newfound faith in Christ, baptized, and with healing of mind and body?

You are entitled to joy, too, because it's listed with the fruit of the Spirit in Galatians 5:22. Letting it into your heart, you'll be the light at home and the mood-lifter at work. Your children will laugh and dance as you praise the Lord together.

Dear God, I know You don't promise constant happiness. But You do offer unending joy. Let me enjoy the joy, in the best of times and amidst the worst of trials. Through Christ, I pray. Amen.

Motive Matters

Simon answered, "Pray to the Lord for me so that nothing you have said may happen to me" (Acts 8:24, *New International Version*).

Scripture: **Acts 8:14-25**
Song: **"I Bring My Sins to Thee"**

No wonder Simon was attracted to Peter and John and all they did through the Holy Spirit. He also knew that almost anyone can be manipulated with money.

We rightly look down on the motives that infused Simon. But even today we might look at ourselves in the mirror and and sometimes admit: "You ask with wrong motives, that you may spend what you get on your pleasures" (James 4:3). Of course, Simon appeared to repent after Peter's fiery rebuke, but his words in verse 24 indicate that he merely wanted to save his own skin!

The Bible doesn't say whether Simon eventually truly repented, or that he never bowed to God's ways. We do know that God celebrates over the heart that stoops to His will, and He would have forgiven Simon any time he asked with a sincere heart.

So it is with us all.

Dear Lord, in the midst of all my busyness today, remind me that what matters most are my reasons. Especially when I work within Your church, let my heart be right and my motives pure. That I might glorify You in all I do, this is my prayer in Jesus' name. Amen.

October 10-16. **Donna Clark Goodrich** is a free-lance writer, editor, and proofreader from Mesa, Arizona. She teaches at writer's seminars across the U.S.A.

Smelly Revenge

Ye have heard that it hath been said, An eye for an eye, and a tooth for a tooth (Matthew 5:38).

Scripture: **Matthew 5:38-42**
Song: **"I Want to Be Like Jesus"**

In this often-quoted verse, Jesus speaks of the Old Testament law of retribution: Whatever someone does to you, do likewise to them. In other words, get revenge. But Jesus' law counters this approach. He came to teach the law of forgiveness instead.

A Sunday school teacher brought a bushel of old potatoes into her classroom. "Take a potato for each person you've been unable to forgive," she instructed her students. Most of them took at least one; however, several took two or three, and some even more.

Then the teacher gave each of them a bag to put the potatoes in. "Carry this bag with you for the rest of the week, wherever you go," she told the students. By Friday, not only were the students complaining of the extra weight, but they and others around them were turning up their noses at the smell.

An unforgiving spirit can do the same to us. We end up carrying around a heavy load, and we certainly do not radiate the sweet aroma of Christ.

Rather than holding to "an eye for an eye," could we not go the second mile with someone today?

Lord, *help us to remember that as You have forgiven us, so should we forgive others. Jesus is our example, and in His name I pray. Amen.*

Quiet Answers

Then some of the Pharisees and teachers of the law said to him, "Teacher, we want to see a miraculous sign from you" (Matthew 12:38, *New International Version*).

Scripture: **Matthew 12:38-42**
Song: **"He Never Has Failed Me Yet"**

The scribes and Pharisees were aware of the miracles Jesus had already performed. The book of Matthew tells us that He had healed all kinds of diseases, cleansed lepers, sent demons into swine, and told a man with palsy to get up and walk. But they weren't satisfied; they wanted more. They wanted a self-defined "sign."

Are we ever guilty of a similar approach to the Lord? Forgetting all the routine prayers God answers for us, we may ask for something approaching the miraculous in order to prove He's really there. He moves stones for us, but we still wait for the mountain to move. He supplies our needs (and many of our wants), He makes a way where there seems to be no way, He opens doors when we didn't even know who opened them.

So many quiet and unpretentious answers! As songwriter Dave Clark put it, "You don't have to move the earth to let me know that You're still there. Just send a quiet answer to my prayer."

Lord, we are grateful for all You do for us every day—especially all the little things we take for granted. You supply us with food and shelter, a job, and the air we breathe. Help us to remember that we don't need a sign when we have You. In Your holy name I pray. Amen.

One at a Time

There was a man of the Pharisees named Nicodemus, a member of the Jewish ruling council. He came to Jesus at night (John 3:1, 2, *New International Version*).

Scripture: **John 3:1-18**
Song: **"Lead Me to Some Soul Today"**

The most quoted verse in the Bible—John 3:16—and Jesus gave it to one person! Why, we wonder, didn't He wait until a big crowd was gathered around Him to share this important truth? And why at night? Surely Nicodemus would have understood if Jesus asked him to come back the next day. But no; Jesus saw one person who had a need, and He met it.

During a writing seminar, I walked into a room prepared to teach my next class. Only one person sat waiting.

I was tempted to cancel the class; however, in speaking with the woman, I began to see that her heart was breaking over a troubling family situation. I offered to sit with her, and for the rest of the hour she unburdened herself until we prayed. A few weeks later she sent me a note of thanks.

When I think of Nicodemus, I think of that woman, that one person in need. Each day we meet such persons as we go about our routines. Do we see them? Do we invite their amazing questions?

Heavenly Father, *as Your Son took the time to present the Word of Life to one person at a time, lead me to do the same. Give me a more open heart of hospitality, in the daytime and even at night. In Jesus' name I pray. Amen.*

Ornamental Only?

This people draweth nigh unto me with their mouth, and honoureth me with their lips; but their heart is far from me (Matthew 15:8).

Scripture: **Matthew 15:1-9**
Song: **"Give Me a Heart Like Thine"**

Raised in a Christian home, I knew all the proper spiritual language. I sounded just right when I prayed. At youth camp, captains chose me for their teams in Bible quizzing. I even took systematic theology and apologetics in college (the only girl in either class). I definitely honored God with my lips, but still it seemed something was missing in my life. It took a 700-mile move when I was 20 to shock me into the realization that much of my relationship with God was based on mere head knowledge.

Suddenly, I was on my own. I couldn't live through my mother's faith anymore. I didn't have my best friend or my beloved Sunday school teacher or my minister. But I did have my Bible and prayer—and a whole new personal relationship with God. Before, I was almost like the oranges found on some Arizona trees—ornamental but useless.

"Useless." That's how the *Amplified New Testament* translates Matthew 15:9: "Uselessly do they worship Me." A secular song from the 50s echoes these words when it asks: "Your lips are so near, but where is your heart?"

Lord, *I do not want to be an ornamental Christian. Let my worship today truly come from the heart. In Jesus' name I pray. Amen.*

Beware a T-Shirt Jesus

What think ye of Christ? (Matthew 22:42).

Scripture: **Matthew 22:41-46**
Song: **"Jesus Is the Sweetest Name I Know"**

This question Jesus asked the Pharisees is similar to the one He asked Peter in Luke 9:20: "But who do ye say that I am?" Unfortunately, our society offers little insight into the biblical Jesus. One author writes, "Today, the Jesus most people hear about is the bumper-sticker Jesus, the Jesus who makes money for us when we put Him on our products, the 'T-shirt Jesus.' "

Leaving our church service one Sunday—after what I felt was a very moving Easter message—my friend turned to me and said, "How can people make such a fuss over just a man?"

So . . . who is Jesus for you? An alarm to ring in time of trouble? Initials on a bracelet? A Santa Claus for your wish list? Perhaps a curse word? Or is He the Son of God, the one who was "despised and rejected" (Isaiah 53:3), your personal Savior and Lord?

Jesus was a good man, but not *merely* a good man. He was a teacher, but not *only* a teacher. He was a healer, but so much *more* than a healer. I pray He is all the world to you; in fact, more than you could ever imagine. Until you see Him, face to face.

Dear Father, *no matter how highly I regard Your Christ, He is greater still than all my imaginings. I bow my knee to Him and His will today, the one in whom I offer my prayer of praise. Amen.*

Just Invite

Understandest thou what thou readest? And he said, How can I, except some man should guide me? (Acts 8:30, 31).

Scripture: **Acts 8:26-31**
Song: **"Make Me a Blessing"**

We see in the early part of this chapter that Philip was having a successful ministry in Samaria, preaching and performing miracles. Then an angel appeared to him and told him to go south to the road to Gaza, "which is desert."

For a man like Philip, familiar with speaking to large crowds, this command must have been puzzling. But God knew there was a man in a chariot who needed some special guidance.

I had just driven 20 miles home from my job one night and was looking forward to hearing a special speaker at our church service. Then a woman—who had made herself a neighborhood nuisance by screaming at her children and constantly borrowing—knocked at my door and asked me to take her to see her daughter who was in the hospital—another 15 miles away. After learning it was the little girl's birthday, I wearily agreed.

On the way I mentioned the church service that night. I will never forget her words. "We used to go to church," she said, "but since we moved here, no one has invited us."

Can you guess what I did then?

Lord, *the least I can do is invite others into Your loving presence. Prepare my heart to do it at the next opportunity. In Christ's name, amen.*

Jesus, the Answer

Then Philip opened his mouth, and began at the same scripture, and preached unto him Jesus (Acts 8:35).

Scripture: Acts 8:32-40
Song: "Jesus Is All I Need"

I was sitting at the breakfast table with several women one morning at a retreat. The friend I came with asked the lady sitting next to me, "Did you sleep well?"

"No," the woman replied. "I was awake most of the night praying. I've been really worried about a family situation."

I was ready to say, flippantly, "Worry is like a rocking chair. It gives you something to do, but doesn't get you anywhere." But before I could speak, my friend gently asked, "And did the praying help?"

Ouch! It's so easy to rattle off a cliché or platitude when a friend is sharing a problem with us. Or we rush to tell them of a similar experience we've had in our own life. Or we dispense some pat answer. However, what most people are looking for is not our attempt to formulate a pleasing answer. They seek the one who *is* the answer.

One woman confessed at a Bible study, "I've read Christian books, listened to tapes, and gone to seminars. While they were all good, one day I realized that the answer wasn't in them. It was in Christ, and Him alone!"

Oh, Lord, *You hear all our questions and know all our deepest desires. Help us to see that these always point to You, the only one who can satisfy every longing. It is in Jesus' name that we pray. Amen.*

Obeying God

He and all his family were devout and God-fearing; he gave generously to those in need and prayed to God regularly (Acts 10:2, *New International Version*).

Scripture: **Acts 10:1-8**
Song: **"I Am Resolved"**

As a military man, Cornelius knew the importance of following orders. He was a centurion in the Roman army, which meant he had one hundred or more soldiers under his command. When he gave an order, he expected his men to follow it without delay. Cornelius himself must have followed the orders of his superior officers on many occasions.

This Gentile believer even practiced obedience in his personal life—obedience to God, that is. The Bible says he prayed regularly and gave generously to charity.

It's not surprising, then, that when Cornelius received instructions from God in a vision, he followed orders and obeyed immediately. He didn't question the angel. He didn't sit and think about what to do. As soon as the angel was gone, he dispatched his men to fetch Peter.

It is our willingness to obey that matters to God, not our race or gender or social status. He is waiting to bless us as we heed His voice.

Dear Lord, *thank You for the example of Cornelius. Like him, when we hear Your voice, let us move quickly to do Your bidding. In Jesus' name, amen.*

October 17-23. **Beth Bence Reinke** is a registered dietitian living in Stewartstown, Pennsylvania, with her husband, Bruce, and their two sons.

Comfort Zone, Good-bye

Do not call anything impure that God has made clean (Acts 10:15, *New International Version*).

Scripture: Acts 10:9-16
Song: **"I'll Go Where You Want Me to Go"**

How would your great, great grandmother have reacted if you told her that people would someday cook food without fire or heat? Imagine trying to convince your great, great grandfather that metal contraptions would orbit the earth and help predict the weather. Although commonplace to us, microwaves and satellites would have seemed quite strange to our family members of four generations ago.

New ideas are especially hard to swallow when they go against traditions ingrained in us since birth. Peter had followed strict Jewish dietary laws all of his life, so he was understandably shocked by the vision he saw while praying. It included a voice from Heaven telling him to eat the forbidden kinds of meat. God was stretching Peter, teaching him to "put on the new" by living in the freedom of grace instead of languishing under the law.

Like Peter, we may face something new that pushes us out of our comfort zone. God sometimes challenges us with the unfamiliar. When we step out in faith, He uses new situations to shape us for future service.

Heavenly Father, *we are thankful that nothing is new or surprising to You. Help us to hear Your voice when we are unsure about what is new and good—and what is only new. Through Christ I pray. Amen.*

He Will Direct

So get up and go downstairs. Do not hesitate to go with them, for I have sent them (Acts 10:20, *New International Version*).

Scripture: **Acts 10:17-23a**
Song: **"He Leadeth Me"**

Have you ever watched a play rehearsal and been distracted by lapses in action or disjointed dialogue? In a theatrical performance, the timing of every word and action is critical to the audience's understanding of the story. If an actor appears onstage too soon, or says his lines out of order, it throws off the sequence of events.

In Acts 10, God directs a precisely timed drama. First, He sets the stage by appearing to Cornelius, who then sends his men on a journey to find Peter. When the men are just a short distance away, God sends a vision to Peter as he is praying on the roof. Then, while Peter is still mulling over the vision, the men arrive at the gate. God scheduled the men's arrival times so they could shed light on the meaning of Peter's vision. God's perfect timing came through at just the right time.

In daily life it is sometimes hard to wait for our heavenly director's cues. Often we desire to rush ahead with our own special performances and plottings. But it is wise to wait patiently, seeking the Lord in prayer. He will lovingly direct every scene of our lives as we follow His lead.

Dear Lord, thank You for loving us enough to keep offering guidance, day by day. We make so many twists and turns in our journeys, yet You meet us right where we are and show us the next step. All praise to You! Amen.

Listening Together

Now we are all here in the presence of God to listen to everything the Lord has commanded you to tell us (Acts 10:33, *New International Version*).

Scripture: **Acts 10:23b-33**
Song: **"We Gather Together"**

How often do you gather your whole family and close friends in one place? Perhaps for Christmas, at weddings, or in celebration of a wedding anniversary? When we commemorate milestones in our lives, we enjoy sharing those special times with loved ones, as many as we can bring together.

In today's Scripture passage, the home of Cornelius buzzed with preparations for receiving an important visitor. Friends and relatives traveled from across the street or from another town to hear what Peter would say. Imagine the women chatting as they prepared food, wondering at what hour the guest of honor would appear. Finally, he arrived and everyone gathered with expectant hearts.

It's not every week that a famous preacher like Peter comes to town. But we do come together each week with our church families for an important event—Sunday worship. Just as God communicated to the crowd through Peter, He speaks through preachers all over the world. What a privilege to be part of the worldwide body of believers who gathers to hear the Word of God each week!

Father God, *we are ever thankful for the privilege of coming together to listen to You regularly. In Jesus' holy name I pray. Amen.*

God Doesn't Play Favorites

God does not show favoritism but accepts men from every nation who fear Him and do what is right (Acts 10:34, 35, *New International Version*).

Scripture: **Acts 10:34-43**
Song: **"In Christ There Is No East or West"**

Most evenings the television news airs a story about people clashing somewhere in the world. Why can't people get along? Sometimes it's because of differences in customs or politics or religions. Often the friction is fueled by prejudices that have been passed on for generations.

Peter and his fellow apostles brought deep-rooted prejudices toward Gentiles into the early church. Historically, Jews did not associate with Gentiles and considered them unclean. But according to Almighty God, that attitude was to be cast aside. With three swoops of a critter-laden sheet from Heaven, the Lord reformed Peter's beliefs about unclean food—and supposedly unclean people. Henceforth, Peter was to preach to *all* peoples.

Aren't you glad that God is no respecter of persons? That He doesn't play favorites? That He loves everyone and desires that all come to faith in His Son?

We would do well to view each person we meet from God's perspective—as someone for whom Jesus died. Cultural bias and prejudice have no place in our lives.

Dear Lord, let us follow Peter's example by pushing bias and prejudicial attitudes aside, extending a hand of friendship and acceptance to all fellow sinners. In Jesus' name I pray. Amen.

Our Mentors

While Peter was still speaking these words, the Holy Spirit came on all that heard the message (Acts 10:44, *New International Version*).

Scripture: **Acts 10:44-48**
Song: **"Holy Spirit, Faithful Guide"**

God blesses each of us with a mentor at the moment we accept Christ. He is, of course, the Holy Spirit. According to my dictionary, a mentor is "a wise and faithful counselor or monitor." The Holy Spirit also comforts, convicts, and sanctifies us. More importantly, He is God within us, which means we are counseled by the Lord himself.

The new believers at the home of Cornelius were doubly blessed—they had a divine mentor and a human mentor. First, the Holy Spirit sealed them. Second, they invited Peter to stay with them for a few more days (Acts 10:48). Can you imagine being taught by someone who had eaten and traveled with our Savior?

A human mentor, like Peter, can play a special role for a new believer. He or she can model prayer, Bible study, and godly living. Scripture gives numerous examples of seasoned mentors supplying wise counsel and instruction— Eli and Samuel, Naomi and Ruth, Paul and Timothy.

If you have recently accepted Jesus as your Savior, will you seek a wise human counselor? Or if you are a mature Christian, will you fill that role for a new believer?

Father, *thank You for the gift of the Holy Spirit, who is our constant companion. Please open our hearts to His prompting. In Jesus' name, amen.*

Miracle of the Gospel

He will bring you a message through which you and all your household will be saved (Acts 11:14, *New International Version*).

Scripture: **Acts 11:1-15**
Song: **"Tell the World that Jesus Saves"**

Beth Ann was in her neighbor's basement attending an after-school Bible club when she made the decision to follow Christ. Mark responded to the gospel invitation at a church banquet. Joe came to baptism after years of seeking.

No matter where or how a person makes the decision to accept the Lord, he or she becomes a child of God, baptized into His body. The gospel still works the same today as it did when Peter shared it at Cornelius's home.

How joyful Cornelius must have been when the Holy Spirit came upon the new believers among his family and friends. How thrilled he must have been when Peter asked, "Can anyone keep these people from being baptized with water?" (Acts 10:47). Cornelius saw the angel's words in Acts 11:14 fulfilled right before his eyes.

Our salvation is a miracle. For a time we are longing creatures, spiritually thirsty, filled with desire, addicted to escaping our pain. Then, through the gospel of grace, God leads us into wholeness, fulfillment, and peace. The gospel is truly a wondrous, life-changing gift.

Loving Father, we praise You for redeeming us through Your Son, Jesus Christ. Help us to share the joy of our salvation with those You place in our paths. In the name of Him who saved us, we pray. Amen.

Spoons, Forks, and Knives

Now in Joppa there was a certain disciple named Tabitha (which translated in Greek is called Dorcas); this woman was abounding with deeds of kindness and charity, which she continually did (Acts 9:36, *New American Standard Bible*).

Scripture: **Acts 9:32-42**
Song: **"Give of Your Best to Your Master"**

Seven-year-old Lindsay was helping me set the table. "I'm glad I'm not a fork," she suddenly announced.

"What's wrong with forks?" I asked.

"Forks like to stab things and try to get everything for themselves," she replied.

I held up a knife. "What about these?"

"Too bossy," she replied, wrinkling her nose. "Knives always cut things up to be the way they want them."

Then she picked up a spoon. "But spoons are your friends," she said, cradling one in her palm. "It's like they say, 'Here, let me help you.'"

I had never analyzed our eating utensils before, but I think my little girl made a good observation about people. Not everyone likes to serve. Not everyone, like Dorcas, abounds with kind and charitable deeds. But where, on this strange table, are you at the moment?

Dear God, *thank You for being patient while we develop into godly "spoons," desiring to give ourselves to others. In the name of Your Son, our Savior, we pray. Amen.*

October 24-30. **Kayleen Reusser** is a freelance writer living in Bluffton, Indiana. She is married with three children.

Practical Worship

It is written, "You shall worship the Lord your God and serve Him alone" (Luke 4:8, *New American Standard Bible*).

Scripture: **Luke 4:1-13**
Song: **"Shout to the Lord"**

Matt, a Christian missionary, had been accidentally killed by a jeepney driver. Filipino law states that someone who causes a death is imprisoned until the matter is resolved, unless the victim's family authorizes his release.

Peggy, Matt's widow, knew the jeepney driver was not guilty and that his family would starve without his daily income. She asked that the driver be released. At Matt's viewing, a native woman and man came up to Peggy. Weeping openly, the jeepney driver and his wife told how their children had gone without food while he was locked up. Now the children could eat, and they were thankful.

It would have been tempting for Peggy not to forgive the driver for killing Matt. In her grief she could have made him suffer as she was suffering. But temptation did not guide Peggy's life; love did.

What does it mean for you to worship and serve the Lord alone? Have you, like Peggy, discovered just how practical it can be? Even how simple? Yet it is usually the most costly to our ego and pride.

Lord, we are so often swept away by passion and selfish desire until our days are ruined. Yet with Jesus' example, You made a way for us to be strong. When temptation is before us, remind us that we need not serve it; let us serve only You. In Jesus' name I pray. Amen.

A Friendship to Go

He came to the disciples and found them sleeping, and said to Peter, "So, you men could not keep watch with Me for one hour?" (Matthew 26:40, *New American Standard Bible*).

Scripture: Matt 26:36-46
Song: "In the Garden"

If there had been coffee shops in Jesus' time, I'm convinced He would have taken one look at the sleepy faces of Peter, James, and John and said, "Hey, you guys, I'm going to need your support in the next several hours, and you don't look like you can hold your heads up much longer. Let's go to the Bohemian Bean in Jerusalem and I'll get you each a super-large caramel latte with caffeine to go!"

Okay, I'm kidding. But it's obvious the disciples had no artificial stimulant to keep them awake. They fell asleep three times, even after Jesus implored them to stay awake and pray. Thus, they lost the opportunity to support their best friend during the most difficult night of His life.

"How could they disappoint Jesus so?" I wonder. Then I consider: "How many times have I disappointed Him?"

Wherever I am, morning or night, I like to talk to God. You see, He's my best friend, and I've failed Him in the past. But He's given me a second chance. Now we have a lot of lost time to make up for!

God, You are patient with us beyond measure. You know we are weak and tired. But please give us wisdom to know when a circumstance needs our full attention for Your sake. In the name of Jesus we pray. Amen.

A Future with Hope

Jesus uttered a loud cry, and breathed his last (Mark 15:37, *New American Standard Bible*).

Scripture: **Mark 15:33-37**
Song: **"Beyond the Sunset"**

When my mother-in-law was dying of liver cancer, it grieved us to see her in such great pain. At her death we were sad. But we were also relieved to know that her suffering was ended and she was living in the glorious presence of our Lord.

Jesus' death would also have been painful to watch. Hanging on the cross as a dead weight meant He could hardly breathe. Unable to move and deprived of oxygen, His muscles would have contracted in wrenching spasms until He died of heart failure or suffocation. Those who loved Him and were present at His death must have been relieved to see Jesus no longer in agony.

During our lifetimes, each of us will probably participate in a loved one's journey from life to death. If he isn't a believer, we need to pray that he will come to know Jesus as Lord. If the loved one is a Christian, we can rest in the hope that, though this life is filled with sadness, pain, and fear, the next life will be filled with hope, courage, and joy.

God, You know how much it hurts to lose a loved one in death. Even though we rest in the assurance that we'll see him or her again someday in Heaven, it still hurts. Comfort us at these times, Lord, and give us courage to face the days ahead. In the precious name of Jesus I pray. Amen.

Suffering for Jesus

Peter was kept in the prison, but prayer for him was being made fervently by the church to God (Acts 12:5, *New American Standard Bible*).

Scripture: **Acts 12:1-5**
Song: **"Were You There?"**

During the 1990s, one of my missionary friends was imprisoned for his faith in Jesus. His family sent prayer requests to Christians around the world. During periods of solitary confinement, he suffered hunger, cold, and loneliness. Yet, when he was allowed contact with other prisoners, he transcended personal discomfort and focused on telling them of God's love for them.

Months later, upon his release from prison, my friend traveled to churches, telling how God had met his needs in prison. Today he carries the message of Christ as a missionary in a different country. Chained or free, this devoted servant will continue to spread the good news of Christ until he hears, "Well done, good and faithful servant."

Herod thought that Peter's arrest would put an end to his ministry. Instead, it united the church members, as they came together to pray on his behalf. Really, can persecution ever dim the light of Christian witness to the world?

God, thank You for courageous men and women around the world who love You and want to serve You, even at risk of death and separation from loved ones. Please show us if there is some way we can help them in their suffering. In the name of Jesus, amen.

What Are You Looking For?

When Peter came to himself, he said, "Now I know for sure that the Lord has sent forth His angel and rescued me from the hand of Herod and from all that the Jewish people were expecting" (Acts 12:11, *New American Standard Bible*).

Scripture: **Acts 12:6-11**
Song: **"You are the Lord, the Famous One"**

Recently, a friend confided that he needed a drummer for his Christian band. Being a non-musical person, I couldn't help or recommend anyone. In fact, the only—and best—thing I could do was pray for his need, which I did. The next morning my sister e-mailed me about a mutual friend, "Did you know Rui plays the bongos? He's great!" I hadn't known. After a flurry of e-mails, I connected the two musicians, and they're planning to meet. God's timing is perfect.

Last week, my neighbor was despairing over his recent diagnosis of a debilitating disease. If he couldn't work, he couldn't make a house payment. Our families prayed together. The next day, he received an unexpected check in the mail, enough to make two house payments. God comes through again!

Do you look for evidence of God at work in your life? Peter wasn't expecting a miracle, but he got one that saved his life. Situations don't always happen the way we want them to, but we can still believe God is there, working it out for His glory.

We trust in You, O God, to guide and keep us. Your ways are perfect and we know You will be there for us at every step. In the name of Christ, amen.

Guess Who's Coming to Dinner!

When she recognized Peter's voice, because of her joy she did not open the gate, but ran in and announced that Peter was standing in front of the gate (Acts 12:14, *New American Standard*).

Scripture: **Acts 12:12-17**
Song: **"Hiding in Thee"**

Some scenes in the Bible are hilarious to me. Today's Scripture is an example. In this scene, God had broken Peter out of jail, so Peter had run to a friend's house for sanctuary. After knocking on the gate, his face must have lit up at hearing a friendly voice on the other side. It was Rhoda, the maid, and Peter relaxed, thinking she would let him in. He would be safe in seconds.

But Rhoda didn't open the gate. Instead, she ran off to tell the rest of the household that Peter, for whom they'd been praying, was outside. Poor Peter! He was left stranded outside the gate. Poor Rhoda! Nobody believed her story about Peter. Those inside the house told her she was crazy, so crazy that the voice she heard was not Peter's but an angel's.

Then they heard knocking at the gate. They must have looked at each other, and thought, "Do angels knock?"

Finally they opened the gate. Guess who!

Lord, thank You for loving all of us, in spite of our tendencies to doubt and criticize each other. And help us to use humor whenever possible to heal our struggling relationships. We pray this prayer in the name of Jesus, our Savior and Lord. Amen.

Faith and Obedience

So they pulled their boats up on shore, left everything and followed him (Luke 5:11, *New International Version*).

Scripture: Luke 5:4-11
Song: "I Surrender All"

"You're going to do what? Have you lost your mind?" Marian stared at her husband. Who was this man?

Howard took a deep breath. "I am going to leave my law practice and join the ministry. I think I'd rather wrestle with the devil than wrestle with the law."

"Me—a minister's wife? I can't imagine," Marian replied. Though her tone was harsh, Howard was pleased to see love and trust in her eyes. "However, I did enjoy running the church carnival last year," she mused aloud.

"I've wanted this for a long time, but you know the ministry is almost pro bono. We've made good investments. I believe God has provided so well for just this reason." He took his wife's hand. "But it really won't be "we," Marian. I am going to seek a prison ministry. I know some of those men can be saved. I want to help them."

Marian recalled that although Howard had sometimes been impulsive, he had never been foolish. Smiling, she squeezed her husband's hand.

"Yes, my love, with God's help, I believe you can."

Dear God, *help me to recognize Your touch and to have the courage to abide by Your will. In Jesus' holy name I pray. Amen.*

October 31-November 6. **Marilyn Kreyer**, of Newton, Kansas, is a mother, grandmother, and great-grandmother who writes to thank God for the blessing in her life.

DEVOTIONS

I rejoiced with those who said to me, Let us go to the house of the LORD.

—Psalm 122:1, *NIV*

NOVEMBER

Photo © Comstock

Gary Allen, editor

Too Clean to Care?

I replied, "Surely not, Lord! Nothing impure or unclean has ever entered my mouth" (Acts 11:8, *New International Version*).

Scripture: Acts 11:1-10
Song: "From Every Tribe and Nation"

Remember the story of the king who wore no clothes? He paraded naked before his subordinates, vainglorious because he believed himself to be attired in the finest garments available. No one appeared more resplendent! He lifted his chin high and then looked down his regal nose at his wretched subjects.

How often do we fool ourselves into believing that we are just about the greatest rooster in the flock? How often do we behave like Peter? Peter had prided himself on his strict adherence to Jewish law. He had known the admiration of Jesus. He had enjoyed the admiration of the crowds who flocked to see his Master. Now Peter felt that, because of his own righteousness and his association with the risen Jesus, he was quite special.

So, quietly and with love, the Lord gave Peter a visionary insight that took his eyes off himself. There were people around him—all kinds of people—for Peter to love and care for. Could Peter reach out to them with the kindness and grace that he himself had received from Heaven?

Lord, pride is such a subtle sin, and I succumb so easily. It is so easy for me to accept flattery as truth and rejoice in my own achievements. Lord, please help me to focus on You and the others You are loving into Your kingdom. In Jesus' name I pray. Amen.

It's Truly Divine!

So then, God has granted even the Gentiles repentance unto life (Acts 11:18, *New International Version*).

Scripture: **Acts 11:11-18**
Song: "Holy Spirit, Truth Divine"

British historian and essayist Thomas Carlyle once said: "Of all acts of mankind, repentance is the most divine. The greatest of all faults is to be conscious of none." In its essence, repentance truly is divine, since it is actually granted by God.

Through the gospel we are allowed to see ourselves as we are, and then we are faced with a choice. We can ignore it and continue on our same ill-fated course. We can start into a program of *self*-improvement. Or we can open our hearts to the salvation that comes only as a gift.

How blessed the Gentiles were! As they heard the promise of the gospel, they believed the message and desired it above all the promises they had heard but never realized from their pantheon of gods. As the Holy Spirit moved upon them, they became willing to change the values of their hearts and minds. They became true believers.

Such repentance is more than just being dismayed or disappointed in ourselves. As another English historian and preacher, Thomas Fuller, put it: "Great is the difference betwixt a man's being frightened at, and humbled for his sins."

Lord, *thank You for the gift of repentance. And please accept my heartfelt thanks for the moving of Your Spirit within me. Through Christ, amen.*

Did You Hear What I Heard?

The men traveling with Saul stood there speechless; they heard the sound but did not see anyone (Acts 9:7, *New International Version*).

Scripture: **Acts 9:1-9**
Song: **"Spirit of God, Descend upon My Heart"**

I came of age just as the hippie movement swept the West Coast. Seeing the young people on the news, so free-spirited and conspicuous in all their youthful abandon, I felt old before my time. Nevertheless, I knew I couldn't be irresponsible toward my family or my God. "Tune in, turn on, and drop out"? No, not for me.

I recall that churches across America reacted against anything bespeaking the New Age, free love, or do-it-yourself religion. And they were correct, for though this was a well-meaning rebellion against the stuffiness of a previous generation, those long-haired youngsters demonstrated a naive and shallow spirit. Extolling exceptional love, they mostly fell into exceptional excess.

I believe those young people did hear the call to love. But how many saw and acknowledged the divine source of love? Saul and his companions, too, heard the sound of God, but only Saul comprehended what they were hearing. But as Paul later wrote, faith comes by hearing . . . and is proved by the *doing*.

Lord, *keep us from being swept up in pseudo-religious fads and writings. Let us hear the Word of God—and see and know the one who gives it. In Jesus' holy name I pray. Amen.*

Your Purpose?

This man is my chosen instrument to carry my name before the Gentiles and their kings and before the people of Israel (Acts 9:15, *New International Version*).

Scripture: **Acts 9:10-16**
Song: **"Lord, Speak to Me"**

Are we really who we think we are? Not only is it common for people to misjudge us, but do we ever really know ourselves? In times of doubt, who hasn't thought, "Why was I born?"

No doubt Saul of Tarsus felt secure in his chosen purpose. He knew he had a real talent for weeding out radicals who called themselves "The Way." They were up to no good, and their rabble-rousing could possibly turn the attention of the Roman government against the Jews. "Yes, I'm doing exactly what I was meant to do," he must have thought.

But God had other plans for him. He struck down the man named Saul of Tarsus, and then raised him up again. And Saul was a new man with a new purpose for living.

Few of us will have such a dramatic conversion, but each and every one of us is here to serve God, whether "instrumental" as king or carpenter. Will you offer your gifts and talents to God this day? Who knows where He will lead you in putting those abilities to use.

Dear God, just as the apostle Paul came to his feet on that Damascus road as a new man with a new purpose, lead me onto the path where I can best serve You. Guide me, Lord! In the name of Christ I pray. Amen.

The First Day

Saul grew more and more powerful and baffled the Jews living in Damascus by proving that Jesus is the Christ (Acts 9:22, *New International Version*).

Scripture: **Acts 9:17-22**
Song: **"He Touched Me"**

"Joanie, you look different today. What's up?" Tammy looked at her friend quizzically. It was lunchtime, and the company cafeteria was filled.

"Find a new man?" Becky teased.

Joanie smiled as she met the gaze of the women at her table. "Yes, I did. I found the Lord last night," she said.

"I didn't know he was missing," Connie chided, and it seemed that everyone except Joanie laughed.

"Seriously," she said. "Last night I went to a church meeting and, after listening to the message, I saw Jesus in a whole new light. I always figured He was a great man, a great teacher in history. Now I believe He really is the Son of God." She smiled warmly as she finished speaking.

Sheryl scoffed. "So are you going to join a nunnery?" Again, everyone laughed, and even Joanie chuckled. "No, Sheryl. I just know I've been forgiven and I'm free to try to do better."

Laughing, they shook their heads, gathered their trays, and left. Only Sally remained, extending her hand: "Welcome, my sister in Christ. It's been so lonely here."

Lord, how can I thank You for not only saving my life but giving me a new life full of Your promises and Your love? In Jesus' holy name, amen.

Time to Rest, Time to Grow

The church . . . was strengthened; and encouraged by the Holy Spirit, it grew in numbers, living in the fear of the Lord (Act 9:31, *New International Version*).

Scripture: **Acts 9:23-31**
Song: **"This Is My Father's World"**

"Gramma, Gramma! My garden is dead." Tommy's voice trembled as his eyes brimmed with tears. She gathered the little six-year-old onto her lap and hugged him tightly.

"Oh Gramma, there's not a green thing out there; just crummy brown dirt." His voice caught again. The old lady quietly chuckled and began rocking.

"Shhh, there, my boy. The garden's not dead; it's asleep. You remember how tired you were last night when I put you to bed?" The boy nodded. "And could you have played anymore?" Tommy shook his head.

"But, Tommy, you could play a lot this morning, right?" Again he nodded. "Well, that's what your garden's doing. Just like we rest, God wants His world to rest from time to time."

It seems the church, too, had its special times for growth. It is our job to pray for those times today, and to wait upon God's power to strengthen and encourage us for nurturing new life among us.

Grant us, Lord, the ability to lean on Your wisdom and to rest in Your love. Please give us the rest that we need for the work to come. In Jesus' name I pray. Amen.

Sharing the Sorrow

Share the sorrow of those being ill-treated, for you know what they are going through (Hebrews 13:3, *The Living Bible*).

Scripture: **Hebrews 13:1-6**
Song: **"Farther Along"**

A venomous Brown Recluse spider had bitten my leg. During the several years that followed, I'd have 12 surgeries and be immersed in nearly constant pain. Though medication sometimes helped, mostly I just had to suffer through each day the best I could.

Many people expressed concern—through kind words, thoughtful acts, and many prayers. But still, most of the time I felt as if I were going through the hurt all alone.

Then one Sunday afternoon—a day when I could hardly get out of bed—a Christian friend stopped by. We talked, and he showed a caring, genuine interest in my feelings. He pulled out a small black case that held two tiny cups, a few wafers, and a little plastic container of grape juice. Then the two of us had Communion. Suddenly I realized that my friend was truly trying to share my pain and was affirming our bond as brothers in Christ. How thoughtful!

Christians around the world are suffering and being persecuted for the sake of the gospel. Let's think how we can share their sorrow.

Father, many of Your children around the world are hurting. Give us hearts of compassion for them. In the name of the Suffering Servant, amen.

November 7-13. **Jeff Friend** is a certified professional in human resources who writes from his home in Clearwater, Florida.

It's Just Not Fair!

Martha was the jittery type and was worrying over the big dinner she was preparing. She came to Jesus and said, "Sir, doesn't it seem unfair to you that my sister just sits here while I do all the work? Tell her to come and help me" (Luke 10:40, *The Living Bible*).

Scripture: **Luke 10:38-42**
Song: **"I Must Tell Jesus"**

If you spend much time around children, you'll find that they all are experts when it comes to justice. If one gets a bigger piece of candy, another will immediately proclaim, "Hey, that's not fair!" This is usually followed by the wronged child explaining what needs to be done to correct the injustice, such as: "Give me the biggest one!"

Adults also tend to cry "Foul!" when things don't go their way, even when talking to God. We plead with Him that it's not fair when a loved one falls ill, or we lose our jobs, or someone gets a pat on the back while our efforts seem ignored. Then we try to tell Him what He needs to do to make it "fair."

Justice originates with God. Does He really need our advice about what He should do to make things right? Or could we learn to rely a little more on our loving Father knowing what is best for us?

Lord, only You are righteous and holy and perfectly fair. We eagerly look for the day when we will be in Your presence, and everything will be made right among us. Even so, Lord Jesus, come quickly. In the name of our Savior, Jesus Christ, I pray. Amen.

Unusual Gift

As each one has received a special gift, employ it in serving one another, as good stewards of the manifold grace of God (1 Peter 4:10, *New American Standard Bible*).

Scripture: **1 Peter 4:7-11**
Song: **"This Little Light of Mine"**

When I was 10 years old, my parents gave me a shiny new gas-powered airplane as a special Christmas gift. My mind swirled with visions of that plane soaring through the air in all kinds of acrobatic moves, bringing untold joy to my brothers and me. Since it was the middle of winter, those flights would have to wait until spring arrived. But, amazingly, once the weather warmed, my thoughts had moved on to other adventures.

Several years later, I found the plane in my parents' garage. It was still in the same unopened box. My special gift had never once flown in the bright sky as it was meant to do. It never had the chance to bring me hours of fun as it should have.

God has given each of us a special gift, and He intends for us to use it to serve one another. If we don't share our gifts with others, the people they were meant to help will never be able to benefit from them, and we will lose many wonderful opportunities to glorify God.

Precious Lord, *thank You for the gifts You have given us to use for Your glory. Help us to develop these gifts to their full potential that we may serve the body of Christ and those who need to know about Your love and grace. I humbly ask all this in Jesus' name. Amen.*

She Kept Urging

She was baptized along with all her household and asked us to be her guests. "If you agree that I am faithful to the Lord," **she said, "come and stay at my home." And she urged us until** **we did** (Acts 16:15, *The Living Bible*).

Scripture: **Acts 16:11-15**
Song: **"I Shall Not Be Moved"**

My wife and I decided to buy a puppy. On our way to the breeder to make our selection, I said: "Now remember, I want a female." Once we arrived, seven little puppies swarmed over us, each vying for our complete attention.

As my wife played with them on the floor, I picked up each female and gently cuddled her. I noticed that one puppy kept following me around the room and staying close by my foot as the others scampered around. Since it was a male, I turned back to the other dogs.

But that puppy would not move from me. No matter how much I tried to ignore him, he wouldn't go away. Finally I gave in and picked him up. He was very affectionate, and I instantly fell in love with him. I told my bewildered wife, "This is the one."

That puppy had something to say to me about my praying, about my "urgings" when I come before the Lord. I know there are times when I need a little more persistence when my heart is heavy with a pressing need. How is it with you?

Almighty God, *may we remain firm and persistent in our intercessions. Through Your strength we will prevail, praying in Christ's name. Amen.*

Dream-Shattering Goodness

Her masters' hopes of wealth were now shattered; they grabbed Paul and Silas and dragged them before the judges at the market-place (Acts 16:19, *The Living Bible*).

Scripture: **Acts 16:16-24**
Song: **"Whispering Hope"**

He was the star pitcher on his high-school baseball team. College recruiters called his home daily. Professional teams contacted his coaches. His dreams of wealth and athletic stardom were soon to be fulfilled.

But during one of his last games before graduating, after hurling a blazing fast ball, he felt a burning, stinging pain surge through his arm. Later, doctors confirmed that he needed surgery . . . and he would never pitch again.

Talk about shattered dreams! The recruiters soon stopped calling, and bitterness crowded his mind. His dreams were gone.

Christians know that God is at work in all the circumstances of their lives. No matter what comes our way, He is still in control. That is why we can recognize: "Sometimes dream-shattering is a good thing." It may or may not have been so in the young pitchers' life. But it was certainly the case with the plans for wrongdoing that the servant girl's masters so cherished. Thank God they were put out of business.

Gracious Father, if we place our hopes in our own abilities, we are destined to be disappointed. May we dream only of Your continued goodness toward us in the days ahead. I pray in Jesus' name. Amen.

Don't Use that Sword!

The jailer woke up, and when he saw the prison doors open, he drew his sword and was about to kill himself because he thought the prisoners had escaped (Acts 16:27, *New International Version*).

Scripture: **Acts 16:25-34**
Song: **"O Perfect Love"**

"Oh, no!" cried the young girl. "Mr. Jackson's rabbit is gone, Mommy! I went next door to feed him, and his cage door was open, and he wasn't in there!"

"Well, he couldn't have gone too far."

"But Mommy! I promised I'd take real good care of his rabbit while he was on vacation, but I didn't lock the cage door. What if something bad happened? What will Mr. Jackson do? It was his prize rabbit."

Being given something valuable to care for, we are honored that we have earned such trust, and we take extra pains to do things right. But when something goes wrong, we immediately expect terrible consequences. We're sure we can never be forgiven.

When we despair of forgiveness, let us consider once again the cross. Which of our sins did Jesus nail there? Only the biggest ones? the little ones? our favorite ones? If not all of them, then was not His eternal sacrifice in vain?

Holy Lord, *I cling to the cross of Jesus when I'm so disappointed in my behavior. Because He was crucified, I need not crucify myself. For this I can only be humbly and eternally grateful. In the precious name of Jesus, my Savior and Lord, I pray. Amen.*

Encourage One Another

After Paul and Silas came out of the prison, they went to Lydia's house, where they met with the brothers and encouraged them. Then they left (Acts 16:40, *New International Version*).

Scripture: **Acts 16:35-40**
Song: **"Through It All"**

Paul and Silas had been beaten and jailed, yet when they were released they went and encouraged their friends. Isn't that amazing? Instead of seeking pity for themselves, they comforted others.

The body of my friend John had been ravaged by cancer, but he still attended church whenever he could. His smile was as charming as ever, but the glimmer in his eyes betrayed the constant pain he felt. He walked slower and with more effort, but he refused to let the disease affect his spirit.

Many people were praying for John's healing, and everyone was supporting him in any way they could. But the amazing thing about John was the way he would walk through the cancer ward and pray with people and encourage them. Despite his failing health, he would actually take the time to help others deal with their own problems. In his time of weakness, he was strengthening others with his words and example.

Dear Father, may we follow Jesus' example of encouraging those around us despite our own circumstances. May we have a servant's heart and realize that we are all pilgrims on a journey to our homeland. In Jesus' holy name I pray. Amen.

Bringing in the Oats

The harvest is plentiful, but the workers are few. Ask the Lord of the harvest, therefore, to send out workers into his harvest field (Luke 10:2, *New International Version*).

Scripture: **Luke 10:1-11**
Song: **"Bringing in the Sheaves"**

I recall the excitement that filled the air on threshing day when I was a child. An uncle would chug up our lane on his threshing machine, and then neighbors joined my father and brothers to harvest oats. As fast as men threw sheaves into the mouth of the contraption, it spit out grain at one place and straw at another. At noontime, the men would line up on our porch to wash their grimy arms and heads in basins of water before eating a huge dinner served by my mother: roast beef, mashed potatoes, corn, and chocolate cake. Then it was back to the fields.

Many hands were needed to harvest grain. Many hands are also needed to harvest souls. Everyone in a congregation has a role to play. Like the threshers of my childhood, some may go into the fields. Others may provide equipment and finances. Then, like my mother who offered physical nourishment, some may nourish workers by keeping in touch and cheering them on. And all may pray that more workers catch the vision.

Lord, only after we've gone into the field can we return rejoicing, arms filled with sheaves. Help us discern Your will for us! In Jesus' name, amen.

November 14-20. **Shirley Brosius** is a Christian education specialist living in Pennsylvania. She and her husband have two sons, and a daughter in Heaven.

Just Say "Yes"

They replied, "The Lord needs it" (Luke 19:34, *New International Version*).

Scripture: **Luke 19:28-35**
Song: **"Open My Eyes, that I May See"**

I love to entertain. I've hosted teas to encourage women going through hard times. On the spur-of-the-moment, I've invited grieving family members home for coffee and doughnuts. Then there are the missionaries, church committees, and friends who have gathered near my hearth.

God has blessed me with a cozy home, and I am happy to offer hospitality. My heart rejoices as I watch people encourage and enjoy one another.

The owners of the colt must also have rejoiced as they watched Jesus' disciples lead it away. All they needed to know was that the Lord had need of their property. They didn't analyze why their colt was needed or why they should be the ones to sacrifice. They simply released what was theirs.

I wonder how often we miss opportunities for rejoicing when we cling to our possessions? Maybe God needs our homes, our cars, or our wallets. Maybe God needs our time, our attention, or our energy.

One thing is sure: God and others will rejoice with us as we share our blessings.

Lord, what do I have that might be used to build Your kingdom? Help me to use my resources to meet the needs. I know as I give to others, You will refill my hands with good things. In the name of Jesus I pray. Amen.

A Nice Funeral

From now on I will go to the Gentiles (Acts 18:6, *New International Version*).

Scripture: **Acts 18:1-8**
Song: **"Christ for the World We Sing"**

Sad, but comforted, we turned from my brother's grave site. We had heard the promises of Scripture and sung the hymns of faith. Two nieces shared remembrances of their father. They described how Robert had always worn a shirt and tie and relished political discussions. They told of how he once grabbed his trademark hat before rushing out the door to douse a car fire. And they told of an affirmation of faith he had made while ill, just weeks before his death. The service uplifted us and reminded us that Robert's earthly suffering had ended; his eternal life had begun.

But how different our funeral services would have been if Paul had not obeyed God's plan to carry the gospel to the Gentiles! What hope would we have for a heavenly home? How could we stand before a holy God without the cross of Christ to cover our sins? Perhaps saddest of all: We would be left wondering what had become of our precious loved ones. I am grateful that God chose to include me and you—whatever our ethnic origin—in His great plan of salvation.

Lord, *we would stand by open graves without hope if Christ had not opened His arms to us all. Thank You for Your generous invitation to eternity! I pray in Christ's precious name. Amen.*

Count Your Co-workers

I am with you, and no one is going to attack and harm you, because I have many people in this city (Acts 18:10, *New International Version*).

Scripture: **Acts 18:9-17**
Song: **"Count Your Blessings"**

Our music director recently listed everyone involved in our worship services, which average around two hundred people. To her amazement, she discovered 119 names. And 38 people serve in more than one capacity.

Too often we focus on unfilled ministry positions. We need teachers. We need a song leader. But if we take time to count, we may be surprised to see how many stand shoulder-to-shoulder with us in our church ministry.

When you're standing in the need of encouragement, remember the promise God gave to Paul after he'd been abused for preaching in Corinth. Although Christ had appeared to Paul on the road to Damascus and at other times since, he was not immune to discouragement as he faced opposition. So God once again spoke to him to remind him of the many other disciples who shared his faith. Through them, God provided a hedge of protection while Paul carried out his ministry at Corinth.

If we carry a heavy burden of ministry, we can identify with Paul. But if we also list those who serve beside us, we may find that God has many people in our "city" too.

Lord, *thank You for those who serve with me. Together we accomplish so much more than we could individually. In Jesus' name I pray. Amen.*

Pass the Spiritual Vitamins

After spending some time in Antioch, Paul set out from there and traveled from place to place throughout the region of Galatia and Phrygia, strengthening all the disciples (Acts 18:23, *New International Version*).

Scripture: **Acts 18:18-23**
Song: **"Pass It On"**

Through a "Secret Sister" program, I've received small gifts, cards, and notes of appreciation. As women in our congregation anonymously contact one another over the course of a year, we get to know each other better. It's fun to guess each other's identity before we reveal our names at Christmas. But to me the most encouraging part of the program comes from knowing that someone is thinking of me and praying for me throughout the year.

As a missionary, Paul did a great job of carrying the gospel to the Gentiles. And he also did a great job of encouraging those who had been converted during earlier missionary trips. He knew that difficult circumstances might cause some to doubt the goodness of God. So he kept checking in with them.

Yes, following Paul's model of ministry may take me places that I would never have visited otherwise. His example may require more patience and perseverance than I feel in my own strength. But that's the idea.

Lord, *Thank You for the gift of encouragement I've received from other Christians. Help me to pass on that blessing to someone who needs a special touch from You this very day. In Jesus' name I pray. Amen.*

Can't Read, or Won't?

[Apollos] vigorously refuted the Jews in public debate, proving from the Scriptures that Jesus was the Christ (Acts 18:28, *New International Version*).

Scripture: Acts 18:24-28
Song: "Break Thou the Bread of Life"

The Bible was the first book to emerge from Johann Gutenberg's amazing invention: the printing press. Its publication in 1456 finally made the Scriptures available to the common people. Up until then, monks had hand-copied the biblical text, a painstaking process that produced few manuscripts. Imagine how awestruck you would have felt the first time you held a freshly printed copy of the Word of God. But with that privilege came a responsibility to accurately interpret the sacred writings.

Apollos, a scholar, treasured Scripture, but he lived before the New Testament was written. While he knew who Jesus was, he evidently did not know the full story of His death and resurrection. So Priscilla and Aquila taught Apollos, who then went on to teach others.

Mark Twain once said, "The man who does not read good books has no advantage over the man who *can't* read them." With a variety of Bible translations and other "good books" available to us today, let's take advantage of our opportunities.

Lord, Your Word is so precious. Thank You that I can read Your Word and use study tools to clarify its meaning. Help me develop sound doctrine so I may help other seekers know You better. In Christ's name I pray. Amen.

Mission of Brotherly Love

Greet one another with a holy kiss. All the churches of Christ send greetings (Romans 16:16, *New International Version*).

Scripture: **Romans 16:3-16**
Song: **"A Common Love"**

On Sunday mornings I sometimes feel as though I'm on a mission. As Christian education chairperson, I rush around checking with this person about teaching Sunday school and that person about returning a library book. I hand a bill to the church treasurer and deliver a cradle roll packet to a nursery worker. In the process I may forget my manners. I concentrate so hard on finding the people I'm looking for that I sometimes miss saying "hello" to those I pass along the way. That is just plain rude.

Paul's letter to the Romans is a lengthy tome. Surely by the time he wrote about all the major Christian doctrines, he was ready to lay down his pen. But he didn't. Writer's cramp didn't stop him from greeting Priscilla and Aquila, Epenetus, Mary, Andronicus, Junias, Ampliatus, and Urbanus. He listed Apelles and a host of other individuals whom he appreciated, stating endearing qualities and relationships. Paul was on a mission, that's for sure. But he didn't forget to take time for the little niceties that build up the church. Neither dare we.

Dear Father, forgive me for the many times I've failed to properly greet my brothers and sisters in Christ. Thank You for the wonderful body of Christ. Bless Kirk, Jeff, Angie, Bryan, Dennis, Renee and all others who bless me with their friendship and support. In Jesus' name I pray. Amen.

Forever Love

Give thanks to the God of heaven. His love endures forever (Psalm 136:26 *New International Version*).

Scripture: **Ruth 1:6-14**
Song: **"His Love Endures Forever"**

An older couple adopted two young girls from China whose parents had abandoned them. The father shared his two greatest challenges: "First is the difficulty of impressing on our daughters that we are really their parents. Second is the challenge of convincing them that our love is forever. We won't leave them like their other parents."

Ruth demonstrated "forever love" for Naomi when she vowed to go wherever Naomi went. She had already lost her husband. How could she leave a mother-in-law who had been such an important part of her life? How could she turn her back on the living God, whom she had come to honor? How could she remain in her homeland?

Have you experienced "forever love"? The Bible tells us this is the kind of love God offers us. In His wisdom, He does not choose to protect us from every adversity. But in the midst of our greatest trials, He refuses to leave us. He gives us grace to cope with our imperfections and peace to overcome our disappointments.

Dear God, *I sometimes feel abandoned when my plans unravel and others fail me. In my times of disappointment, reassure me of Your presence and give me a renewed sense of Your enduring love. In Jesus' name, amen.*

November 21-27. **Larry Jones** is senior minister of Northside Church of Christ in Yorktown, Virginia. He and his wife, Jane, have two children, Nathan and Laura.

No Greater Love

Greater love has no one than this, that he lay down his life for his friends (John 15:13, *New International Version*).

Scripture: **1 Samuel 20:32-42**
Song: **"No Not One"**

In 1943 Lt. Col. Joseph P. Duckworth flew his single-engine AT-6 trainer into the eye of a category one hurricane. It was the first time anyone had intentionally done so. This event ushered in a new era in storm research, enabling forecasters to provide life-saving information to communities in harm's way.

Receiving information can be a matter of life and death. Jonathan risked his life to warn David of his father's murderous threats. The two knew David's only hope was to run from King Saul and hide. After a tearful goodbye, both friends parted to realize their uncertain destinies.

Good friends may willingly die for one another. But what about the friendless, or those reaping the consequences of sinful behavior? Jesus gave His life for His friends—and His enemies. The apostle Paul once wrote, "God demonstrates his own love for us in this: While we were still sinners, Christ died for us" (Romans 5:8).

How do you define ultimate love? For your answer, look at Jesus' sacrifice of His own life on the cross of Calvary. No love is greater or more complete.

Heavenly Father, thank You for sending Your Son to die for me when I least deserved it. Fill me with His love toward my friends and the friendless. Make me Your ambassador of grace. In Jesus' name, amen.

The Real Thing

Encourage one another and build each other up, just as in fact you are doing (1 Thessalonians 5:11, *New International Version*).

Scripture: **Acts 20:1-6**
Song: "For You I Am Praying"

Every day, hundreds of Americans receive military honors at their funerals. A two-person uniformed honor guard folds and presents to a surviving family member the United States flag, followed by a solemn rendition of Taps. To address concerns over a shortage of qualified buglers, the Defense Department recently approved an electronic bugle that plays the song automatically when a soldier places the horn on his lips.

Sometimes innovative substitutes will suffice, but nothing beats the real thing when it comes to relationships. Paul rarely passed up an opportunity to meet with believers on his missionary journeys. Why? God created each of us with a deep desire for relationships with real people. Thus He put followers of His Son into a family called "the church" and asked them to make meeting together a high priority.

As a believer, are you involved in a church family where you can share your life and blessings with others? Watching worship on television and listening to Christian music may meet a need in your spiritual life. But consider how it compares to real life, face-to-face encouragement, and the opportunity to reach out and serve.

Dear God, *remind me of my need to serve and be served. Thank You for the church and the opportunity I have to use my gifts in a family of faith.*

You Had to Be There

I rejoiced with those who said to me, Let us go to the house of the Lord (Psalm 122:1, *New International Version*).

Scripture: **Acts 20:7-12**
Song: **"Surely the Presence of the Lord Is in this Place"**

In a small country church, wasps regularly buzzed around the sanctuary during worship. One Sunday morning a single wasp came to rest on the pew behind an unsuspecting sister. The young man behind her raised his hymnbook, paused briefly, and then slammed the book against the back of the pew with all his might. This produced a loud smacking sound that resonated throughout the room. The woman rose to her feet with a scream! As the startled congregation turned to look, the young man brushed the wasp carcass off of his hymnbook, and everyone enjoyed a round of uncontrollable laughter.

You never know what is going to happen in a church service. One night as Paul preached to believers at Troas, a young servant by the name of Eutychus fell asleep in a window and plunged to his death below. Paul rushed to his side and miraculously raised him up.

Maybe you've never seen a man raised from the dead, or even a wasp brushed from a hymnbook. But would you like to observe what amazing, unpredictable things God does in the lives of His people, week after week? If so, perhaps I will see you next Sunday morning.

Dear God, *thank You for the opportunity to experience Your power and might in worship. In the name of Your Son, our Savior, I pray. Amen.*

Dying to Live

I eagerly expect and hope that I will in no way be ashamed, but will have sufficient courage so that now as always Christ will be exalted in my body, whether by life or by death (Philippians 1:20, *New International Version*).

Scripture: **Acts 20:17-24**
Song: **"Living for Jesus"**

A young father of two underwent surgery to remove a large cancerous mass resting between his heart and lung. The procedure was so rare that he was able to find only one doctor willing to take the risk of doing the surgery. Nevertheless, the tumor was successfully removed, and the thankful young father returned to his family.

My point is this: *sometimes we have to be willing to die if we want to keep on living.* This is the logic behind many medical treatments, but it also applies to other areas of our lives. We need to put past failures to rest if we want healthy emotions in the present. We also need to bury certain cherished sinful habits in exchange for a new walk with God.

So consider what keeps you from living a full, healthy Christian life. Can you take the risk of giving yesterday's burdens to the Lord? He will skillfully cut out the deadly sin and make you whole again.

Dear Lord, sin and disappointment easily weigh me down. Take my sorrows and turn them to joy. Help me find the courage to leave yesterday behind so I will be free to run the race You have set before me. In the precious name of Jesus I pray. Amen.

Beware the Doctrinal Stowaway

The time will come when men will not put up with sound doctrine. Instead, to suit their own desires, they will gather around them a great number of teachers to say what their itching ears want to hear (2 Timothy 4:3, *New International Version*).

Scripture: **Acts 20:25-31**
Song: **"Thy Word"**

On a Saturday morning in September, 2003, Charles McKinley was discovered inside a crate being delivered to his parents' home in DeSoto, Texas. McKinley had shipped himself as cargo from New York City to avoid the cost of an airplane ticket! When a delivery man unloaded the crate at its destination, he noticed eyes staring at him between two slats. He frantically opened the crate, only to find McKinley, who politely thanked him and walked inside his home.

Sadly, many people devise schemes to take advantage of others. Even the church is vulnerable to scams and falsehoods because of the trusting nature of believers. Yes, it's true that Jesus warned His followers not to judge others, and to turn the other cheek when threatened. Yet the Lord never expected His people to be passive in their defense of doctrine. He knew evil people would try to "stowaway" in church families, hoping to twist God's Word for selfish reasons. Beware!

Dear Lord, *give me the wisdom to know when Your Word is being misused for selfish gain. Help me resist the temptation in my own life to use Your truth as a vehicle for my own purposes. I pray in Jesus' name. Amen.*

In the Lord's Hands

The Lord is my rock, my fortress and my deliverer; my God is my rock, in whom I take refuge. He is my shield and the horn of my salvation (Psalm 18:2, *New International Version*).

Scripture: **Acts 20:32-38**
Song: **"God Will Make a Way"**

At the age of three, Michael May was blinded in a chemical accident. Forty-three years later, a surgical procedure restored his sight in one eye, but he was still not able to see his children's faces clearly. Doctors determined this unusual impairment was a result of his brain's inability to process information. Michael May could see, but his mind had not yet learned to recognize what it saw.

Similarly, have you noticed how we may see God at work in our lives but fail to comprehend His purposes?

The apostle Paul and the elders from Ephesus wept and embraced one another because they were convinced they would never be together again in this life. They also knelt and prayed. They could not predict what the future held, but they knew God was in control, and they wanted to put everything in His hands. Their faith helped them see God's glorious future for the church, even as their time together came to an end.

What's your vision of the future? Look to God, and He will show you more than you ever dreamed possible.

Dear God, I often become obsessed with trials and disappointments and forget You are in control. Give me the eyes of faith to recognize what human eyes cannot see. In Christ I pray. Amen.

Renewing, One Believer at a Time

Be silent before me, you islands! Let the nations renew their strength! (Isaiah 41:1, *New International Version*).

Scripture: **Isaiah 41:1-7**
Song: **"God of Our Fathers"**

How does a nation renew its strength? A nation is renewed as its Christians are renewed. Too often we look at the negative things all around us, wring our hands in dismay, and wonder, "What can just one person do?"

Tony Izzi is a quiet, humble businessman in Shelby, North Carolina. He doesn't like the spotlight. But when he heard of a campaign to place the national motto ("In God we trust") in school classrooms, he wanted to help.

He began by working with public school officials, churches, and ordinary citizens in his home county. Tony's work resulted in more than 1,600 motto posters being displayed in schoolrooms and public offices throughout the county. A year later, he had gone to the adjacent county and secured permission to put posters in three thousand classrooms there.

Scripture calls us to be salt and light in our culture. Tony is doing it. We can, too, by going to our churches and other Christian groups to discover new ways of expanding our influence.

God of our Fathers, help me to seek You and find ways to be salt and light in my own neighborhood. I pray in Jesus' holy name. Amen.

November 28-December 4. **Randall Murphree** is editor of the American Family Association Journal in Tupelo, Mississippi. He writes frequently about missions.

A Friend Is a Masterpiece

You, O Israel, my servant, Jacob, whom I have chosen, you descendants of Abraham my friend, I took you from the ends of the earth, from its farthest corners I called you (Isaiah 41:8, 9, *New International Version*).

Scripture: **Isaiah 41:8-13**
Song: **"What a Friend We Have in Jesus"**

Early American essayist Ralph Waldo Emerson wrote, "A friend may well be reckoned the masterpiece of nature." Many others through the ages have agreed that a true friend is marvelous: the friend accepts us, loves us, endures trials with us, and serves as our advocate in trying situations. Yet for such a friend to stick with us through the years, there must be a two-way relationship. Both parties must be equally loyal to one another.

Amazingly, God called Abraham His friend. And God wants each of us to be His friend today. He has already proven that He's ready for a committed relationship with us. That's a comforting thought for believers, but will we return the kind of love and loyalty we receive?

At times I feel compelled to do a "friendship inventory" in my life. I carefully consider: Do I love God above everything else? Do I enjoy spending time with Him each day? Do I look for opportunities to introduce Him to others? I'm convinced that this masterpiece of friendship with God requires commitment on my part too.

Lord, *may we thoroughly enjoy our friendship with You while never taking it for granted. Keep us faithful, Lord! In Your name I pray. Amen.*

Let Living Water Flow

The poor and needy search for water, but there is none. . . . But I the Lord will answer them . . . I will make rivers flow on barren heights (Isaiah 41:17, 18, *New International Version*).

Scripture: Isaiah 41:14-20
Song: "Fill My Cup, Lord"

Missionary David Heady walks with a voodoo priest through a dusty village in Haiti's desert. David is not intimidated. After all, he's already been framed and jailed for his faith; he's survived two heart surgeries, typhoid fever, and malaria. For him, a voodoo priest holds no fear.

Heady and his wife, Judy, work with Global Outreach, and they've been in Haiti for more than 20 years. Drilling and maintaining wells is a big part of their ministry in this small land where potable water is rare.

They especially wanted to provide water to remote villages on the huge mountain behind their ministry site. Driving up the stony mountain, David told me, "Every driller I talked to said, 'Don't go up on that mountain and look for water. You won't find anything but rocks up there.'" He then showed me two of eleven mountaintop wells he maintains.

"We never drill a well without presenting the gospel," he said. And they never taste fresh water without thanking the one who so faithfully makes rivers flow on barren heights.

Lord, *I pray that You will, indeed, fill my cup and use me to bring Your living water to those who thirst for life. In Your holy name I pray. Amen.*

My Prayer Notes

DEVOTIONS

Gary Allen, editor

Watch out for those who cause divisions and put obstacles in your way that are contrary to the teaching you have learned. Keep away from them.

—Romans 16:17, *NIV*

DECEMBER

Photo by Dale Meyers

© 2004 STANDARD PUBLISHING, 8121 Hamilton Avenue, Cincinnati, Ohio, 45231, a division of STANDEX INTERNATIONAL Corporation. Topics based on the Home Daily Bible Readings, International Sunday School Lessons. © 2002 by the Committee on the Uniform Series. Printed in the U.S.A. Scripture taken from the King James Version unless otherwise identified. Scripture taken from the HOLY BIBLE, NEW INTERNATIONAL VERSION®. NIV®. COPYRIGHT © 1973, 1978, 1984 by International Bible Society. Used by permission of Zondervan Publishing House. All rights reserved. Scripture quotations are taken from the Contemporary English Version copyright © 1991, 1992, 1995 American Bible Society. Used by permission.

No Idols in Your Life?

See, they are all false! Their deeds amount to nothing; their images are but wind and confusion (Isaiah 41:29, *New International Version*).

Scripture: Isaiah 41:21-29
Song: "Jesus Calls Us"

Like many Christians in the West, I thought: "What could idols have to do with me?" I figured idolatry reigned only in the dark jungles and remote tribal villages of Latin America, Africa, or Asia.

I needed a broader view. So I took the opportunity to teach freshman composition to a class of 26 eager students at Discipleship University in Eldoret, Kenya. In Kenya, 64 percent of the people profess Christianity, but 26 percent still hold fast to deep-rooted native religions.

Some of my young students, most preparing to be preachers or missionaries, wrote stories about the personal pain of being disowned by their families after they received Christian baptism. They gave up their idols and much more to follow Jesus Christ.

But no idols in your life? Think again. Money? Prestige or position? Comfort? Your children? A beautiful home? Relaxing hobbies? Idols have always been, and will always be, any temptation that diverts us from heartfelt devotion to the one true God.

Lord, *You graciously spread before us all good things. May we enjoy them with gratitude and thankfulness—and not a hint of idolatry. In the name of Jesus I pray. Amen.*

Creative, Freeing Witness

To free captives from prison and to release from the dungeon those who sit in darkness (Isaiah 42:7, *New International Version*).

Scripture: **Isaiah 42:1-9**
Song: **"O Spread the Tidings 'Round"**

During the 1970s, Miguel Robles languished in a Paraguayan prison because of his Christian faith and ministry. One day he learned that a woman inmate had attempted suicide. He never saw her, but he witnessed to her through a tiny hole in the wall between their cells. Miguel tore pages from his Bible, pushed them through the little hole, and urged her to read. Soon after that, Miguel was freed.

Years later, living in Buenos Aires, he received a telephone call from the head of Argentina's government TV station. The man wanted to meet Miguel. "Do you remember a woman in jail who wanted to commit suicide? Are you the one who pushed pages of Scripture through the wall to her?" the television executive asked.

"Yes, I'm the one."

"You saved that woman's life."

"How do you know this?"

"She is now my wife." The man and his wife were both vibrant Christian witnesses in their community.

Father, You are in the business of freeing people. Not only did You free Miguel from prison, You used him to lead someone else to freedom in Your Son. I praise You in Jesus' name. Amen.

Stringed Proclamation

Let them give glory to the Lord and proclaim His praise in the islands (Isaiah 42:12, *New International Version*).

Scripture: **Isaiah 42:10-17**
Song: **"Praise Him! Praise Him!"**

Harpist Christina Sonnemann lives in Tunbridge, Tasmania, an island off Australia's southern coast. She recently visited the ministry where I work in order to share her music and lead our morning devotions. Her skilled hands on the harp strings created a moving spirit of worship. "Worship is something we should be doing every minute of life," she said, "in everything we do."

Christina was four years old when her parents moved to Australia as missionaries. At an early age, she longed to play the harp for God's glory, and she told us how He prepared the way for her to study the instrument.

"I live at the end of the earth," she said. "The nearest traffic light is 60 miles away. Yet I've been able to study with world-class musicians." Her first teacher was principal harpist for the Queensland Symphony Orchestra.

Later, Christina studied under Michael Jefferies, former principal harpist for London's Royal Philharmonic. Jefferies retired in Tasmania. "We live in a town of 80 people," Christina said. "And Michael Jefferies moved 15 minutes away! The Lord is so faithful."

*How great and awesome You are, **Lord of all!** May we commit our talents to Your glory and praise, every minute of our lives. This I pray in Jesus' name. Amen.*

Seeing the Trapped Ones

This is a people plundered and looted, all of them trapped in pits or hidden away in prisons. They have become plunder, with no one to rescue them (Isaiah 42:22, *New International Version*).

Scripture: Isaiah 42:18-25
Song: "Rescue the Perishing"

Scotty West saw many "trapped" men in his church in Tupelo, Mississippi, and he wanted to do something about it. He went to his church elders and told them of his burden. "I want to begin a group for men who have started on the road to recovery from their addictions but have hit some potholes," Scotty said.

After prayerful consideration, the church leaders agreed, and Restoration Class was born. Two years later the group is a strong brotherhood of men who challenge, encourage, and depend on each other for daily support. Their weekly meeting draws men from several church fellowships. "We just want to help hurting men who need Christ-centered recovery," Scotty says. Participation is anonymous, and the group now includes men who are gaining victory over various substance-abuse problems, as well as sex and pornography addictions.

Are you feeling trapped, "plundered and looted" these days by a seemingly impossible addiction? First, fully and candidly admit your need. Then look up for rescue.

Father, *let me hear Your voice and respond when You call me to help rescue those in need. In Christ's name, amen.*

Heart Repair Needed?

A voice of one calling: "In the desert prepare the way for the Lord; make straight in the wilderness a highway for our God" (Isaiah 40:3, *New International Version*).

Scripture: **Isaiah 40:1-5**
Song: **"Come, Thou Long-Expected Jesus"**

Have you felt the pressure to get everything done early, before the crowds set in and Christmas shopping becomes an ordeal? Today's passage isn't about holiday shopping, but it is about the need to be prepared. Through Isaiah, God called His people to prepare for an event that wouldn't take place for centuries into their future: the coming of the Savior.

In that culture, whenever a king visited from a distant land, people prepared by smoothing the road. They got rid of the big rocks, filled the potholes, and removed all the debris to make it safe for the royal procession. Isaiah's prophetic analogy encouraged the people of Israel to be spiritually prepared. Then, some six hundred years later, John the Baptist proclaimed the message once again.

John warned of the need to repent—to clear hearts of sinful attitudes and other "debris"—and be open to the arrival of the great King from a heavenly country. So may I ask: What is the condition of your heart at the moment?

Holy Spirit, prepare our hearts for worship. Give us a sense of wonder and thankfulness as we contemplate the gift of the Messiah. In His name, amen.

December 5-11. **Linda Washington**, a former staff editor at a Christian publisher, now works as a freelance writer from her home in Carol Stream, Illinois.

Rest and Move

Those who hope in the Lord will renew their strength. They will soar on wings like eagles (Isaiah 40:31, *New International Version*).

Scripture: **Isaiah 40:27-31**
Song: **"Be Still, My Soul"**

Ever seen an eagle fly? They say that bald eagles can fly up to 60 miles per hour. But they don't flap their wings the whole time. Their pattern of gliding and soaring on thermals helps them conserve energy.

Today's passage provides another way to conserve energy: putting hope in God. Just as a wind current enables a mighty bird to both rest and still keep moving, God supports and renews those who trust Him.

Believe it or not, worrying takes a great deal of energy. Perhaps you're fully convinced of this already, yet many of us try to justify our fretting: "At least I'm doing *something!*" But as Jesus once asked, "Who of you by worrying can add a single hour to his life?" (Matthew 6:27). In other words, worrying is a waste of time.

But what about hope in God? Hardly a waste, it provides energy to soar to greater heights in spiritual growth. Often this means gaining patience and confidence when it would be so easy to give up in exhaustion. Like the eagle, in a blessed paradox, when we rest we move forward.

Give me the courage, O God, to hope in You this day. Help me to avoid running after the approval of others or walking to the beat of my own agenda. Instead, Lord, may I wait on Jesus, in whose name I pray. Amen.

His Rejection, My Reward

I have labored to no purpose; I have spent my strength in vain and for nothing. Yet what is due me is in the Lord's hand, and my reward is with my God (Isaiah 49:4, *New International Version*).

Scripture: **Isaiah 49:1-7**
Song: **"Jesus, Name above All Names"**

Should we expect rejection whenever we do anything for God's kingdom? Yes.

And should we expect reward? Yes, that too. But rejection and reward, as the prophet tells us, come from completely different sources.

In today's Scripture, Isaiah previews the coming and mission of God's suffering servant, the Messiah. In response to God's plan, formulated in response to the acts of people in Genesis 3, the Savior would come to bring God's people back to himself. The New Testament reveals how perfectly Jesus did the job. Yet His ministry was that of both triumph and rejection. He excelled in the task appointed Him by His Father. But the rejection of His people led Him to the ultimate sacrifice.

In all of this, here is what warms my heart: "It is finished" (John 19:30)—Jesus' last statement before death—isn't a cry of defeat. It is a cry of triumph, since the rejected one now has the reward: "all authority in heaven and on earth" (Matthew 28:18).

Lord, *let me truly believe this triumph today, demonstrated through every thought, word, and deed! In Your holy name I pray. Amen.*

No More Thirst

They will neither hunger nor thirst, nor will the desert heat or the sun beat upon them. He who has compassion on them will guide them and lead them beside springs of water (Isaiah 49:10, *New International Version*).

Scripture: **Isaiah 49:8-13**
Song: **"I'd Rather Have Jesus"**

Thirsty? I've been there. I experienced several scorching summer days during my mission trip to WuJiang, a city in China. Lifting boards and driving nails, hour after hour, I felt as if I'd never get enough liquids into me to satisfy my raging thirst.

A kind of dryness characterizes people in need of spiritual renewal, as today's Scripture implies. As desert dwellers, the people of Palestine were familiar with the body's need for water. They'd already survived decades of hunger and thirst while camping in the wilderness.

So . . . never be thirsty again? For them, what a radical concept! Yet the Lord promised that someday He would lead His people to the ultimate place of satisfaction at every level of longing: Heaven.

During this holiday season, why not take some time to think carefully about your own thirst? What is your deep desire today? Could this longing help you hear the heavenly calling to seek refreshment in God?

Giver of living water, daily we need Your compassion. During the hustle and bustle of the season, we often thirst for times of quiet and restoration. Lead us, Lord, to your quiet, quenching springs. In Christ's name, amen.

Long-Lasting Tattoo

See, I have engraved you on the palms of my hands; your walls are ever before me (Isaiah 49:16, *New International Version*).

Scripture: **Isaiah 49:14-18**
Song: **"The Steadfast Love of the Lord"**

Giving an engraved item is a wonderful way to commemorate an important event like an anniversary or birthday. It's also more permanent than, say, a card or a bouquet of flowers. After all, things "written in stone" aren't easily changed.

"Written in stone." The phrase can often apply to Israel's history. The Ten Commandments came down from the mountain chiseled in stone (see Exodus 31:18). Even the garment of the high priest displayed stones upon which were engraved the names of Israel's tribes (see Exodus 28:21). But God had a special way of remembering Israel, as this passage from Isaiah reveals. His hand-engraving was one "tattoo" that would never be removed!

God would one day restore the people to their land. He would respond to their cry that the Lord had forsaken them with the assurance of His permanent presence.

He provides that assurance for us, as well: "Never will I leave you; never will I forsake you" (Hebrews 13:5). You and I are safe and secure in the palm of His hand. The promise is as sure as if written in stone.

Father God, we're comforted by Your promise never to leave us. Thank You for engraving Your sons and daughters in the palm of Your hand. Help us to share that blessing with others. In Jesus' name I pray. Amen.

Our Banner

I will lift up my banner to the peoples; they will bring your sons in their arms and carry your daughters on their shoulders (Isaiah 49:22, *New International Version*).

Scripture: **Isaiah 49:22-26**
Song: **"His Banner over Me Is Love"**

Amidst ancient battles, the colorful, unfurled banner was always a rallying force. A king's banner usually displayed an image related to his particular reign. Seeing the king's banner lifted the spirits of scattered troops and helped them courageously assemble for another stand.

Each tribe of Israel had a banner that was carried to many victories in war (see Numbers 1:52-2:34, for example). But Israel's cry in the verse preceding today's passage was anything but the voice of the victorious: "I was bereaved and barren; I was exiled and rejected" (v. 21). Now, this destruction and subsequent exile had not yet happened! Nevertheless, discouragement would win the day unless God rallied His people back to their homeland.

But even after that time had come and gone, God would send a more permanent banner for His people to gather around. Jesus is the ultimate standard, or banner, of salvation for all peoples. As he told a crowd, "When I am lifted up from the earth, I will draw all men to myself" (John 12:32). That's why we can all triumphantly sing: "His banner over me is love" (Song of Songs 2:4).

Victorious Lord, *You are Jehovah-nissi ("Yahweh is my banner"). May we rally to Your Son, our banner of salvation. In His name I pray. Amen.*

Not Ashamed

Because the Sovereign Lord helps me, I will not be disgraced. Therefore have I set my face like flint, and I know I will not be put to shame (Isaiah 50:7, *New International Version*).

Scripture: **Isaiah 50:4-11**
Song: **"Better Is One Day"**

I'm usually the most determined to do a task when others try to stop me from doing it. Often adversity is the "yeast" that causes determination to rise within me.

Here Isaiah details the determination of the Lord's servant. Nothing would stop him from accomplishing his purpose, not even the humiliation heaped upon him by adversaries (see 50:6, 8). Suffering would, in fact, sharpen his determination.

Jesus later fulfilled the events predicted in this chapter. First, He set out for Jerusalem, knowing that humiliating trials and the agony of the cross lay before Him. But the approval of the Father outweighed this humiliation.

Thankfully, because Jesus was disgraced, His people will not be disgraced. This doesn't mean we'll never have to suffer another embarrassing moment again. After all, Jesus also promised that His followers would suffer persecution. But He has already won for us the ultimate victory: eternal life without sorrow or disgrace. In gratitude, what will we determine to do for God?

Jesus, because of You, we will never suffer permanent disgrace or separation from the Father. Thank You for Your willingness to suffer so much on our behalf. I pray this in the name of Jesus, our sovereign Lord. Amen.

Who Will Understand?

Kings will shut their mouths because of him. For what they were not told, they will see, and what they have not heard, they will understand (Isaiah 52:15, *New International Version*).

Scripture: **Isaiah 52:13—53:3**
Song: **"The King of Glory"**

When I was in Pakistan, I visited the beautiful Faisal Mosque in Islamabad. Its white marble minarets and space-age pinnacle seemed to celebrate God's holiness with special power. But as I stood inside, in the visitor's corner, praying, I wondered how many of the men kneeling around me could see the truth of the true Lord of all. The words of Isaiah came to me: "Who has believed our message, and to whom has the arm of the Lord been revealed?" (Isaiah 53:1)

Actually, I have had these same thoughts praying in some of the palatial yet vacant Christian cathedrals in Europe. And I have had them strolling through our plastic suburban shopping malls.

Yet Isaiah's words encourage me. The prophet is reaching out to the very places in the world where we are least likely to see Jesus. And . . . am I willing to confess that my own heart is sometimes less alive to Him than a mosque, or an ancient church, or a modern mall?

Lord, *inhabit the citadel of my heart today and infuse my life with Your power and goodness. In the name of Jesus, amen.*

December 12-18. **Larry Brook,** a missionary kid, has served for decades as a cross-cultural communications expert to various businesses and ministries.

It Was Bad!

He was pierced for our transgressions, he was crushed for our iniquities; the punishment that brought us peace was upon him, and by his wounds we are healed (Isaiah 53:5, *New International Version*).

Scripture: Isaiah 53: 4-12
Song: "Amazing Love"

My boss in a previous job was like the wicked kings of the Old Testament. I'm sad to say that he "did evil in the sight of the Lord." I will never forget the pain I felt when, after encouraging me to trust him, he betrayed me completely for his own selfish gain. Have you been there, too?

Isaiah uses words about the Messiah that seem to describe my own suffering: "pierced," "crushed," "despised," "rejected." I wanted to retaliate, to get revenge. But I held my anger for Jesus' sake.

Isaiah's words meant a lot to me in those days. First, I was reminded that Jesus could empathize with my own suffering. Second, I learned to appreciate firsthand what Jesus must feel like when I betray Him and let Him down.

But Jesus not only brings empathy and reminders. Through the terrible cross, Jesus completely overcame evil and suffering. He carried on Him all our sins and exchanged them for peace with God. Does that comfort you in whatever suffering or conflict you face today?

Father, forgive me of my trespasses just as I try to forgive those who trespass against me. Take my infirmities and carry my sorrows close to Your heart this day. In Jesus' name I pray. Amen.

Don't Be Afraid

Do not be afraid, Zechariah; your prayer has been heard. Your wife Elizabeth will bear you a son, and you are to give him the name John (Luke 1:13, *New International Version*).

Scripture: **Luke 1:5-17**
Song: **"O Come All Ye Faithful"**

During the Vietnam War missionary nurse Betty Olsen was captured by the Viet Cong and kept in a cage. To survive, she and the other prisoners ate manioc leaves. For months, the Viet Cong marched their prisoners, chained together, through two hundred miles of jungle. Covered with fungus, leeches, and ulcers, Betty grew weak from starvation and dysentery. After seven months of grueling marches, she died and was buried along the trail.

One of the prisoners survived. He reported later that it was Betty Olsen, with her love and courage and prayers, who kept him alive. But what about Betty Olsen herself? Were her daily prayers for delivery answered? In human terms, certainly not. She died a terrible death. In contrast, God answers yes to Zechariah and Elizabeth's specific prayers for a son. Though we are sad for Betty Olsen, we are happy for Zechariah and Elizabeth.

What does this mean for us? Do we let our fear and questions paralyze us? Or do we respond in faith to the angel's call, "Do not be afraid"?

God of Zechariah, John, and Betty Olsen, *give us faith today to rise above our fear and our worry. Give us the strength to obey, no matter what You allow. In Christ's name, amen.*

You Can't Be Serious!

The angel went to [Mary] and said, "Greetings, you who are highly favored! . . . Do not be afraid, Mary . . . You will be with child and give birth to a son and you are to give him the name Jesus (Luke 1:28, 30, 31, *New International Version*).

Scripture: Luke 1:26-38
Song: "Here I Am, Lord"

"Because the real Jesus is such a terror," wrote Kristen Johnson Ingram in *Weavings*, "we make him into Gentle Jesus, Meek and Mild." Ingram adds that, of course, the real Jesus is gentle and kind and a healer. But Jesus is also an "outsider," a "scruffy wild man." Jesus is the one who says to "turn the other cheek, to pray for our enemies, to forgive seventy times seven."

When Jesus breaks into Mary's life, she is not cheerful; she is terrified. In other words, the real Jesus shocks us with the unpredictable, the impossible. And though Mary's story is unique in history, I suspect that Jesus, the alarming Miracle Baby, has turned her experience into a model for each of us. For example, today I imagine that I am Mary and, at a surprise moment, Jesus breaks through my crust of doubt and routine with a totally life-changing love. Will my reaction be, "How can this be?" Or will I overcome my fear and narrow-mindedness? Will I exclaim along with a transformed, receptive Mary, "May it be to me as you have said"?

Awesome Lord, open my heart today to Your surprising love. Shock me with Your power, Your impossible peace. In Jesus' precious name, amen.

Jumpy Baby

In a loud voice [Elizabeth] exclaimed: "Blessed are you among women, and blessed is the child you will bear!" (Luke 1:42, *New International Version*).

Scripture: **Luke 1: 39-45**
Song: **"All Hail the Power of Jesus' Name"**

A friend of ours lives quietly in the suburbs of Chicago, but she shines with the bright light of the Holy Spirit. Often she says, "I was praying, and these people came to my mind, and I knew God wanted me to call them." Many times she has brought blessing or hope to people because she listens intently and allows the Spirit to work through her.

Zechariah's wife, Elizabeth, must have been like this. If she had been preoccupied with her own strange pregnancy, or with her daily tasks, she may not have noticed anything special about her baby making a sudden move inside her. In fact, the child leaped for joy, and Elizabeth, "filled with the Holy Spirit," knew immediately that the mother of God's Son was paying her a visit.

What might the Holy Spirit be saying to us today? Will we be too busy with our own concerns? Or will we go through the day, however quiet or busy, with our hearts tuned to what God is trying to say to us? Maybe, if we listen carefully, our hearts too will leap for joy.

Heavenly Father, make me aware of Your Spirit's guidance. Teach me to discern Your truth and Your message that I may serve the Christ child, born of Mary. In Jesus' name I pray. Amen.

Who, Me?

Mary said . . . "my spirit rejoices in God my Savior, for he has been mindful of the humble state of his servant" (Luke 1:46, 47, 48, *New International Version*).

Scripture: **Luke 1: 46-55**
Song: **"Angels, We Have Heard on High"**

Elizabeth Canham, a North Carolina writer, once traveled to Brazil for a religious conference. When she landed in Rio de Janeiro, she was frightened by the crowds. Since she spoke no Portuguese she wondered how she would find transportation to her hotel. Her fear increased as she moved outside. "Am I safe among these strangers?" she wondered. "Will I be exploited by a ruthless cab driver?"

Elizabeth suddenly noticed a young woman holding up a sign in English. The sign was for her! As Elizabeth approached, the young woman smiled and said, "Welcome to Rio."

The biblical Mary was also greeted—and reassured— by a special sign in a language she could understand. The angel Gabriel called her by name and told her she was highly favored and would give birth to God's baby.

No wonder Mary rejoiced. She had personally witnessed the fact that God can do anything, from calling out to a humble virgin, to scattering those who are proud. It makes me wonder: "Is God choosing me out of the crowd to do something special for Him today?"

Father, please perform a good work through me today, that I may rejoice in Your power and goodness! In the holy name of Jesus, amen.

Live Lives of Hope

Hope does not disappoint us, because God has poured out his love into our hearts by the Holy Spirit, whom he has given us (Romans 5:5, *New International Version*).

Scripture: **Romans 5:1-11**
Song: **"Love Divine, All Loves Excelling"**

Festo Kivengere, bishop of Kigezi in Uganda, once had to flee for his life because of his faith in Christ. During a reign of terror, Ugandan dictator Idi Amin not only murdered Archbishop Janani Luwum, but executed Christians in public and shamelessly vandalized churches.

Later, after Amin was overthrown, Festo returned to Uganda to preach love and reconciliation. In one of his early sermons, Festo stated, "It is Christ, the one crucified, who wins rebellious lives, melts stony hearts, brings life to the dead. People are to be drawn by the power of the self-sacrificing love of God in Christ into new life in him."

Festo Kivengere is echoing Paul's words in Romans. Paul, too, says that we can live lives of hope, even amidst sufferings, because "God has poured out his love into our hearts" through Christ's death on the cross.

Do we take Jesus' love for granted? Or do we, like the apostle Paul and Festo Kivengere, continually rejoice in the reconciling power of His life and death?

Father of the crucified and risen Christ, I praise You for offering access by faith into grace, in which I now stand. You have brought peace, rejoicing, and hope into the world and into my life. For this, I rejoice. In Jesus' holy name I pray. Amen.

A Wasteland Garden

He will make her deserts like Eden, her wastelands like the garden of the Lord (Isaiah 51:3, *New International Version*).

Scripture: **Isaiah 51:1-6**
Song: **"The Beautiful Garden of Prayer"**

My friend Al was a Minnesota farmer turned preacher. His heart for missions, along with his administrative gifts, landed him a job with a missions staff in Chicago. Those of us who knew Al wondered how this gentle, gardening-loving bachelor could possibly find contentment in a huge, bustling city.

To the south of the headquarters building a narrow, weed-infested strip of earth lay discretely hidden from the sidewalk by a hedge. Al saw something in that ugly strip of land that we all had missed. Early mornings and late afternoons found him clearing away weeds and debris. He erected a wooden fence and hauled in dark topsoil.

Soon gorgeous hybrid irises appeared. A perky rose bush budded by the gate. As summer wore on, flowers, green peas, yellow beans, and cucumbers appeared on secretaries' desks—then fat, red tomatoes and golden squash. We were amazed to see what tender loving care could produce on a strip of wasteland. Al, a gentle man of God, knew what it took to turn a desert into a garden.

Lord, help me do whatever it takes to turn my heart's weed patches into gardens that will enrich and feed others. In Jesus' name, amen.

December 19-25. **Lloyd Mattson** is a retired minister and author of Christian camping books. He and his wife, Elsie, live in Duluth, Minnesota.

Watch that Thumb!

Be pure, you who carry the vessels of the Lord (Isaiah 52:11, *New International Version*).

Scripture: **Isaiah 52:7-12**
Song: **"I Would Be True"**

It was late in the day, and we were hungry. We found a table in the Lemon Drop, a new restaurant in town, eager for a good meal. When the waitress finally approached, we saw that her apron was soiled. She took our order with little enthusiasm, and when she returned with our food, she had her thumb in the gravy. The meal tasted fine . . . but we never returned. One tired waitress toward the end of her shift cost the Lemon Drop a customer.

In food service, presentation is vital. Similarly, we who present the bread of life to a hungry world must package it attractively. Bearing the vessels of the Lord is a high honor, and we must never grow careless, no matter how weary we become. Indifferent, brassy, or intrusive "witnessing" alienates, as does any hint of spiritual compromise.

We carry the priceless gospel, God's year-round Christmas gift. Such a gift demands a pure life and thoughtful presentation. Wear a clean apron . . . and keep your thumb out of the gravy.

Heavenly Father, help me always to remember what Christmas cost Your Son and what a high honor you have granted me to be His servant. Remind me that my life is my primary witness to Your goodness and grace. In Christ I pray. Amen.

Christmas Lights

Your sun will never set again, and your moon will wane no more; the Lord will be your everlasting light, and your days of sorrow will end (Isaiah 60:20, *New International Version*).

Scripture: **Isaiah 60:17-22**
Song: **"The Light of the World Is Jesus"**

In my youth, our Christmas trees bore real candles. We cut a ceiling-high spruce in the snowy woods and hauled it home on Father's Model T. The tree took up one corner of our small living room, filling the house with a woodsy smell. Tinsel, shiny balls, red and green paper rope—all joined the popcorn we strung liberally in the branches. What a beautiful sight!

Finally, Father carefully placed small, twisted candles in special clip holders on the far end of limbs. On Christmas Eve he lit them one by one, standing on a ladder to reach the top. The candles flickered brightly, but briefly. Mother saw to that. Christmas fires were legendary among country folks. Then brave Father pinched each flame to death, beginning at the bottom.

Somehow, small bulbs strung on green wire never evoked that candle magic. When one bulb failed, the whole string failed. Candles never did that. How good to know that one day we will enjoy Christmas all the time, in everlasting light.

Thank You, Father, *for Christmases that remind us of more than feasts and gifts. May our memories of Your Son's birth glow the more dear as decades pass. In the name of our Savior, Jesus Christ. Amen.*

A Hammer, My Pulpit

You will be named ministers of our God (Isaiah 61:6, *New International Version*).

Scripture: **Isaiah 61:1-7**
Song: **"Lord, I Want to Be a Christian"**

My friend Odin lifted his hammer. "This is my pulpit," he said. Coffee-break conversation had turned to the subject of witnessing. Some work crew volunteers found it difficult to speak to friends about salvation. One man envied the minister, who could witness every Sunday from his pulpit. That's when Odin lifted his hammer.

We hired Odin to help build a modest addition to our church building. He was a skilled craftsman, though short on patience and sometimes mildly profane. His part of the work had ended, but he stayed on without pay to guide the volunteers who would complete the project. Odin joined the friendly banter and felt the love the volunteers had for each other. One evening, in conversation with the pastor, he asked to be baptized.

Providence connected Odin to a mission building project on a nearby Indian reservation. He left his construction business in mid-season to guide volunteer builders. That would be the first of many such projects, costing him thousands of dollars in lost business. Odin would be hard pressed to preach a sermon, but his hammer-pulpit spoke eloquently and led to many lives changed for Christ.

Heavenly Father, *teach me how I can use my skills and experiences to serve Your kingdom! In Christ's name I pray. Amen.*

Christmas Clothes

My soul rejoices in my God. He has clothed me with garments of salvation and arrayed me in a robe of righteousness (Isaiah 61:10 *New International Version*).

Scripture: **Isaiah 61:8—62:3**
Song: **"I Would Be Like Jesus"**

Christmas often brings new clothes, but how should a Christian dress? Years ago a preacher friend met me on the street and chided me for wearing work clothes in public. "If you want to succeed as a minister," he advised, "you must look the part." That good man never appeared without jacket and tie, trim haircut, and a freshly shaven chin. I took no offense; however, I wasn't only a pastor. I was church custodian, plumber, builder of kites for neighborhood kids, repairer of aging cars . . . and an addicted fly fisherman. I felt quite comfortable in work clothes.

My preacher friend was right, of course. He became a seminary president while I served a string of small churches. I built many kites, took kids camping, and wrote stories that have gone around the world. I still appear in work clothes, having given up on certain forms of success. But I trust I look like a Christian. I wear the garments of salvation with gratitude, be they blue collar. And over all, I don the robe of Christ's righteousness. From on high, don't all God's children look alike?

Thank You, Lord, *that Your children of every place and culture are dressed alike, wearing the garments of salvation. And thank You that each one has the supreme Christmas gift, a robe of righteousness. In Jesus' name, amen.*

The Lamb King

She gave birth to her firstborn, a son. She wrapped him in cloths and placed him in a manger (Luke 2:7, *New International Version*).

Scripture: **Luke 2:1-7**
Song: **"Away in a Manger"**

We can't fully appreciate the Christmas story apart from its historical and cultural setting. All Scripture tells us is that Mary gave birth and laid her Son in a Bethlehem manger. Yet we chide a mythical inn keeper for blowing a great opportunity. We locate the manger in a stable of our imagining, complete with imaginary animals. Church pageants bring on the Magi (however many there were) more than a year ahead of schedule. We conveniently set Jesus' birth date to coincide with winter solstice.

Our gentle imaginings hide the grim facts of that holy night, the pivotal event in human history. It must have been a hard night for Mary and Joseph, alone in a strange town with a new baby to care for. Shepherds came, but no celebrities. Little wonder; royalty doesn't visit stables.

Jesus' birth place speaks to us in a loud, fast-paced world. The stable was probably quiet. Jesus? Just another peasant baby. Nothing to draw a crowd. Yet the closing words of an old folk song provide a Christmas Eve thought full of theological insight: "A stable is not a fit birthplace for a king, but it's a perfect place for a lamb."

Heavenly Father, help us to understand the lesson of the manger, birthplace of the Lamb slain for our salvation. In His mighty name, amen.

Borrowed, or Really Yours?

When they had seen him, they spread the word (Luke 2:17, *New International Version*).

Scripture: Luke 2:8-21
Song: "Do You Know My Jesus?"

It was just before closing on Christmas Eve. A few procrastinators were still browsing when a ragged lad rushed into the department store, close to tears. "Can we borrow your Jesus?" he blurted to a clerk. "Ours got busted."

The store manager learned that the boy had toppled the Christmas tree in a nearby mission, smashing baby Jesus beyond repair. With the children's pageant hours away, the lad was devastated. He promised to find another Jesus.

Smiling, the manager gently removed an ornate Baby Jesus from the creche in the front window and handed it to the lad. He stared at the holy figure. "Whoa!" he said. "Thanks! I'll bring Him back." Tucking the borrowed Jesus under his arm, the lad dashed off for the mission.

We smile at a small boy's ingenuity. A borrowed Jesus saved the pageant. However, we need more than a borrowed Jesus to meet life's needs. When the shepherds told about their hillside encounter with angels, they weren't spreading hearsay. They had hunted out the manger and found their very own Jesus.

Help me, Lord, to look beyond Christmas tradition to know Your present reality. Lead me often back to the manger and the cross. I pray in Your Son's precious name. Amen.

Down, and Looking Up

I am at the point of death. Let your teachings breathe new life into me (Psalm 119:25, *Contemporary English Version*).

Scripture: **Psalm 119:25-32**
Song: "Thy Word Is a Lamp Unto My Feet"

Frustrated? Down in the dumps? Think it can't get any worse? We've all been there. The one who wrote Psalm 119 understood and offered us some simple but powerful ways to get out of the dumps. Furthermore, it seems the worst of times can, in fact, be the best of times.

The psalmist begins by admitting he's in the dumps. He tells God his story and troubles. That's step one. Next, he knows an immediate source of help: the Bible. God gives fresh insight and perspective through His Word.

It's one thing to know God's Word can help; it is quite another to allow it to change us. The psalmist asks God to help him understand His Word and obey it. He admits he is weak and can deceive himself. With honest humility, he is ready to learn from God and allow God to change him.

The Lord is ready and able to lift us, too, from frustration and despair. No, He may not change our circumstances. But He can certainly change our attitude and choices. And think how far that can go in getting us through our difficulties.

Lord, I feel stuck and need help to get moving again. In the days ahead, may I go to Your Word for insight and strength. In Jesus' name, amen.

December 26-January 1. **Glen Elliott**, now a minister in Tucson, has served as a missionary to the Ukraine, starting several churches and a Christian college there.

December 27

Watch the Company You Keep

I urge you, brothers, to watch out for those who cause divisions and put obstacles in your way that are contrary to the teaching you have learned. Keep away from them (Romans 16:17, *New International Version*).

Scripture: **Romans 16:17-27**
Song: **"Blest Be the Tie that Binds"**

It's amazing how just being around a negative person can rub off on me. After a short while I'm negative, too. Or if I'm around a gossip, I catch myself joining in. People do affect us, and we are often unaware of their influence.

In today's verse, Paul reminds us to watch out for troublemakers. Yes, even in the church. And when we spot them, we are to make a conscious choice not to associate with them. Paul knows how easily those with whom we keep company influence us. Not only are we not to associate with negative people, we are to seek those who have a Christ-like character instead.

Romans 16 is an impressive chapter, isn't it? Paul contrasts those we should fellowship with and those we are to avoid. In verses 17 and 18 he warns of the troublemakers. But almost all the rest of the chapter Paul devotes to commending some wonderful Christians. These are the kind of people to hang around with. Keep good company so that you can be in good company with God.

Dear Lord, today my desire is to let You shine in and through me. Help me find those who will encourage me to stick with this goal as You empower me. In Jesus' name I pray. Amen.

Don't Be Unsettled

[We sent Timothy] so that no one would be unsettled by these trials. You know quite well that we were destined for them (1 Thessalonians 3:3, *New International Version*).

Scripture: **1 Thessalonians 3:1-5**
Song: **"Holy Father, Grant Us Peace"**

When my wife and I took birthing classes in anticipation of our first child, the nurse taught us what would happen and what to expect during each stage of birth. The classes didn't take away the pain or the difficulty of childbirth, of course. But we both were better able to handle all that happened. We weren't unsettled as we encountered each step of the process.

Satan will throw trials at us in order to knock us off balance. He wants to distract us from daily worship and giving honor to God. So, as Paul says, we should expect difficulties but not let them unsettle us.

When the difficulties come (and they will come), let us all the more draw near to our God. While we might be tempted to blame God for the tough situations, let us instead seek Him for strength to endure. After all, have you noticed that you often experience God in a much more profound way in the midst of your trials?

The trials will come. But He has promised to be with us in their midst.

Dear God, I pray to be at peace, even during my tough trials. Remind me of Your abiding presence, and may Your love and grace always fill my heart to carry me through each challenge. In Jesus' holy name I pray. Amen.

Graded, but Gifted

Timothy has just now come to us from you and has brought good news about your faith and love (1 Thessalonians 3:6, *New International Version*).

Scripture: 1 Thessalonians 3:6-13
Song: "Change My Heart, Oh God"

Since I was a poor student in elementary school, I'd dread report card time. I usually struggled just to make a passing grade each quarter. Then, the final report card of the year would state whether I was promoted to the next grade or not. Did I fear that one! My eyes immediately zeroed in on the promotion section: thumbs up or thumbs down? I dreaded that first peek.

As much as I once hated grades and report cards, I now understand that evaluation is an essential part of life. We can't earn God's favor by getting good "spiritual grades," for God's grace and mercy are gifts we can't earn. But do you realize that God does, nevertheless, grade us? (See 2 Corinthians 5:10.) He grades our character, our actions, and our devotion to Him. What kind of report would you get on your faith, your love, or your devotion to God?

Now matter how you answer, today is an opportunity to draw nearer to God. Enter this time of quiet with an open heart and a desire to know and please Him. The beautiful thing is that He is truly looking forward to fellowship with His beloved child. That would be you!

*May my thoughts, prayers, plans, and actions bring honor to **You, Dear Lord.** In the name of Christ I pray. Amen.*

Beaming Attraction

You will be the pure and innocent children of God. You live among people who are crooked and evil, but you must not do anything that they can say is wrong. Try to shine as lights among the people of this world (Philippians 2:15, *Contemporary English Version*).

Scripture: **Philippians 2:14-23**
Song: **"Shine, Jesus, Shine"**

In my favorite picture of my children, the kids are just one and three years old. They're on the couch in their pajamas, smiling and having fun. In fact, they are beaming. I can't remember what was happening at the time, but the joy radiates through the photograph. It's a picture of innocence and joy. I'm just drawn to it.

While none of us can be purely innocent, Paul reminds us to live in such a way that those who don't know God can't say anything bad about us. Further, when God's presence is truly alive in us, others will just naturally be drawn to Him.

Jesus said it simply: "Let your light shine before men, that they may see your good deeds and praise your Father in heaven" (Matthew 5:15, *New International Version*).

I want my life to be like that picture of my children. I want people to so clearly see God in me that they are irresistibly attracted to Him.

I want to be pure, and innocent, and a shining light for **You, Lord.** *May others see only Your love beaming through in my life today. I pray this in Jesus' precious name. Amen.*

Recommit to the Basics?

You must teach people to have genuine love, as well as a good conscience and true faith (1 Timothy 1:5, *Contemporary English Version*).

Scripture: **1 Timothy 1:1-11**
Song: "More Love to Thee"

I came home one day to find my daughter washing her car. Great, but the hose she was using knocked over a new cactus I had just planted. And I was really angry that she wasn't more careful.

A classic example of misplaced priorities? Apparently. The cactus (which could easily be replanted) could never be more important than my daughter's tender heart. This story, with different details, can be retold over and over in all of our lives, right?

Jesus said the main thing is to love God with all our being and to love others as ourselves. That's it! That covers it all. Paul reminds Timothy that the core of all teaching is to love others genuinely. That kind of love, the genuine kind, can't be manufactured out of sheer willpower. It comes only from true faith in God.

So keeping the main thing is the main thing in life—loving others, putting them first, and focusing on their needs. As you end this year, will you recommit to the basics with me?

Dear God, *forgive us for not loving others wholeheartedly but putting our own needs first. Help us be a people who genuinely and consistently shine forth Your love. I pray through our Deliverer, Jesus. Amen.*